Come Now, Let Us Reason Together

Come Now, Let Us Reason Together

Uncovering the Torah's Liberal Values

Mark D. Friedman

RESOURCE *Publications* · Eugene, Oregon

COME NOW, LET US REASON TOGETHER
Uncovering the Torah's Liberal Values

Copyright © 2024 Mark D. Friedman. All rights reserved. Except for brief quotations in critical publications or reviews, no part of this book may be reproduced in any manner without prior written permission from the publisher. Write: Permissions, Wipf and Stock Publishers, 199 W. 8th Ave., Suite 3, Eugene, OR 97401.

Resource Publications
An Imprint of Wipf and Stock Publishers
199 W. 8th Ave., Suite 3
Eugene, OR 97401

www.wipfandstock.com

PAPERBACK ISBN: 979-8-3852-2333-6
HARDCOVER ISBN: 979-8-3852-2334-3
EBOOK ISBN: 979-8-3852-2335-0
VERSION NUMBER 12/26/24

Unless otherwise noted, all Biblical quotations are: Reprinted from the Tanakh: The Holy Scriptures by permission of the University of Nebraska Press. Copyright 1985 by The Jewish Publication Society, Philadelphia. The author is grateful to the Jewish Publication Society for granting him permission to quote its copyrighted material.

Unless otherwise noted, all quotations from the Babylon Talmud are taken from William Davidson Talmud: Text from The William Davidson digital edition of the Koran Noé Talmud, with commentary by Rabbi Adin Even-Israel Steinsaltz, License CC-BY-NC https://creativecommons.org/licenses/by-nc/4.0/.

*For Aracelly, my wonderful wife,
who combines the wisdom of Solomon with the patience of Job.*

I know that when I stand before God on Judgment Day, I shall not be asked the question posed to Cain—where were you when your brother's blood was crying out to God?

—Imre Bathory (Hungary), recognized by Yad Vashem: The World Holocaust Remembrance Center (Jerusalem), as a Righteous Among the Nations (quoted by Yad Vashem).

Contents

Acknowledgments | ix
Abbreviations | xi
Introduction | xiii

1. A Theological Framework | 1
2. Autonomous Ethics, Liberalism, and Judaism | 23
3. Liberalism and Critical Rationalism | 40
4. The Ten Commandments, the Oral Law, and the Decline of the Generations | 51
5. Rabbinic Innovation and Pluralism | 80
6. The Fractious Canon | 98
7. Making Peace with the Torah's Immoral Commandments | 130
8. The Tragedy of Rabbi Eliezer | 147

Glossary | 163
Selected Bibliography | 167
Subject Index | 181
Scripture Index | 199

Acknowledgments

I WISH TO TAKE this opportunity to express my heartfelt gratitude to those individuals who provided invaluable assistance to the author in the writing of this book. First, I thank Professor Ari Ackerman, President of the Schechter Institute of Jewish Studies (Jerusalem), for his continuing encouragement and for his thorough and penetrating critique of an early version of my manuscript, prompting me to make what I hope are substantial improvements. Second, I owe a tremendous debt to my late friend Danny Frederick, a widely published independent scholar, who patiently introduced me to Karl Popper's thought, thus providing the conceptual basis for a key element of this book. His untimely death left many brilliant books and papers unwritten.

I also wish to thank Professor Daniel Statman (University of Haifa) and Professor Dan Baras (Bar-Ilan University) for taking their valuable time to answer my questions regarding certain aspects of their views relevant to this book. Finally, I wish to commend my excellent copy editor, Nicole Halper, for her hard work, and to thank Matthew Wimer for guiding me smoothly through the publishing process at Wipf and Stock.

Abbreviations

BCE	Before Common Era
CE	Common Era
Babylonian Talmud	b. [+ tractate + page], e.g., b. B. Bat. 24b
Jerusalem Talmud	y. [+ tractate + section], e.g., y. Shabb. 1:2
Mishnah	m.[+ tractate + paragraph]
Midrash Rabbah	MR [+ canonical book + chapter:verse], e.g., MR (Gen) 6:18
Pirkei de-Rabbi Eliezer	PRE [+ chapter:verse]

The Jewish Bible (books cited in text)

Pentateuch

Genesis (*Bereshis*)	Gen
Exodus (*Shemos*)	Exod
Leviticus (*Vayikra*)	Lev
Numbers (*Bamidbar*)	Num
Deuteronomy (*Devarim*)	Deut

Prophets

Samuel	Sam
Kings	Kings
Isaiah	Isa
Jeremiah	Jer
Amos	Amos
Jonah	Jonah
Micah	Mic

Writings

Proverbs	Prov
Job	Job
Lamentations	Lam

Mishnah and Talmud Tractates (cited in text)

Bava Batra	B. Bat.	Menahot	Menah.
Bava Metzi'a	B. Metz	Mo'ed Qatan	Mo'ed Qat.
Berakhot	Ber.	Nedarim	Ned.
Eduyyot	Ed.	Sanhedrin	Sanh.
Eruvin	Eruv.	Shabbat	Shabb.
Gittin	Git.	Sotah	Sotah
Hagigah	Hag.	Sukkah	Sukkah
Hullin	Hul.	Ta'anit	Ta'an.
Ketubbot	Ketub.	Yadayim	Yad.
Kiddushin	Kid.	Yevamot	Yevam.
Makkot	Mak.	Zevahim	Zevah.
Megillah	Meg.		

Reference Works

EJ — *Encyclopaedia Judaica*. 2nd ed., 22 vols. Edited by Fred Skolnik. Macmillan Reference USA, 2007, (cited in notes by volume, page). Available online: https://ia903008.us.archive.org/12/items/EncyclopediaJudaica_201905/Encyclopedia%20Judaica.pdf.

Sefaria.org — Library of classic Jewish texts, open access, subject to a creative commons license agreement (cited in notes to named text). Available online: sefaria.org.

SEP — *The Stanford Encyclopedia of Philosophy. Edited by Edward N. Zalta and Uri Nodelman*. Philosophy Department, Stanford University (cited in notes to specific entry). Available online: https://plato.stanford.edu/.

Introduction

ONE OF JUDAISM'S CENTRAL tenets is that God is perfect in all respects, including in the moral realm. This is illustrated by God's dialogue with Abraham, the prophet he selected to bring monotheism to the world. God, like a dramatist breaking the fourth wall, confides to his audience that, before obliterating the grotesquely wicked cities of Sodom, Gomorrah, and neighboring communities, he will explain himself: "Shall I hide from Abraham what I am about to do, since Abraham is to become a great and populous nation and all the nations of the earth are to bless themselves by him?"[1]

God then elaborates: "For I have singled him out, that he may instruct his children and his posterity to keep the way of the LORD by doing what is just and right, in order that the LORD may bring about for Abraham what he has promised him." In other words, God wants to reassure his prophet that the utter destruction he is about to rain down on these cities is warranted so that Abraham understands God's true nature and can convey it to the wider world.

It seems clear that the Almighty not only anticipates but welcomes his prophet's forthcoming challenge. And upon learning of God's intention, Abraham does, in fact, protest: "Will you sweep away the innocent along with the guilty . . . Shall not the Judge of all earth deal justly?"[2] God is not at all offended by Abraham's questioning. After patiently negotiating with him regarding the number of righteous people it would take for God to spare these five wicked cities for *their* sake, it turns out that there are none; only Abraham's nephew Lot and his immediate family, who are ultimately saved, not on their own merit but because of their relationship to Abraham.

---

1. Gen 18:17–19.
2. Gen 18:23–25.

Introduction

The Torah records that, before destroying these communities, God investigates whether they are beyond redemption and confirms that they are: "Then the LORD said, 'the outrage of Sodom and Gomorrah is so great, and their sin so grave, I will go down and see whether they have acted altogether according to the outcry that has reached Me; if not, I will take note.'"[3] Thus, God's harsh retribution on the residents of these five cities is vindicated.

It may well seem odd that an omniscient and omnipotent God needs to "go down and see" whether these communities are indeed as wicked as he has heard. Would he not just *know*? The answer seems to be that this is the first of many occasions where the author of a biblical or talmudic narrative has elected to "humanize" God in order to model virtuous conduct: in this instance, the necessity of making a thorough investigation for the purpose of obtaining reliable evidence before passing judgment.

God's commitment to what we regard today as the most exalted ethical standards is also on display in the command of Leviticus 19:18 that "you shall love your fellow as yourself." Notable in this regard is the conclusion of Rabbi Aharon Lichtenstein (1933–2015), indubitably one of the most respected Orthodox *halakhists* (experts on Jewish law) of his generation. He argues convincingly in his 1975 essay, "Does Judaism Recognize an Ethic Independent of Halakhah?" that—based on a comprehensive examination of rabbinic discourse and medieval commentaries—the ethical demands of Jewish law extend far beyond such obviously necessary prohibitions on physical violence, theft, and deceptions of various types to include positive mandates of common decency and benevolence of the sort Kant terms "imperfect duties." Such moral demands arise either under the letter of the law or its unmistakable spirit.[4] For the reasons adduced throughout this study, it is evident that R. Lichtenstein's conclusion is true, *in the abstract*.

However, in this same highly influential essay, R. Lichtenstein holds that all "natural morality" (moral principles that would be binding even in the absence of biblical commandments) is incorporated into the Torah's 613 mitzvot, so that there can be no possible conflict between the Torah's commands and our best moral judgment.[5] Accordingly, on R. Lichtenstein's account, God's genocidal decree against the Amalekites—including all their

---

3. Gen 18:20–21.
4. See Lichtenstein, "Does Judaism Recognize," 51–52.
5. See Lichtenstein, "Does Judaism Recognize," 37–38.

Introduction

descendants[6]—is morally permissible, a conclusion he forthrightly affirms in a subsequent essay:[7]

> I said to [a critic], "Wiping out Amalek does not conform to what we would normally expect a person to do. Normally, you should not be killing 'from child to suckling babe.' But I'm not saying, God forbid, that it is immoral in our case, where God has specifically commanded the destruction of Amalek—'A faithful God, without iniquity, righteous and upright is He' [quoting Deut 32:4]."

In addition to this repugnant command, the Pentateuch mandates capital punishment for a variety of victimless crimes such as Sabbath desecration, sexual immorality, witchcraft, idol worship, and so on. Moreover, it prescribes gender roles that now seem oppressive and unjust. These horrific commands, coupled with the failure of leading Orthodox rabbis to repudiate them as anachronistic holdovers from an ancient phase of Judaism, appears to be a primary reason for the common, firmly held view that authentic Judaism is deeply repressive and illiberal.[8]

Obviously, the blatantly unjust mandates just cited are inconsistent with liberal values, which, as discussed more fully below, insist on a strong presumption of liberty and preclude the application of force or coercion against innocent persons absent a compelling justification. Accordingly, if the thesis described in this work's title is to be vindicated, a way must be found to harmonize the exalted Jewish ethics identified by Rabbi Lichtenstein with the Torah's sometimes barbaric commands. In other words, it must be shown that the existence of the latter does not impugn the former.

Broadly speaking, there appear to be three strategies for resolving this challenge: (i) view these problematic texts as reflecting the oral traditions of morally primitive Bronze Age people that can now be dismissed in light of humanity's more advanced ethics; (ii) pretend that no conflict exists between our best secular ethics and these repellent laws because human beings are simply not equipped to second-guess God; and (iii) acknowledge

---

6. Exod 17:14–16; Deut 25:17–19; 1 Sam 15:1–9.
7. Lichtenstein, "Being Frum."
8. Additionally, because the ultra-Orthodox follow age-old Jewish traditions and rigorously study and adhere to *halakhah* (Jewish law), this often leads to the erroneous belief that the repressive, rigidly hierarchical norms and social institutions that characterize their communities represent the "real" face of Judaism. See the discussion in chapter 7, note 164, below.

the immoral nature of these commands yet argue that they nevertheless are compatible with God's perfection.

The first option does not, unfortunately, seem to provide a benign explanation for the existence of the "distasteful" elements of the Torah that readers may now wish to ignore. Couldn't the Almighty have "skipped ahead" and provided an ethics that would have advanced humankind to a more civilized social order? The apparent absence of a satisfying answer calls into question the traditional conception of God as a perfect being, and thus threatens to strip Judaism of the transcendence that inspires awe, reverence, worship, and ritual observance: what Rudolph Otto (1869–1937) famously described as religion's "numinous" character.[9]

The second alternative is, as argued below, inconsistent with the Torah's axiomatic stance that human beings are created by God as moral agents; that is, with the capacity—in contrast to all other known animals—to grasp the moral law and act accordingly. In fact, abundant Scriptural evidence shows that, when God declares that he will make humankind "in His image,"[10] he is referencing our moral autonomy. Thus, a refusal to admit to, for example, the gross immorality of the command to exterminate the Amalekites is not only indefensible as a matter of moral reasoning but is also contrary to the Torah's own values.

This study defends the third approach, using the evidence found in the Tanakh, as these texts have been expounded in the Talmud and Midrashim and by many of Judaism's leading commentators through the generations. It argues that, notwithstanding the blatant immorality of many of the Pentateuch's commandments, Judaism's sacred literature is infused with liberal values. The central idea is that, accepting "Sinai" as metaphor, what God gave the Jewish people there was not the ultimate moral truth but the best and surest means of getting to it.

Rabbi Nathan Cardozo, a leading Modern Orthodox philosopher, articulates something close to this idea when, after acknowledging the litany of immoral commandments, he says:[11]

> Just as in the creation chapter (Gen 1), God provides the main ingredients and then asks humanity to fashion the world and

---

9. Otto, *The Idea of the Holy*, 5–7. See also Wynn, "Phenomenology of Religion" and Rowe, *Philosophy of Religion*, chapter 5.

10. Gen 1:27.

11. Cardozo, "The Deliberately Flawed," section 5 ("Sages' Responsibility to 'Update' the Text") (endnote omitted).

improve it, the Torah is presented as the main ingredient that the Sages must engage with and improve. The text was meant as a point of departure, not as an arrival, and the Sages are the ones required to adapt the text.

It is likely that the arguments presented here are simply incompatible with a literal reading of the Five Books of Moses. However, most Jews do not take the Pentateuch to be an accurate historical record of the triumphs and travails of their ancient ancestors and do not consult it for this purpose. Rather, they honor and study these texts to understand the fundamental tenets of their faith; the terms of the covenant between God and the Jewish people; and for the profound ethical lessons imparted.[12] Further, a figurative and metaphorical interpretation of the Torah need not weaken the faith that it accurately expresses God's will. Accordingly, it is worthwhile to examine what it gained and lost by the radically more naturalistic reading of these texts set forth in chapter 1.

To proceed further with the defense of Judaism's essential liberalism, it is necessary to flesh out the meaning of this term, which is grounded in two fundamental moral principles: (i) Kantian respect for persons as moral agents, which places severe constraints on how people may be treated; and (ii) pluralism, meaning the tolerance of a wide variety of new ideas and ways of living. The firm commitment of rabbinic Judaism to the former is discussed in chapter 2, while chapter 3 examines the Rabbis' dedication to pluralism from the perspective of Karl Popper's critical rationalism.[13]

---

12. It seems clear that the Rabbis themselves had no interest in "history" in anything approaching the modern sense but rather, as Prof. Yosef Yerushalmi (1932–2009) puts it, they felt called to an "ongoing exploration of the meaning of the [biblical] history bequeathed to them, striving to interpret it in living terms for their own and later generations." Yerushalmi, *Zakhor*, 18 and see generally chapter 1.

13. Prof. Menachem Fisch, a Talmudist and distinguished philosopher of science, appears to have been the first to draw parallels between Popper's epistemology and the discursive methods of the Rabbis. See Fisch, *Rational Rabbis*. Fisch enlists Popper's writings to formulate a standard of "rationalism" as a heuristic for clarifying and elucidating many of the debates and discussions recorded in the Gemara, specifically the Rabbis' surreptitious defense of what he terms "anti-traditionalism"; that is, the idea that long-established dogmas should be examined "with a view not to following them indiscriminately, so much as to seriously putting them to the test." See Fisch, *Rational Rabbis*, 43. In contrast, this monograph employs Popper's critical rationalism, in conjunction with Kantian respect for moral autonomy, to construct a robust understanding of "liberalism" that is used as a heuristic for understanding and evaluating the full range of Judaism's classical sources. It is fair to say that Fisch's and this book's respective debts to Popper lead them in substantially different, although not opposite, directions.

Introduction

By drawing on Scriptural depictions (and rabbinic interpretations) of encounters between the Almighty and biblical personalities, these chapters describe the sort of ethical progress that can be expected when the parties proceed with mutual respect and epistemological humility.

Clearly, various biblical texts seem in conflict with the sort of dialectical interpretation being proposed here. These include Deuteronomy 4:2 and 17:11. The former mandates that "[y]ou shall not add anything to what I command you or take anything away from it, but keep the commandments of the LORD your God,"[14] while the latter enjoins the Israelites to "act in accordance with the instructions given you . . . you must not deviate from the verdict . . . either to the right or the left. Should a man act presumptively and disregard the priest . . . or the magistrate, that man shall die."[15] Tradition holds that these pronouncements and others mean that the Torah's 613 commandments are flawless, eternal, and immutable, like the basic axioms of logic and mathematics that have always been and will always be true.[16]

This idea does much to explain the deeply conservative ethos of Orthodox Judaism that threatens to elevate dogma at the expense of ethical progress. Chapter 4 critiques two important doctrines that are cited in its favor: first, that, together with the commandments and laws found in the text of the Pentateuch, God conveyed to Moses at Sinai definitive answers to all questions that may arise in the application of the Torah's written laws (the "Oral Law from Sinai"); and second, that each generation following the one that personally experienced the miraculous Sinaitic revelation is, by virtue of this distance, less spiritually committed and wise (the "Decline of the Generations"). These doctrines tend to insulate the halakhic decisions of the earliest Sages from the sort of constructive criticism that generates steady advancement in all intellectual endeavors.

This study argues that both precepts conflict with the highly abstract and universal values enunciated in the Ten Commandments, which delineate the basic principles that undergird any civilized society and the essential elements of the covenant between God and the Jewish people. That these laws are set forth in highly general terms, without specifying the details of compliance or corresponding punishments for violation, signifies their open-ended character. This structure strongly suggests that they were

---

14. Deut 4:2.
15. Deut 17:11–12.
16. See Wurzburger, "Orthodoxy," 15:494.

Introduction

designed to leave space for the Jewish people's understanding of them to evolve over time alongside their ethical consciousness.

Further, an examination of Jewish history reveals that both conservative canons are relatively recent additions that only became widely accepted in the Amoraic era (Oral Law from Sinai) or in the Geonic era (Decline of the Generations), well over a millennium after the Torah was given, according to Orthodoxy's own timeline. Moreover, as outlined in the balance of this study, this spirit of stasis is at odds with the liberalism evident in Scriptural texts and their rabbinic interpretations. Therefore, it seems clear that these doctrines are not inherent in Jewish theology but were grafted on in response to threatening external developments; specifically, the perceived existential threats posed by Christianity, the Karaite heresy, and Islam.

Chapter 5 traces the development of Jewish law and ethics from the Mishnah through the closing of the Babylonian Talmud, and then analyzes the effect of its codification, first by Maimonides in the *Mishneh Torah* and then by Joseph Karo in the *Shulchan Aruch*. This review reveals the Rabbis' firm commitment to the virtue of controversy, respect for minority opinions, pluralism, and tolerance, shown by their history of modifying halakhah in response to new social conditions. This spirit of innovation was constrained during the Geonic era and thereafter by the existential threats mentioned above, and by the transition from an essentially common law system of jurisprudence to a statutory one.

Chapter 6 maintains that the Tanakh, in its diverse genres and perspectives, exhibits precisely the sort of ideological tension that would be expected from Judaism's embrace of critical rationalism. Thus, the Pentateuch evidences an evolution of legal norms between the law code given to the just-liberated Israelites in Exodus and the more humanistic version proclaimed by Moses in Deuteronomy after their forty years in the Wilderness. Further, a distinct contrast is apparent in this text between its generally patriarchal worldview and the frequent depiction of the matriarchs and other heroines as fully formed, active participants in shaping key events in Jewish history.

Also evident is a pronounced conflict between the Pentateuch and the prophetic books regarding the relative importance of ritual observance and ethics. Finally, an analysis of the wild cacophony of discordant voices heard in the *Ketuvim* (Writings) reveals their subversive effect on incumbent doctrines, with special attention paid to the books of Jonah[17] and Job.

17. For seemingly arbitrary reasons, Jonah is included in Prophets as one of the

Introduction

Chapter 7 directly addresses the repellant and problematic Torah mitzvot identified earlier and argues that the none of the solutions offered by leading rabbis and scholars are satisfactory. It is posited that this is the result of the failure to recognize that these commandments were unavoidable, given the Israelites' existing ethics and the supreme value God accords moral autonomy. An interpretation of Scripture grounded in respect for autonomy and critical rationalism is proposed as a superior means of resolving this difficulty.

Chapter 8 concludes this work with a presentation and analysis of the famous talmudic saga of the "Oven of Akhnai," which is not only a brilliant literary creation but also serves as a fitting illustration and summary of the Torah's liberal values as seen through the Rabbis' eyes. By showing that these attitudes and norms are also "from Sinai" and have been transmitted faithfully from generation to generation down to the present moment, Judaism's authority and majesty are preserved. In short, it is possible to humanize the Torah without emasculating it.

"minor prophets." See discussion below in chapter 6, footnote 4.

1

A Theological Framework

FOR AT LEAST THREE reasons, it is advisable at this point to outline the theological assumptions that govern this study. First, because the arguments presented are based on these ideas, it is only fair to identify them and acknowledge that their wholesale rejection will likely invalidate the resulting conclusions. Moreover, if the reader finds it impossible to accept, even for the purpose of argument, one or more of the basic premises set forth here, then they need not waste any further time. Finally, readers may not have had occasion to deeply consider some of the issues touched on in this chapter and thus may find this discussion useful in formulating their own thoughts.

The Torah as Literature, Not History

For many Jews, their religious commitment is independent of any belief in the Torah's historical accuracy. In fact, it seems probable that for those with a decent secular education, a dogmatic insistence on viewing the Pentateuch as a factual, divinely authored account of ancient Judaism would constitute an unfortunate distraction that interferes with their appreciation of its true meaning.

Historians of the ancient Near East are satisfied that they have sufficient evidence to establish the existence and exploits of many of the region's great kings of the late Bronze Age.[1] However, despite centuries of archaeological, epigraphical, and historical research, there is no material, extra-biblical evidence for the existence of any of the Pentateuch's main characters: Abraham, husband of Sarah, father of Isaac, who left the land of Ur at God's command to spread monotheism; Moses, son of Amram and Jochebed, desperately cast into the Nile and raised in Pharoah's palace; Jacob, father of the brothers and half-brothers who would head the twelve tribes; etc. Nor is there credible evidence of any of the major events described: God leading his people out of bondage in Egypt with "a strong arm" and "with signs and wonders"; the revelation at Sinai; the Israelites wandering for forty years in the Wilderness; and so on.

Accordingly, this study takes it as a given that the Pentateuch was neither written nor intended as a work of history in anything resembling the modern sense, so this text will not devote any further effort to debunking this idea. Most secular scholars regard the first eleven chapters of Genesis as entirely mythic.[2] Regarding the other Pentateuchal narratives, as Professor Robert Alter observes, "prose fiction is the best general rubric for describing biblical narrative."[3]

There is no apparent reason why the Torah's ahistoricity should rob it in the slightest degree of its value as a guide for living an ethically conscious, spiritual, and fulfilling life.[4] This is certainly not a novel observation. As Professor Jon Levenson, an outstanding Bible scholar, puts it: "Can it not be the case that the literary form of the Torah conveys a truth which is not historical in nature? Is not fiction a valid mode of knowledge?"[5] To this point, Alter and other leading practitioners of "the Bible as literature"

---

1. See Abo-Eleaz, "Did Kings Meet?"

2. See Davies, "Introduction to the Pentateuch," 33. In this text, Davies distinguishes between narratives of "pure imagination" (myths) and those "constrained by a particular historical situation" (legends and folklore).

3. Alter, *The Art of Biblical Narrative*, 27.

4. It is worth noting at this point that the discipline of history, however carefully and scrupulously it may be practiced, is incapable of producing a unique, objectively true, and complete account of any complex event. There are simply too many apparently insoluble conceptual obstacles standing in the way—the nature of historical causation; the value-laden nature of historical evidence; and the ontology of historical events (was the French Revolution a "thing" or simply a name we apply to describe countless discrete human actions?)—to permit anything like an objectively "best" explanation of, say, the causes of the American Revolution. See Little, "Philosophy of History," §3.

5. Levenson, *Sinai and Zion*, 8.

school have demonstrated the technical sophistication and deep insights conveyed by Judaism's sacred texts.

Indeed, it is intriguing that the collection of canonical texts traditionally known as the Former Prophets (the books of Joshua, Judges, Samuel, and Kings) are qualitatively more conventionally historical than the Pentateuch. These books present a theologically driven story regarding the Jewish people, from Moses' death to the Babylonian exile. Broadly, these texts attempt to reconcile and justify the social reality of their day with God's promises and demands from hundreds of years before.

These texts are commonly referred to collectively as the "Deuteronomistic history" because many scholars believe that they consistently reflect and echo certain themes earlier sounded in Deuteronomy, including the harsh and unforgiving condemnation of the worship of "other gods"; the necessity of centralizing all collective religious practice exclusively at the Temple in Jerusalem; and the recognition of the Davidic dynasty as the only legitimate temporal rulers and as the ultimate source of the final messianic redemption.[6] The Deuteronomistic history describes both people and events that are known to be real, albeit not generally portrayed in an objective or accurate way.[7] Yet, despite its greater verisimilitude, for the observant, this corpus has nothing like the holiness and authority of the Pentateuch.

As mentioned above, it is evident that the insistence by some on a literal reading of the Torah distracts us from God's message, and to illustrate this point, consider the creation narrative set forth in Genesis. Here, the Torah says that the world and everything in it were created in six days, and on the seventh day, "God finished the work that He had been doing, and He ceased . . . And God blessed the seventh day and declared it holy."[8] According to Chazal,[9] the Almighty did this—as of this writing—5,784 years ago.

However, if this is true, God must be, at best, some sort of strange prankster, intentionally warping or distorting the empirical evidence (or our

---

6. See Gottwald, "Book of Samuel," 17:759–63; and Brettler, *How to Read the Jewish Bible*, 99–102.

7. For a useful summary of what archaeologists believe they have confirmed regarding biblical personalities, see Mykytiuk, "53 People." Since the publication of this survey, plausible evidence has been unearthed that seems to establish the historicity of the eighth-century BCE prophet Isaiah. See Mazar, "The Prophet Isaiah."

8. Gen 2:2–3.

9. An acronym derived from the Hebrew *chachamim zichronam levracham*, literally "rabbis of blessed memory." Typically used to refer to the sages and rabbis of the talmudic era.

understanding of it) to deceive the world's leading scientists, who estimate the age of the universe at roughly 13.8 billion years. As will be seen, the Torah depicts humankind as curious, truth-seeking beings, so there is no reason to believe that the Almighty wished to subvert the scientific enterprise by deceiving humanity regarding the true age of the world. The biblical version may have seemed plausible 500 years ago, but today it invites mockery, thus diverting readers from the Torah's spiritual and ethical values.

Accordingly, Genesis's narrative of six days of creation followed by a seventh day of rest is not, in this interpretation, intended as cosmology. Instead, it is meant to instill in Jews such essential values as the imperative to emulate God to the best of one's finite ability; the importance of periodically engaging in sincere reflection about conduct toward loved ones and the larger community; the sanctity of human life even above the sanctity of the Sabbath,[10] as well as more esoteric insights. One example of the latter is Rabbi Abraham Joshua Heschel's (1907–1972), the famous Orthodox-trained rabbi, exegete, and civil rights icon, view that the Sabbath represents and proclaims the superiority of the realm of time (spirit) over the realm of space (material objects).[11]

It is also the case that adopting an interpretative approach that regards the narrative portions of Pentateuch as moral philosophy in the guise of literature frees the reader from the futile effort to reconcile the text's literal meaning with its radically open-ended hermeneutics.[12] By way of example, if Abraham and Isaac are understood as literary characters employed allegorically, the reader need not accept that God actually demands the sacrifice described in the *Akedah* (the "binding of Isaac," see Genesis, ch. 22). Accordingly, they may proceed to more abstract and penetrating readings, such as the one proposed by Professor Israel Knohl, a highly respected

---

10. See b. Yoma 84b.

11. See Heschel, *The Sabbath*, 79.

12. The extent to which Chazal holds that allegorical, symbolical, metaphorical, and other figurative readings of Biblical texts are *constrained* by their literal or plain meaning is a very complicated question that is not going to be sorted out here. However, it may be said that, while Tradition gives free reign to non-literal heuristics, such that each verse is said to be subject to 70 different interpretations, the general understanding is that none of these interpretations are mutually exclusive. See Altman, "Bible, Allegorical Interpretations," 3:643–45. Yet, as a literary device, deliberate contradictions in the narrative are often the key to unlocking its meaning.

scholar of the Hebrew Bible, who opines that this story is intended to resolve a fundamental conflict in Judaism's conception of God:[13]

> In this story, the rational and ethical dimensions of God, symbolized by the name "YHWH," overrule the numinous dimensions, symbolized by the name "Elohim."... the child intended for the sacrifice is replaced by the ram, and understanding the import of the story more broadly, the practice of child sacrifice can by replaced in Israel by animal sacrifice. The *Akedah* story can thus be seen as an allegory of this momentous change in the religion of Israel.

In the words of Howard Wettstein, one of Judaism's leading philosophers, "The Bible's theological concepts and implicit beliefs remain *uncrystallized*. They are formulated by way of literary tropes . . . poetically infused, not propositionally articulated."[14]

Faith and Evidence

Most people like to think that their beliefs are generally rational; that is, adequately supported by evidence and logic. A random stroll through the world of social media conclusively falsifies any such conceit. There is a school of thought that seems to have been founded by W.K. Clifford in his 1876 essay that holds that such false confidence is culpable: "it is wrong always, everywhere, and for anyone, to believe anything upon insufficient evidence."[15]

His reasoning is that, while such unfounded personal beliefs may in and of themselves be harmless, an ingrained habit of uncritical thinking is dangerous:[16]

> But I cannot help doing this great wrong towards Man, that I make myself credulous. The danger to society is not merely that it should believe wrong things, though that is great enough; but that it should become credulous, and lose the habit of testing things and inquiring into them; for then it must sink back into savagery.

And, since one sloppy thought can lead to others, even the most apparently harmless mental lapses become a sort of thought crime:[17]

13. Knohl, *The Divine Symphony*, 107–8.
14. Wettstein, "Against Theology," 226.
15. Clifford, "The Ethics of Belief," 295.
16. Clifford, "The Ethics of Belief," 294.
17. Clifford, "The Ethics of Belief," 292.

> No real belief, however trifling and fragmentary it may seem, is ever truly insignificant; it prepares us to receive more of its like . . . and so gradually it lays a stealthy train in our innermost thought, which may some day explode into overt action, and leave its stamp upon our character for ever.[18]

Critics of theism often cite Clifford's argument against it, asserting that, since there is no evidence for God's existence, rational persons should, at the minimum, be agnostic. For the reasons presented below, Clifford's thesis is unconvincing.[19] First, notice that Clifford is not just finding fault for harboring *false* beliefs, but also for those not supported by at least a preponderance of the evidence. Notice further that he is making an extraordinarily strong claim, and that such claims require extraordinarily strong evidence.

However, his only "evidence" consists of two hypothetical examples where careless or motivated thinking could have foreseeably produced tragic results for other innocent people. Obviously, a more rigorous epistemic standard may be demanded in such cases, while mistakes that present no risk of harm should be judged more leniently. While it is theoretically possible that an agent's acceptance of one or more unfounded beliefs might make them "credulous" in general, there is no empirical basis for concluding that this is anything resembling a universal rule of human psychology.

Moreover, it may be the case there are unsupported beliefs whose *positive* effects on the agent and society at large outweigh Clifford's postulated harm. If there were a belief—about which we should, according to his theory, be strictly agnostic—that would dramatically decrease the level of violence and aggression in the world, why would we not eagerly embrace it? Since Clifford is not entitled to assume that evidence-supported belief is an absolute value trumping all others, this objection appears very powerful. As argued in the remainder of this study, because Judaism, properly

---

18. It appears that a follower of Clifford would be required to fault Anne Frank for harboring the following dubious belief: "It's really a wonder that I haven't dropped all my ideals because they seem so absurd and impossible to carry out. Yet, I keep them, because in spite of everything I still believe that people are really good at heart. I simply can't build up my hopes on a foundation consisting of confusion, misery, and death." Frank, *Diary*, 220. The reader may decide for themselves whether Clifford's stance is morally defensible.

19. The arguments against Clifford's proposal advanced in this section are largely anticipated by the famous American "pragmatist" philosopher William James (1842–1910) in his 1896 essay, "The Will to Believe." They are reformulated here in the interests of concision and, it is hoped, clarity. See also Bishop and McKaughan, "Faith," §§6–9.

understood, is both a belief system that can neither be proven nor falsified and one that promotes liberal, benign values, no culpability is attached to accepting its principles as true.

Finally, adherence to Clifford's rule will not lead society closer to the truth but away from it, which seems to be a rather paradoxical and undesirable result. As quoted above, the point of his rule is that people should not "lose the habit of testing things and inquiring into them." However, this rationale ignores Popper's principle of human fallibility (discussed in chapter 3), which holds that most of our current beliefs in both the realm of science and other domains are almost certainly false and destined to be replaced by better theories that are not themselves true but are merely closer to the truth. What were once regarded as "crazy" ideas often supplant conventional wisdom. Accordingly, agents can never know what constitutes "sufficient evidence," and if public attitudes discourage researchers from pursuing radical theories, much progress will be hindered or lost.

If this dismissal of Clifford's argument is correct, and if it is right that, as asserted below, the proper philosophical stance regarding God's existence is agnosticism, and that the practice of authentic Judaism will produce virtuous behavior, then people are not to be faulted for believing that God exists. However, what if one does not believe this in the propositional sense (the sort of belief that is true or false) but simply has faith that God exists; that is, has a "belief in" God. Can one have faith without belief? It appears the answer is "yes."

In contrast to a "belief that," a "belief in" something can express a *commitment* rather than a factual claim. Precisely because a "belief in" something is fundamentally distinct from a "belief that," it can peacefully coexist with doubt. Just as one would expect a person who says that they "believe in" justice to act accordingly, it is sincere behavior consistent with faith—prayer, ritual observance, acts of loving-kindness, etc.—that makes it possible to truly say of a person that they "believe in" God or are a person of faith without their necessarily believing "that" he exists. As two prominent religious philosophers express it:[20]

> The "venture" models of faith [roughly, a "leap of faith"] (with or without belief) and the model of faith as a venture in hope all fit the view that faith is consistent with doubt, and, indeed, impossible without doubt of some kind, though they allow that persons who have faith may give firm and sustained commitment to the

20. Bishop and McKaughan, "Faith," §9.

truth of faith-propositions in practice ... The "certainty" of faith on these models is more a matter of the certainty that persons of faith find themselves *conferring* on the foundational claims of their faith, rather than a matter of discovering in themselves a certain knowledge or intellectual conviction of the truth of these claims.

However, it is clearly possible to "believe in" obviously irrational things, such as contrived deities like the Flying Spaghetti Monster. So, it seems that for those who hold themselves accountable in the court of reason, the issue comes down to whether belief in Judaism's God is implausible in this sense. It is important to understand when approaching this question that conjectures favoring theism or atheism are metaphysical, not scientific theories, and are therefore not testable empirically by the procedures used in the natural sciences. This does not imply that, for critical rationalists, they are pointless, nor that all are equally plausible.[21] Furthermore, there can be no persuasive *philosophical* arguments in favor of or against God's existence because, as the influential philosopher Leo Strauss (1899–1973) argues, if God does exist, he is not the sort of "being" (if that is even the right term) whose nature will be comprehensible to us, nor about which one can necessarily speak without introducing contradictions.[22]

Nevertheless, since at least the Middle Ages, Jewish, Christian, and Islamic philosophers have formulated "proofs" of God's existence based on the implications of what it means for a being to be "necessary" or "perfect." Enlightenment philosophers responded with counterarguments debunking these supposed proofs, and the consensus of academic philosophers is that the skeptics are right. More recently, atheists have essayed arguments against the existence of God based on comparisons between the actual world and their speculations regarding what a divinely created world *should* resemble. It would take the reader too far afield to say much more than this: that all the arguments reviewed for this book either supporting or denying God's existence seem to be flimsy at best.[23] Accordingly, sincere faith need not be motivated by the dictates of logic or evidence but may be a personal choice or preference.

Although certainly not "proofs," there are several considerations that make faith in the God of Judaism far more plausible than faith in the likes

21. See Gattei, *Karl Popper's Philosophy*, chapter 3.
22. See Strauss, "Interpretation of Genesis," 6–7.
23. For those interested in greater detail regarding such controversies, see Rowe, *Philosophy of Religion*, chapters 2–4 and 7).

of the Flying Spaghetti Monster. For one thing, a deep dive into the Hebrew Bible might convince even a skeptic that a corpus of such astonishing depth, subtlety, profundity, and grandeur is not entirely the product of human minds. Thus, a believer may simply invoke the legal doctrine *res ipsa loquitur* and suggest that people carefully study the Tanakh and the related rabbinical literature, and decide for themselves.

It is also rather remarkable that Jewish Scripture, given to a politically insignificant, rather obscure people, has had an impact on Western civilization that is impossible to overstate. This is evident in the influence exerted on the other two Abrahamic faiths—especially Christianity, which adopted and incorporated the entire Jewish canon as a part of its own. Through Christianity, Judaism's fundamental commitment to human dignity and autonomy radiated outward into the larger world.[24]

Examples of this effect would include, in the realm of philosophy and theology, that a university library could be stuffed to the rafters with just the books and papers devoted to the exegesis of the book of Job, only one of the twenty-four canonical texts.[25] In art and culture, museums around the world are chock full of paintings and sculptures depicting biblical personalities and stories that encapsulate essential aspects of our common humanity. In literature, one scholar observes: "What is beyond amazing is that is that a several-thousand-year-old-story [the Exodus], which posits future readers . . . should turn out to be the most widely and continuously read story in all history."[26]

Moreover, viewed without any metaphysical preconceptions, the history of the Jews might well seem miraculous. This people have never been more than a small minority, often hated, despised, and murderously persecuted both in *Eretz Israel* (the "Land of Israel") and the diaspora; yet, while countless other nations, ethnicities, and religions have entered and then exited the stage of history, the Jews—against all odds—remain. Not only have they survived, but also have returned to and rebuilt their ancestral homeland; continue their religious traditions; govern themselves in an independent state with Jerusalem as its capital; and have revived their ancient

---

24. See Vermes, *Jesus the Jew*, 26–29, 223–25; Wigoder, "Christianity," 4:686–93; and Fitch, "Common Ethic."

25. See, e.g., Batnitzky and Pardes, *The Book of Job*.

26. Segal, "God's Project," 176–77.

language, once dead outside of Torah study and the liturgy. At a minimum, this is unprecedented in human history.[27]

Finally, Judaism, to greatly understate the matter, is a complicated religion. The analysis by the Sages and Rabbis of the biblical commandments produced the encyclopedia-length Talmud and other rabbinic literature, followed by legal codes, innumerable halakhic commentaries, and rulings from medieval times until today.

There is an equally rich and extensive collection of aggadah and related discourse that articulate the values and philosophical background that shape the law. It may be a mere coincidence that God happened to select as his emissary a people whose future contributions in science, law, mathematics, medicine, literature, music, chess, and other intellectual arenas is wildly disproportionate to their numbers; but then again, it may not.

It seems unlikely that human beings are equipped to comprehend or understand God in any deep way. If the God depicted in Jewish Scripture exists, he is certainly as far beyond people's knowledge as a person is beyond a cat's. However, it is basic to Jewish theology that, as the Talmud holds, "the Torah spoke in the language of people [often translated "men"]."[28] In other words, the Bible reveals to readers all they need to know—what the Almighty wants them to know—as people of faith.

Modern Biblical Scholarship

At this point, a few (admittedly abbreviated) words regarding what modern biblical scholarship has to say regarding the composition of the Pentateuch are in order, since these findings are often used to question its divine origin. The now-eroding scholarly consensus, known as the "documentary hypothesis," is that it is comprised of four distinct, identifiable sources that were

---

27. Mark Twain seems to have noticed:
   The Egyptian, the Babylonian, and the Persian rose, filled the planet with sound and splendor, then faded to dream-stuff and passed away; the Greek and the Roman followed, and made a vast noise, and they are gone; other peoples have sprung up and held their torch high for a time, but it burned out, and they sit in twilight now, or have vanished. The Jew saw them all, beat them all, and is now what he always was, exhibiting no decadence, no infirmities of age, no weakening of his parts, no slowing of his energies, no dulling of his alert and aggressive mind. All things are mortal but the Jew; all other forces pass, but he remains. What is the secret of his immortality?

   Twain, "Concerning the Jews," point no. 6.

28. b. Zevah. 108b.

edited or redacted into the received text.[29] These strands consist of the "J" source (thought to be the oldest, based on its frequent use of the ineffable "YHWH" name for God); the "E" source (for "Elohim," a second name for God, associated with certain divine attributes); the "D" (Deuteronomist) source; and the "P" (priestly) source, which is generally thought to be the most recent one. Proponents of this theory also hold that each of these sources express what seems to be a distinct theological viewpoint that, in conjunction with other characteristics, makes it possible to identify their influence in most Pentateuchal passages.

Support for the documentary hypothesis has waned in recent decades because, among other reasons, its basic premise has been undermined by the intense and increasing dissensus regarding the exact number of original sources and the assignment of various textual passages to them.[30] This has brought renewed interest in two rival theories: that the Five Books were built up chronologically from various separate layers (the "supplementary hypothesis") or that they were assembled and stitched together from a multitude of fragmentary oral traditions (the "fragmentary hypothesis") until each book, then the Pentateuch as a whole, reached its final form.[31] However it was composed, most secular scholars date the final redaction of the Pentateuch to the late sixth or early fifth century BCE.

For those who regard the Pentateuch as divinely inspired but not dictated to Moses at Sinai, the documentary hypothesis presents little threat. This was the "daring" idea famously propounded by Rabbi Louis Jacobs (1920–2006) in the middle of the last century:[32]

---

29. The non-Pentateuchal canonical books, which often equal the Five Books in their literary quality, each have their own unique and complicated compositional history, much of which is unknown and highly controversial, and so apart from the commentary in chapter 6 on specific texts, no more will be said on this subject.

30. See Davies, "Introduction to the Pentateuch," 42–52 and Blenkinsopp, "Documentary Hypothesis in Trouble."

31. Some insight into the complexities of the scholarly debate about the merits of the main competing theories regarding the Torah's composition may be found in Davies, "Introduction to the Pentateuch," 18–34, 42–52; Schwartz, "Scholarship's Critique," 3–16; and Berman, *Inconsistency in the Torah*, 236–68.

32. Jacobs, *Reason to Believe*, 81. Jacobs was educated and ordained as an Orthodox rabbi and held the pulpit of a large, prestigious London synagogue until he lost his position because of statements such as the one just quoted. He is generally regarded as the primary inspiration for the English Masorti branch of Judaism, roughly equivalent to the Conservative movement in the U.S.

> The new knowledge [of biblical criticism] need not in any way affect our reverence for the Bible and our loyalty to its teachings. God's power is not lessened because He preferred to co-operate with His creatures in producing the Book of Books . . . We hear the authentic voice of God speaking to us through the pages of the Bible . . . and its truth is in no way affected in that we can only hear that voice through the medium of human beings.

However, for large numbers of traditional Jews, the documentary hypothesis poses a severe challenge to their theology both because (i) it is inconsistent with the faith's age-old commitment to God's single, verbatim revelation of the Torah to Moses at Mt. Sinai; and (ii) it purports to offer a coherent, overarching explanation for the existence of many of the contradictions and inconsistencies found in the Torah, both glaring and relatively inconspicuous.[33] Moreover, it can frequently suggest a credible ideological basis for these conflicts.

There is, in fact, a startling narrative inconsistency in the very first two chapters of Genesis that seems to offer distinctly different accounts of creation. In chapter 1, the Almighty forms the world and all that lives in it over the course of six days, starting with "Let there be light."[34] After the table has been set on the previous five days with all "lower" life forms, on the sixth day, "God created man in His image, in the image of God He created him; male and female he created them."[35] Although the exact details of the Almighty's handiwork remain obscure, it seems clear that man and woman were "born" together as part of the same generative act; and that the Almighty's work was completed in six days.

Although chapter 2 of Genesis includes elements that might be read as a continuation of the narrative of the prior chapter, it also includes strikingly discordant material that strongly suggests an alternative creation story. Thus, it begins with the report that "On the seventh day God finished the work that He had been doing and He ceased on the seventh day from all the work He had done."[36] It goes on to describe that no shrubs and grasses had yet sprouted, as "there was no man to till the soil . . . [but] a flow would well up from the ground and water the whole surface of the earth."[37] Apparently

---

33. See Bazak, "Replications," for a list of eighteen well-known examples.
34. Gen 1:3.
35. Gen 1:27.
36. Gen 2:2.
37. Gen 2:5–6.

to fill this void, "the LORD God formed man from the dust of the earth. He blew into his nostrils the breath of life, and man became a living being."[38]

God then plants "a garden in Eden" and places man there "to till and tend it," commanding him not to eat from "the tree of knowledge of good and bad," lest he die. The Master of the Universe then observes that "[i]t is not good for man to be alone; I will make a fitting helper for him."[39] Accordingly, after creating "all the wild beasts and all the birds of the sky" and allowing the man (*Adam* in Hebrew) to name them,[40] God "took one of his ribs . . . And the LORD God fashioned the rib that He took from the man into a woman," later named *Chavah* (in English, "Eve") by Adam.[41] Thus, chapter 2 varies significantly from chapter 1 in the sequence of God's creation (whether the shrubs and grasses and wild beasts and birds preceded man); whether Adam and Eve were created together or Eve was subsequently taken from Adam's rib; and whether creation continued past the sixth day, including the creation of Adam.[42]

Less consequential discrepancies in Genesis include the Torah's account of the timing and circumstances of God's commandment to Abraham in Genesis 12:1 to "go forth [*lech lecha*] from your native land and from your father's house" to serve God.[43] Since Abraham's native land and father's house is in Ur Kasdim, this implies that he was still there when he received this order. However, the preceding *parshat*[44] (Torah portion) indicates that, at the time of this command, Abraham had already traveled with his father to the land of Charan. A second example of a "minor" conflict is the apparently incompatible reports that Joseph was sold into Egyptian slavery by both the Midianites[45] *and* the Ishmaelites.[46]

Of course, the Rabbis noticed and discussed these inconsistencies but struggled to resolve them without abandoning the plain meaning of the Torah's text by, for example, assuming important new facts not found there

38. Gen 2:7.
39. Gen 2:18.
40. Gen 2:19.
41. Gen 2:21–22.
42. Although it will not be discussed at this point, a second major, obvious case of inconsistent Pentateuchal narratives is presented by the versions of the Sinaitic revelation in Exodus and Deuteronomy. (see chapter 4),
43. Gen 12:1.
44. Gen 11:31–32.
45. Gen 37:36.
46. Gen 39:1.

or by reading the text in a forced and unnatural way.⁴⁷ For example, the rabbinic explanation of the distinct accounts in the first two chapters of Genesis is that, in the words of the late Chief Rabbi Sacks: "originally God created the world under the attribute of justice but then He saw that the world cannot survive on justice alone and, therefore, God had to create it all over again, joining to justice His attribute of mercy. Hence the two creations."⁴⁸ Not only does this rely on extra-biblical sources, but the suggestion that God erred initially sits in great tension with the traditional notion of God's perfection.

With respect, specifically, to the different accounts of Adam and Eve's creation found in the first two chapters of Genesis, the Gemara quotes Rabbi Abbahu: "At first, the thought entered God's mind to create two, and ultimately, only one was actually created."⁴⁹ Again, this appears to be a rather makeshift solution. Regarding the circumstances of God's order to Abraham to "go forth," the Rabbis artificially construe "*lech lecha*," contrary to its literal meaning ("go forth"), as "distance yourself even further" (from your father's house) in order to harmonize this command with Abraham receiving it in Charan.⁵⁰

There is nothing amiss with the Rabbis offering creative interpretations of Torah verses. Indeed, as mentioned above, Tradition holds that they are so rich in meaning that there are seventy legitimate interpretations of every verse. However, these are supposed to enhance and vivify the text's plain meaning, not erase it. As Rav Bazak writes in his illuminating discussion of these rabbinic tactics, "in many instances the solutions are less than satisfactory, since . . . one who seeks to understand the literal meaning of the text has trouble reconciling the various explanations with the plain meaning."⁵¹

Apparently, the problematic nature of such "solutions" under the traditional paradigm led Mordechai Breuer (1921–2007), a very prominent Orthodox rabbi and scholar, to propose a *frum* (religious) variant of the documentary hypothesis: "The traditional belief, which we advocate, holds that the Torah is directly authored by God. Since we acknowledge the phenomena

---

47. See Bazak, "Replications," for an excellent summary of the Rabbis' responses to these conflicting passages.

48. Sacks, "What is Faith?" part 1.

49. b. Ber. 61a; also in b. Eruv. 18a; and b. Ketub. 8a (where it is attributed to Rav Yehuda).

50. See Bazak, "Replications," 2, 4, and endnote 2.

51. Bazak, "Replications," 3–4.

uncovered by the scholars, this means that God provided J, E, P, D, and R [the redactor] the editorial layers."[52] However, Breuer rejects the idea that the authors of the four strands were transmitting God's word at different times and places, in a prophetic manner; rather, he retains Chazal's view of the unitary revelation to Moses at Mt. Sinai, while now *interpreting* the Torah in a manner that accommodates the different voices or (what he terms) "aspects" identified in the documentary hypothesis. Of course, inasmuch as R. Breuer embraces the division of Torah passages into the four streams posited by the documentary hypothesis, his theory is subject to the same objections.

Pentateuchal inconsistencies of the type just noted present much less of a challenge to believers who adopt a non-historical perspective. To accept Alter's recommendation to treat the Torah's narratives as akin to "novels of ideas" or "philosophical novels" would be to read such conflicts and inconsistencies as a literary device intended to nudge the reader to dig deeper into the story, probing for the esoteric levels of meaning intimated by these discrepancies. This storytelling technique is sufficiently commonplace in film and literature to have a name: the "Rashomon effect," after Akira Kurosawa's famous 1950 film that employed it so brilliantly.[53] For example, both Rabbi Joseph Soloveitchik (1903–1993), generally regarded as the leading Modern Orthodox theologian of his generation, and Leo Strauss have each offered elaborate metaphorical readings of Genesis's dual creation stories that go far beyond the strained rabbinic explanation cited above.[54, 55]

---

52. Breuer, "The Study of Bible," 174.

53. See Deguzman, "The Rashomon Effect."

54. See Soloveitchik, *Lonely Man of Faith*; and Strauss, "Interpretation of Genesis." R. Soloveitchik sees in the dual creation stories not an embarrassing contradiction of narratives but "a real contradiction in the nature of man. The two accounts deal with two Adams, two men, two fathers of mankind, two types, two representatives of humanity, and it is no wonder that they are not identical." Soloveitchik, *Lonely Man*, 10. From the four significant discrepancies Soloveitchik identifies in the two accounts, he derives the opposing natures of these two faces of mankind. "Adam the first" seeks to control, dominate, and subdue nature; he is brilliant and creative but also arrogant and narcissistic; and has no time for religion beyond his own self-interest. Soloveitchik, *Lonely Man*, 17–19. "Adam the second," in contrast, is a thinker and seeker, with little interest in the workings of the material world. His quest for meaning pulls him towards life within a covenantal community of worship. According to Soloveitchik, Genesis's dual narratives challenge humankind to harmoniously integrate these two personalities, but the modern world ever more closely resembles Adam the first, dooming Adam the second to a life of loneliness and alienation. Soloveitchik, *Lonely Man of Faith*, 93–102. See Ziegler, "Lonely Man of Faith," part 1, for a deeper and more thorough analysis of Soloveitchik's interpretation.

55. Strauss's interpretation is grounded in highly abstract arguments that are

Scholars may never determine exactly how Scripture was composed, but if God created the universe *ex nihilo*, as Judaism holds, then authoring the Tanakh through human consciousness must not have been overly challenging. Accordingly, whatever the process, believers will hold that the final version of the canonical books bears God's imprimatur. Thus, this work approaches each of the canonical texts as a literary unit, then examines the unifying themes that emerge when integrating the teachings of these disparate books into a coherent theological whole.

Miracles

To reject the historicity of the Pentateuch is to also necessarily deny the existence of the miracles recorded therein; that is, divinely directed events that plainly suspend or violate the laws of nature, such as the traditional account of the Sinaitic revelation, the Ten Plagues sent against Egypt, etc. This perspective does not exclude the idea that the universe itself—and all the life within it—is a miracle. Remarkably, at least as early as medieval times, Jewish rabbis and scholars expressed a certain unease regarding overt displays of God's supernatural power. Proceeding from the assumption of God's omniscience and omnipotence, they ask, in effect, does God's open intervention in the ordinary operation of the world not suggest a flaw in the original design? Thus, Maimonides posits that these miracles were encoded in the natural processes at the time of creation.[56]

Nachmanides (the "Ramban," 1194–1270), another important Jewish theologian, saw all of creation as an ongoing miracle performed by God. The rare open miracles were necessary to sensitize the Jewish people to the hidden ones that they otherwise might miss. He also observes that, were God to regularly perform miracles in a revealed manner, it would

---

impossible to adequately summarize in a few words. See Strauss, "Interpretation of Genesis," 16. He understands the crux of the first account as a "depreciation of heaven," meaning a devaluation of cosmology and philosophical speculation "in favor of [a commitment to] human life on earth, and ultimately, [faith] that the origin of the world is divine creation." "Interpretation of Genesis," 16. In Strauss's conception, the second narrative supplements the first by cautioning humanity that the weakness of will depicted in the Tree of Knowledge episode cannot be overcome by a resort to human reason in the form of philosophy but only by "life in obedience to revelation." "Interpretation of Genesis," 19.

56. See Maimonides, *Ethical Writings of Maimonides*, 87.

eliminate moral agency, since everyone would be intimidated into obedience.[57] Eliezer Berkovits, one of the last century's great champions of liberal Orthodoxy, made a similar observation: "In the interest of religion itself, the Almighty has to be a 'hiding' God."[58] Just as Jews lose nothing by abandoning the historicity of the Pentateuch, they lose nothing by adopting a healthy skepticism regarding the open miracles described there. People of faith see miracles everywhere they look; atheists see none. Many philosophers are agnostic.

An Alternative Revelation

The relationship between God, his Torah, and the Jewish people seems eternally recursive. Yochanan Muffs (1932–2009), a noted scholar of the ancient Near East, brilliantly likens it to a playwright who not only provides the theater, stage, scenery, and props for the performance, but has also crafted a drama that distills his "very essence" and "inner vision." He gives the gifted actors permission "to improvise that which was not spelled out, and to interpret the ambiguous and translate the hints into sentences and chapters." If, perchance, they deviate too far from the author's vision, God is forever waiting in the wings "to set them on the right path by means of hints delivered by His agents." Until this day, "[t]he dramatist . . . haunts the wings of the theater, desperately worried about the fate of His play."[59]

Perhaps a friendly amendment to Muff's ingenious metaphor is in order, turning it in an even more radical direction. This would propose that the Almighty has not only licensed the Jewish people to fill in lacunae with improvisation but, with respect to matters of ethics, he is *expecting* that his people will rewrite those portions of the play no longer appropriate for an audience whose moral consciousness has dramatically evolved over time.

Just as in the domain of the physical sciences, better moral theories are built by improving the formerly prevailing ones. Newtonian physics was the best theory for some three centuries until it was superseded by Einstein's general relativity, which offered a more complete and satisfactory explanation of the observable evidence. Now, the current scientific consensus is that general relativity's account of gravity has been falsified by certain

---

57. See Nachmanides, *Commentary on the Torah*, Exod 13:16.
58. Berkovits, "Encounter with the Divine," 228.
59. Muffs, *Love & Joy*, 45–46.

aspects of quantum mechanics.[60] Whereas at one time, humans understood that their moral duties were owed only to immediate family and kin, it has gradually expanded to an ever-widening circle of people, moving from clan to tribe, tribe to nation, from nation to all humanity, and even (to a lesser degree) animals.

This perspective suggests that God did not reveal the ultimate moral truth to the authors of the Torah for the same reason he "neglected" to reveal all scientific knowledge: this is for humans to discover. Thus, Samuel Luzzatto (1800–1865), a prominent Italian-Jewish philosopher and defender of Tradition, wrote that "cosmology of Moses is not and ought not to be a tractate of physics . . . for it would have been incomprehensible to mankind during many generations and would have been more harmful than beneficial to their religious and moral education."[61]

It is a given in Jewish theology that the Jewish people are the Almighty's "partner" in purifying the world both spiritually and materially: by making peace, expanding the moral community, curing diseases, eradicating hunger, extending the duration and quality of life, etc. As expressed in a medieval midrash: "The Holy One, blessed by He, gave the Torah unto Israel like wheat from which to bring forth fine flour; or like flax from which to make a garment."[62] If God were to do this for people, humanity would be deprived of the pleasures, merit, and well-earned pride and self-esteem arising from such discoveries.

The Nature of Scripture

In light of the above, it seems deeply implausible that God would limit himself to history as a means of conveying profound spiritual and ethical truths. To the contrary, it appears likely that the Almighty would use every available tool to pierce the seemingly impenetrable barrier standing between his infinite wisdom and humans' finite understanding. This conjecture would nicely explain why, as noted above, the Bible contains a dizzying

60. See Hossenfelder, "Einstein's General Relativity," para. 5: "But we already know that [General Relativity] cannot ultimately be the correct theory for space and time . . . We know this because General Relativity does not fit together with another extremely well confirmed theory, that is quantum mechanics."

61. Rosenbloom, *Luzzatto's Ethico-psychological Interpretation*, 38, quoted and discussed in Solomon, *Torah from Heaven*, 177.

62. See the medieval Midrash, Seder Eliyahu Zuta, ch. 2, quoted and discussed in Heschel, "Understanding the Bible," 248.

array of literary genres of the highest artistic merit. As the ever-quotable Alter writes, these books "vividly remind us that the biblical world was far from monolithic, that it tolerated and perhaps sometimes even encouraged a bracing variety of value systems expressed through a wide spectrum of styles and literary modes."[63]

The Hebrew Bible is customarily divided into three groupings: the Five Books of Moses (Torah), Nevi'im (Prophets), and the Ketuvim (the Writings). Since the Middle Ages, the entire collection of canonical books has been referred to by the acronym "Tanakh," derived from "Ta" (Torah), "Na" (Nevi'im), and "Kh" (Writings). Traditional Judaism endows the Pentateuch with a fundamentally superior holiness to that of the other books, expressly including Nevi'im, due to its status as the literal word of God to Moses, heard and witnessed by the entire community at Sinai. As one prominent Chabad rabbi writes on this movement's website:[64]

> Although all the books of Tanach are revered as divine works, the Chumash [Pentateuch] holds a unique place . . . All other prophecies in Tanach, whether Samuel or Isaiah or Daniel, were the testimony of a single individual. They are believed only because Moses instructed us—in G‑d's name—to believe and to obey prophets who fulfill the conditions set out clearly for them . . . Obviously then, no prophet can add or detract from anything Moses taught—since their credibility rests entirely on his authority. The prophets come only to explain, elaborate and admonish the people to keep "the Torah of Moses."

However, one important implication of the theological framework set out in this chapter is that the fundamental dichotomy between the Pentateuch and the balance of canonical texts cannot be sustained. Neither the Pentateuch nor the books comprising Nevi'im and Ketuvim were dictated by God word-for-word to a human secretary. All of Judaism's holy texts are the product of divine communication filtered through the human consciousness of their authors. Because the Pentateuch records the "gestation and birth" of the Jewish people and details the provisions of the eternal covenant between them and the Almighty, it is entitled to pride of place, but has no superior ontological status. The non-Pentateuchal canonical texts equally express the authors' experience of the divine spirit and accordingly must be accorded due weight, including their revisions to Pentateuchal doctrines.

63. Alter, *The Hebrew Bible (Writings)*, xlv.
64. Freeman, "What is Torah?" see section, "Torah in 24 Books."

This stance is already widely accepted by leaders of Judaism's non-Orthodox streams, who are deeply inspired by the classical prophets. In the words of one prominent Reform rabbi, published on the website of the Union of Reform Judaism: "To be a Reform Jew is to hear the voice of the prophets in our head; to be engaged in the ongoing work of *tikkun olam*; to strive to improve the world in which we live."[65] Similarly, Heschel, one of the leading lights of the Conservative movement in the 1950s and 1960s, was heavily influenced by the classical prophets. His daughter, Professor Susannah Heschel, in discussing her father's personal and theological kinship with Dr. Martin Luther King Jr., writes that "Their common understanding of the prophets and of the connection between faith and political engagement was the motivation that brought both men to speak out against the war in Vietnam, despite the political consequences."[66]

Ritual and Observance

The Torah's ethics are the primary concern of this study, but it is nevertheless necessary to say a few words regarding ritual, which is an essential and irreplaceable aspect of Judaism. First, ritual and ethics do not occupy parallel universes, never to intersect. As Professor Berkovits argues, obedience to the non-rational commandments serves a moral purpose by disciplining our physical needs and desires in service of something higher and more noble:[67]

> The purpose of the inhibitive rules is to practice saying "no" to self-centered demands: whereas the fulfillment of positive commands is the exercise of saying "yes" in consideration of an order different from one's own. By such training, one breaks down the exclusiveness of man's organic selfishness. The obedience to the rules and commands is itself an exercise in behavior that is not purely self-regarding and orients a person towards the other.

Of equal importance, believers are aware of the presence in the world of something far greater than themselves, and typically feel the urgent need to express this awe in individual and communal worship and observance:

---

65. Feldman, "Why Advocacy is Central," paragraph 1. The liberal streams of Judaism typically define *tikkun olam* as "repairing the world" in the material sense (eliminating poverty, curing disease, etc.) while the Orthodox see the spiritual elevation of the world as an indispensable aspect of this notion.
66. Heschel, "Theological Affinities," 138.
67. Berkovits, "Law and Morality," 25–26.

A Theological Framework

by, for Jews, prayer and atonement, lighting Sabbath and Hanukkah candles, eating only unleavened bread on Pesach, affixing *mezuzot*, saying *Kaddish* for a deceased loved one, etc. Accordingly, any theology that claims to represent and express Judaism's core values must affirm the importance of ritual, although not necessarily in the manner prescribed by any particular stream of the faith.

Somewhat ironically, perhaps, given his great reputation as an eloquent exponent of Jewish ethics, Rabbi Heschel expresses the most eloquent appreciation of ritual's value:[68]

> The mitzvot are forms of expressing in deeds the appreciation of the ineffable. They are terms of the spirit in which we allude to that which is beyond reason. To look for rational explanations, to scrutinize the mitzvot in terms of common sense is to quench their intrinsic meaning. . . . The purpose of religion is not to satisfy the needs we feel but to create in us the need of serving ends, of which we otherwise remain oblivious.

Authenticity

There can be little doubt that Orthodoxy regards itself as the sole authentic and thus legitimate form of Judaism, primarily because its adherents alone are deeply committed to living a life governed by halakhah, with little regard for the clear-cut division that more secular Jews make between the ethical and ritual commandments. Thus, Samuel Lebens, an Orthodox rabbi and respected philosopher of religion, writes that:[69]

---

68. See Heschel, "The Meaning of Observance," 182. The author's attitude towards the commandments is beautifully expressed by Arnold Jacob Wolf (1924–2008), a prominent Reform rabbi and theologian:

> In principle, no commandment is inferior to any other. But some are in fact unavailable to me, some are dependent on a land in which I do not live, some on a world which is not my world. Some are just too heavy for me to lift. That is no reflection on them or, perhaps, even on me; it is just so. Any Orthodox insistence that every Jew must do the same thing at the same time in the same way is oblivious of human differences. Liberal subjectivism which lets every Jew be his own god forgets our deepest need to become what we are not yet by serving a very great Master. Neither Orthodox nor liberal, I try to be a Jew.

See Wolf, "State of Jewish Belief," 268–69; quoted in Dane, "Yoke of Heaven," 385.

69. Lebens, *The Principles of Judaism*, 187.

> [O]ne of the key distinctions between Orthodox and Conservative Judaism is that the rulings of the Conservative rabbinate are, on the whole, addressed to a halakhically apathetic laity . . . The Orthodox rabbinate, by contrast, addresses itself, on the whole, as halakhically *observant* laity.
>
> More progressive movements—to the left of Conservativism—are unlikely even to *claim* deep commitment to life in accordance with Torah law . . . This all indicates that the warrant of Sinai flows most forcefully today in the direction of Orthodoxy.

Although most Orthodox public figures are too circumspect to say such things out loud, the Israeli Chief Rabbinate has no qualms about asserting, "If you look at the assimilation that has spread throughout the Jews of the world who are connected with these [Reform] bodies . . . the uprooting of everything of holiness, you will see clearly that they have no connection to original Judaism."[70] Unfortunately, the authors of such pronouncements almost invariably help themselves to the assumption that they already know Judaism's essence, and then proceed to ignore the liberal philosophical and ethical commitments that lie at its heart.

To avoid arbitrariness of this sort, the value structure of Judaism must be derived from its canonical texts and the interpretations given them by the Rabbis, who were forced to completely reorient their faith away from long-established cultic practices towards new rituals and ethics appropriate to life in the diaspora. The meta-halakhic principles that evolved in the talmudic era were intended to guide all contemporary and future legal decision-making. They are of such central importance that no "Judaism" that contravenes them can rightly be considered authentic.

---

70. Sharon and Sokol, "Chief Rabbinate in Fierce Attack," paragraph 6.

2

Autonomous Ethics, Liberalism, and Judaism

THE OVERARCHING CLAIM OF this volume is that authentic Judaism, as represented in the Hebrew Bible and in the Rabbis' legal and ethical discourse, is essentially liberal. This and the following chapter will flesh out the meaning of "liberalism" by characterizing it in terms of two central principles. This chapter argues that Judaism is committed to the first of these, Kant's notion of moral autonomy and the corresponding respect and dignity owed persons as moral agents. The following chapter analyzes Judaism from the perspective of the second, Popper's critical rationalism, contending that it shares with this worldview an unshakeable devotion to tolerance and pluralism in both thought and religious practice.

Defining "Liberalism"

The claim of liberalism does not enlist the Torah in any sort of partisan political project. "Liberal" and "liberalism" are used here in a broad sense, denoting that constellation of moral principles that produce and sustain those polities recognized as liberal democracies. These include a commitment to the rule of law and such basic rights as free expression and association, due process, equal protection, political participation, and various economic liberties. Such societies also incorporate institutional checks and balances, including separation of powers and regular free and fair elections.

Members of a liberal state will hold a wide variety of conflicting opinions and beliefs regarding every imaginable topic; thus, any such entity will establish and defend a robust marketplace of ideas where essentially all views may be expressed, heard, criticized, and refined. Naturally, these citizens will also have diverse lifestyle preferences, which will be respected by the state so long as they do not infringe on the right of other innocent people to live as they please.

A liberal society will employ force or coercion against its members only when necessary to accomplish important objectives that cannot be achieved by consensual means. It will also recognize an unhindered right of exit so that its members may, if they desire, relocate to jurisdictions they believe are more conducive to their flourishing. No current or past state has ever realized this ideal, but liberal ones come qualitatively closer than illiberal ones.

There is a rich vein of philosophical literature explicating and defending the values just described that would certainly include the writings of such luminaries as Adam Smith, Montesquieu, Locke, Hume, Kant, Jefferson, and Mill. In more recent times, the received view that stringent property rights are essential to the realization of liberty has been widely criticized, making the task of defining "liberalism" harder. Nevertheless, all liberals agree that competent adults enjoy the presumption of freedom, such that, "If citizens are obliged to exercise self-restraint, and especially if they are obliged to defer to someone else's authority, there must be a reason why. Restrictions on liberty must be justified."[1] Under this formulation, a wide array of prominent modern political philosophers qualify as "liberal," including John Rawls (1921–2020), Robert Nozick (1938–2002), Ronald Dworkin (1931–2013), F.A. Hayek (1889–1992), Thomas Nagel, Amartya Sen, and Karl Popper (1902–1994), whose views are analyzed in the following chapter.

Kantian Autonomy and Liberalism

The concept of moral autonomy has been enormously influential in secular philosophy's theorizing about liberalism. This chapter approaches this subject by asking, as have many philosophers, "What is it about human beings

1. Courtland et al., "Liberalism," §1.1.

that requires us to assign a radically greater moral weight to their welfare than to that of say cows or chickens?"[2] Of course, the theist's answer—"because human beings are made in God's image while other animals are not"—is unavailable to philosophers, as it plainly begs the question against non-believers. Theorists have therefore searched for rationales that do not rely on God's existence and commands.

Immanuel Kant (1724–1804) appears to have been the first to draw the connection between the capacity of competent adults to recognize and apply the moral law and the severe constraint this imposes on the use of force or coercion against them. In a pistachio-sized nutshell, he holds that all rational and morally impartial persons of goodwill, conscious of the value of their own autonomy, are under the duty to "[a]ct in such a way that you always treat humanity, whether in your own person or in the person of any other, never simply as a means, but always at the same time as an end," which is the second and best-known formulation of his Categorical Imperative.[3] Or, as Judith Jarvis Thomson (1929–2020), a highly respected moral philosopher, succinctly expresses Kant's idea: "the capacity to conform your conduct to moral law is a necessary and sufficient condition for the moral law to apply to you."[4]

A clear implication of Kant's argument is that all persons, as moral agents, are entitled to equal respect, with no special pleading permitted. Accordingly, he holds that, "*Right* is the limitation of each person's freedom so that it is compatible with the freedom of everyone, insofar as this is possible in accord with a universal law."[5] Kant's conception of rights has been enormously influential in moral and political philosophy, and liberals as diverse as Rawls and Nozick have employed it in developing their own theories. In fact, the late Gerald Gaus (1952–2020), himself an important figure in this field, has held that "the most plausible understanding of the fundamental liberal principle presupposes a Kantian conception of moral autonomy."[6] It will be argued in the balance of this study that the paramount value the Rabbis and subsequent commentators place on autonomy is a critical heuristic in their interpretation of Judaism's canonical texts.

---

2. See Nozick, *Anarchy, State, and Utopia*, 35–39.
3. Kant, *Groundwork of the Metaphysics*, 96.
4. Thomson, *The Realm of Rights*, 215.
5. Kant, "That May be True in Theory," 72.
6. Gaus, "The Place of Autonomy," 305.

Unsurprisingly, the Hebrew Bible does not read like a collection of secular moral or political philosophy textbooks, with carefully wrought theories, thought experiments, clever counterexamples, and so forth. This is because it is dedicated to the higher purpose of inspiring its readers to lead a God-centered life and, to this end, employs a wide variety of styles and genres to bridge the vast chasm between the finite human mind and the divine spirit. The Tanakh's ethics are gleaned from, among other things, the multiplicity of meanings encoded in its narratives, including intertextual disputes; the Pentateuch's law codes, including their evolution over time; the oracles of the classical prophets; the Rabbis' halakhic and aggadic discourse; and more modern commentary on the above.

Accordingly, to hear the canon's inner message is to attend not only to the Torah's laws but also to the Bible's stories, employing the literary methods of such scholars as Robert Alter, Adele Berlin, and Meir Sternberg. This process will reveal Judaism's underlying commitment to tolerance and pluralism, having as its mainspring the dignity and respect owed persons as moral agents. This observation is supported by numerous Scriptural passages and rabbinic texts that describe dialogue and arguments between God on the one hand and biblical personalities, Rabbis, and even angels, on the other.

The episodes identified in this chapter show that the Almighty is neither a tyrant nor a bully; and that God permits people to question, debate, defy, and even persuade him. Because humankind is created "in His image," these texts imply that persons are required to act with the same deference towards their fellows. The texts also serve to demonstrate that God regards humanity as possessing sufficient moral knowledge to engage in reasoned debate.

As discussed below, the first four chapters of Genesis, including God's dialogues with Cain, and Adam and Eve, may be seen as establishing the existence and value of autonomy; and is thus the rationale for individual responsibility. Within the context of moral philosophy, the concept of autonomy "requires that we utilize a law to guide our decisions, a law that can come to us only by an act of our own will . . . This self-imposition of the moral law is autonomy."[7] In turn, accountability presupposes an objective morality that can be comprehended and applied. The biblical stories reviewed in this chapter and various related midrashim record a series of encounters or "arguments" that—although they frequently do not involve

---

7. Christman, "Autonomy," §2.

efforts to persuade by rational means—all relate in some way to the significance and implications of moral autonomy.

In God's Image

As previously suggested, the best explanation for the biblical assertion of *imago Dei* ("image of God") is humankind's moral agency. However, according to various midrashim, the creation of Man was not a foregone conclusion but was the subject of heavenly controversy. These tales were composed in response to the strange language of Genesis 1:26—"Let's make man in *our* image, after *our* likeness" (emphasis added)—that appears to call into question Judaism's monotheism. A variety of solutions for this problematic verse are offered, including that God is merely consulting with Heaven and Earth, the other days of creation, or the souls of the righteous.[8]

It seems, however, that the most developed and interesting exegesis depicts God conferring with his ministering angels, who formed into "various parties and groups" representing different Platonic attributes.[9] The angels representing Kindness and Righteousness favor Man's creation, as he would act kindly and perform righteous deeds, while the angels representing Truth and Peace oppose it, as he is "all falsehoods" and "all quarrel." God then "took Truth and threw it to the ground" so that a majority now favored creation.[10]

This story holds much of interest. First, it seems that God is demonstrating exactly the process of truth discovery advocated by critical rationalists; that is, the testing of ideas and theories by subjecting them to criticism and objection. The authors of this midrash understood full well that God is, by definition, omniscient and thus not in need of advice from his attendants. Nevertheless, it appears that the Rabbis wish to employ God as a model; if even the Almighty felt it prudent to consult with lesser beings before acting, how much greater is the need for deeply flawed human beings, especially leaders and legislators, to act accordingly?

Moreover, it is notable that Truth, and not Peace or some other angelic stand-in, is ejected from the debate. One might surmise that God is suggesting that, of all the attributes that humankind might aspire to, truth is secondary, because for persons to live together harmoniously it is not

8. MR (Gen), 8:3–8 and n82.
9. MR (Gen), 8:5.
10. MR (Gen), 8:5.

necessary for them to agree on any ultimate or final truth; rather, all that is required is that the community embraces the liberal principle of equal right, mentioned above. In other words, a sincere commitment to tolerance and pluralism is sufficient for society to flourish.

After humankind is created, the question of moral responsibility, and thus implicitly the existence of human autonomy, comes front and center. The Adam/Eve and Cain/Abel pericopes, which unfold long before the revelation of God's laws at Sinai, seem designed, in part, to address this issue. Thus, Adam and Eve are "punished" for disobeying God's injunction not to eat from the "tree of knowledge of good and bad [often translated "evil"]."[11] Because of their disobedience, they become mortal, are exiled from the Garden of Eden, and will be afflicted by those hardships and challenges that befall all flesh and blood: the pain of childbirth; the need to earn a living by the "sweat of your brow"; and so forth.[12]

However, this story is clearly paradoxical. Since Adam and Eve decided to partake of the forbidden fruit *before* they gained knowledge of good and evil, how can God hold them to account for this sin? Everything about them, including their asexuality, paints them as moral innocents. Accordingly, any "punishment" seems, on its face, manifestly unjust, but this may not be the correct frame of reference.

As many scholars have previously conjectured, an alternative, better reading is to regard the Tree of Knowledge episode as etiological, meaning that it was intended to explain key human attributes; namely, suffering, disease, death, and, above all else, moral agency.[13] With respect to the last attribute, Maimonides, the preeminent medieval Jewish theologian, writes:[14]

> As it is written in the Torah, "And so, man has become as one of us, knowing good and evil" (Gen. 3:22); that is, this human species has become singular in the world, and no other species resembles it with respect to this matter: that he, of himself, in his wisdom and understanding knows the good and the evil and does what he wills, and there is none to restrain his hand from doing the good or the evil.

---

11. Gen 2:17.

12. Gen 3:16–17.

13. See Ngo, "Should We Take Creation."

14. *Mishneh Torah*, Hilkhot Teshuvah 5:1, quoted and discussed in Rabinovitch, "The Way of Torah," 3.

The noted Jewish philosopher Abraham Kaplan (1918–1993) expresses a similar idea: "Morality is the link between man and God, having its seat in what is divine in man, and being intrinsic to divinity itself."[15]

If autonomy is the essential trait shared by God and Man, it becomes apparent why "punishment" may be an inapt description. As Benjamin Sommer, a prominent biblical scholar, observes: "some modern scholars . . . have argued cogently that the story involves ascent to moral agency rather than (or as much as) a fall from grace."[16] This reading seems almost compelled by the circumstance that it is only Adam and Eve's new ethical consciousness that validates God's statement that Man is created "in His image." There is also talmudic support for this view, as the Rabbis hold that God created both the human inclination for good (*yetzer ha-tov*) and evil (*yetzer ha-ra'*) and gave humanity the Torah as a means of understanding and choosing the former.[17]

Human autonomy also best explains God's purpose in creating the world. He is by hypothesis omnipotent and thus does not need mankind to erect grand edifices or otherwise improve the world in a purely material way. The only thing that human beings can possibly offer God is their dedication to building a world modeled on the lessons of Scripture.[18] This involves using humans' creative powers and compassion to make peace, expand the moral community, conquer disease, banish hunger and deprivation, and build a society that provides everyone the opportunity to flourish and thrive up to the maximum extent of their ambitions and talents. As memorably stated by the prophet Micah: "He has told you O man, what is good; And what the LORD requires of you: Only to do justice; And to love goodness; And to walk modestly with your God."[19]

---

15. Kaplan, "The Jewish Argument," section II.
16. Sommer, *Revelation and Authority*, 20, and sources cited there.
17. See b. Kid. 30b.
18. It might be thought that God desires to be worshipped. However, it seems very likely that this is simply a projection by humans of their own psychological needs. It is far more plausible that worship is the means provided by a benevolent God through which humans can connect with and draw closer to him; in other words, a gift.
19. Mic 6:8.

Respect for Autonomy in Classic Texts

The story of Cain and Abel raises additional pressing questions regarding autonomy. There is no indication that Cain is "officially" on notice that murder is a sin that will subject him to severe punishment. Yet, this is precisely what he receives after he, apparently becoming enraged by God's preference for Abel's sacrificial offering over his own, kills his brother.[20] When God confronts him over this murder, Cain famously asks, "Am I my brother's keeper?"[21]—which appears to be an attempt to evade responsibility. The punishment that God metes out to him implicitly establishes both that Cain possesses free will[22] and that he knew that this killing was wrong: "the culpability of Cain rests upon an unexpressed assumption of the existence of a moral law operative from the beginning of time."[23] Accordingly, Cain is accountable for his sin.

However, the Tannaim are troubled by certain aspects of this story. The great sage Shimon ben Yochai questions why an all-powerful deity allowed this murder to occur. Could not God have arranged for Abel to prevail over Cain, or at least to escape?[24] It seems that the only satisfactory answer is a theodicy invoking the paramount value of free will and moral agency.[25] The capacity for virtue and beneficence implies an equal capacity for wickedness and cruelty. In other words, the supreme value of autonomy outweighs the harms that spring from it.

In contrast to the unbounded wickedness of the Sodomites, who are obliterated, Cain is merely condemned to be "a restless wanderer on earth."[26] Moreover, "the LORD put a mark on Cain, lest anyone who met him should

---

20. See Gen 4:11–15.

21. Gen 4:9.

22. Tradition is quite insistent on the existence of free will and the justice of individual responsibility. When confronted with the apparent incompatibility of free will with divine omniscience, the Rabbis and medieval commentators consistently hypothesized limits on God's powers rather than circumscribe free will. See Pines, "Free Will," 7:230–34.

23. Sarna, *Understanding Genesis*, 31 (endnote omitted). See also Kaufmann, *The Religion of Israel*, 233: "The Bible itself recognizes the existence of a universal moral law from primeval times, to which all men are subject. Cain, the generation of the Flood, and Sodom are all punished for violations of this law."

24. See MR (Gen), 22:9.

25. See Holtz, *Back to the Sources*, 194–97.

26. Gen 4:14.

kill him."[27] There are various midrashic theories regarding this leniency, but the most credible appears to be that Cain had so little knowledge or experience of death that he did not understand that his attack would actually *kill* Abel, and thus the murder was not premeditated.[28] However, the mark placed on Cain symbolically places humankind on notice that all future murderers will be punished, even up to death.[29]

In a story set many centuries after Cain, a midrash probably written in the fifth century CE illustrates the transcendent value that Jewish theology places on autonomous ethics.[30] It builds on two Scriptural passages. The first is the report in Genesis[31] that, as Jacob travels from Haran to Eretz Israel with his entire household, his beloved wife Rachel dies in childbirth, and he buries her "on the road to Ephrath," near Bethlehem (which believers hold to be the site venerated today as Rachel's Tomb), rather than in the Cave of Machpelah (with the other patriarchs and matriarchs). Tradition explains that he did so because he foresaw that her tomb would be situated alongside the route taken by the Babylonian exiles, whom she would comfort and offer hope.[32]

The second is from the book of Jeremiah,[33] in which this prophet, mourning the destruction of the First Temple, articulates a vision: "A voice is heard on high, wailing bitter weeping, Rachel weeps for her children." Jeremiah then prophesizes that God will comfort her: "Restrain your voice from weeping and your eyes from tears, for there is reward for your accomplishment . . . your children will return to their border."[34] From the premises just described, the author of the above-referenced midrash weaves an elaborate fantastical drama that is evidently intended to explicate Jeremiah's

---

27. Gen 4:15.
28. MR (Gen), 22:12, n180; see also Sarna, *Understanding Genesis*, 31.
29. See MR (Gen), 22:12, n181.
30. See MR (Lam) Proem XXIV.
31. See Gen 35:16–20, 48:7.

32. See Sivan, "Rachel Weeps in Ramah," note 5. There is a "technical" problem with this drama, as the more popular translation of Jeremiah's oracle (Jer 31:14) is that a "cry is heard in Ramah," rather than a cry from "on high," as in the Scherman/ArtScroll edition. Ramah is substantially north of Rachel's Tomb in Bethlehem and adjacent to the shorter, more likely route of Jewish exiles headed for Babylonia. In other words, if the exiles went by way of Ramah, they would *not*, as Jeremiah foretells, pass by Rachel's Tomb. See Medan, "Vayechi," part B.

33. Jer 31:14–16.
34. Jer 31:14–16.

prophesy, justify Jacob's decision to bury Rachel "on the road," and explain the seemingly miraculous return of the Babylonian exiles to the Holy Land (pursuant to the decree of Cyrus the Great in 528 BCE).

To do so, this midrashic author conjures up a scenario in which God, although permitting these events to occur, nevertheless suffers inconsolable grief over the Temple's destruction and the exile of his people.[35] In this scenario, God orders Jeremiah to summon the souls of the three patriarchs and Moses to share his anguish; one might say to sit *shiva* with him. Naturally, these great leaders cannot stand idly by while the Jewish people suffer, and each makes a heartfelt plea for God's mercy on the Jews' behalf.

Abraham begs God to recall his willingness to sacrifice his spiritual heir and beloved son Isaac, and the latter describes how he willingly offered himself for this purpose. Jacob reminds God of the suffering he endured in raising his twelve sons and now pleads with God to spare their descendants. Moses beseeches God to remember how he lovingly tended his Jewish flock in the Wilderness for forty years and was still denied entry into the Promised Land. God is unmoved.

Then Rachel, apparently uninvited, steps forward with what seems to be more in the nature of a demand than a plea. First, she recalls that Jacob loved and desired to marry her, rather than her older sister, Leah. And, fearing that Laban, her devious father, would substitute Leah for her on the wedding night, she agreed with Jacob on signs that would distinguish her. Rachel then reminds God that she "relented, suppressed [her] desire, and had pity upon [her] sister that she should not be exposed to shame."[36] She continues:

> In the evening they substituted my sister for me with my husband, and I delivered over all the signs which I had arranged with my husband so that he should think that she was Rachel. More than that, I went beneath the bed upon which he lay with my sister; and when he spoke to her she remained silent and I made all the replies in order that he should not recognize my sister's voice. I did her a kindness, was not jealous of her, and did not expose her to shame.

Rachel then concludes, appearing almost to scold God:

> And if I, a creature of flesh and blood, formed of dust and ashes, was not envious of my rival, and did not expose her to shame and contempt, why shouldest thou, a King Who liveth eternally and

---

35. See Sivan, "Rachel Weeps in Ramah," for a valuable overview of this midrash.
36. All quotations of this midrash are from MR (Lam), Proem XXIV.

art merciful, be jealous of idolatry in which there is no reality, and exile my children and let them be slain by the sword, and their enemies have done with them as they wished!

God immediately relents: "For thy sake, Rachel, I will restore Israel to her place. 'And so it is written, *Thus saith the Lord: A voice is heard in Ramah . . .*'"

This midrash presents a theologically audacious tale that confounds the reader's expectations. While the other biblical figures cite the great sacrifices they made for God or the immense suffering they endured in his service, Rachel's deed was for the benefit of a single person, prompted by her refusal to be used as a means of her sister's disgrace. Crucially, Rachel's self-sacrifice was not in obedience to God's commands because the events of this narrative precede Sinai and, unlike Moses and the patriarchs, God had never appeared to Rachel.

Accordingly, she acts in response to an ethical obligation she alone identifies. Rachel had, in fact, grown up in a household headed by Laban, an extremely unscrupulous person. It appears that this midrash is best understood as an expression of the utmost value the Rabbis place on autonomous moral judgment. It is also worth noting that this story undermines the dominant patriarchal worldview of the Tanakh, a subject explored in chapter 6.

Various Pentateuchal episodes in which Moses either disregards God's instructions or argues with him confirms the supreme value the Torah assigns to autonomy. One example is God's initial encounter with Moses at the burning bush.[37] Here, God briefly outlines his plan to rescue the Hebrews and bring them to the Promised Land, then summons Moses to act as his instrument: "Come, therefore, I will send you to Pharoah, and you shall free My people, the Israelites, from Egypt."[38]

There follows an extended dialogue in which Moses raises every conceivable objection, including "Why me?" "Nobody will listen to me," "I have a speech impediment," and more.[39] Finally, after patiently addressing all his concerns, God commands him a second time: "Now go, and I will be with you as you speak." Then, in what can only be described as a breathtaking act of defiance, Moses tells the Almighty, "Please, O Lord make someone else your agent."

37. See Exod 3:4–22.
38. Exod 3:10.
39. Exod 4:12–13.

Remarkably, the Torah then reports, "The LORD became angry with Moses, and He said, 'There is your brother Aaron the Levite. He, I know, speaks readily . . . and he shall speak for you to the people.'" With this concession, Moses acquiesces in God's requested mission. Despite the prophet's obstinance and God's "anger," nowhere does the Torah report that Moses is punished for it.[40] This extended engagement, which, according to Rashi, lasted "for a full seven days"[41] not only highlights Moses' possession of the abject humility that the Almighty sees as an essential characteristic for his leadership role but also speaks to the dignity owed persons. Despite his obvious exasperation, God appears to have accepted that Moses is sincere and entitled to refuse; therefore, he—modeling liberal values—eschews coercion in favor of compromise.[42]

A second instance is Moses' catastrophic decision to send spies into Canaan to ascertain the most efficient means of conquest, rather than simply proceeding straight away, as God commands. When the twelve spies return, all but Joshua and Caleb give a pessimistic report that disheartens the people, causing them to lose their will. Consequently, the Almighty requires the Israelites to wander in the Wilderness for forty years until this faithless generation dies off.

---

40. There is an inconclusive talmudic debate in which R. Yehoshua ben Karchah holds that this is the unique instance of a biblical report of "God's anger" that did not result in a plague or other punishment, while R. Shimon ben Yohai counters that the reference in the verse to Aaron, and the circumstance that the office of High Priest was ultimately bestowed on Aaron and his descendants, rather than on Moses and his, indicates that this loss of office was God's punishment. See b. Zevah. 102a. But, even if God decided to award this office to Aaron for this reason, since the Torah reports that Moses "was a very humble man, more so than any other man on earth" (Num 12:3), he may well have counted the loss of this office more as a blessing than a punishment.

41. Rashi, *Commentary on the Torah* (Exod) 4:10.

42. Nahum Rabinovitch (1928–2020), a prominent Orthodox rabbi and educator, argues—citing several important talmudic debates, including the rabbis' abolition of capital punishment in virtually all cases and their preference for compromise settlements in litigation—that if the Great Sanhedrin were reconstituted, it would eschew coercion, except in defense of the rights of others:

> The Torah authority should never use compulsion, except with the consent of the community that accepted it as authoritative and granted it that power. Even then, compulsion should be used only in instances where harm may be inflicted on others, such as in family law matters related to divorce, support, and the like. It is desirable that the Torah authority never employ force.

See Rabinovitch, "The Way of Torah," 32.

This story is twice told: in Numbers (13:1–3 and 17–33) and in Deuteronomy (1:19–40). In Numbers (13:2), God instructs Moses: "Send out men for yourself to scout the land of Canaan." Contrary to the apparent plain meaning of this verse, Rashi (c.1040–1105), the preeminent medieval Torah commentor, understands the words "for yourself" as meaning "by your discretion: As for Me, I do not command you; if you so desire, send."[43] That Moses bears responsibility for this tragic decision is substantiated by the corresponding verse in Deuteronomy, where the prophet recalls that "I approved of the plan, and so I selected twelve of your men, one from each tribe."[44] Accordingly, the text reveals that God preferred that Moses and the people make a disastrous decision of their own free will than to intervene to alter their course.[45]

It must be said that there is one incident described in the Pentateuch that the Rabbis construe as Moses receiving punishment for questioning God, but even this verdict seems to have been reconsidered by later authorities. Namely, Moses' bitter complaint to the Almighty after his and Aaron's initial demand of Pharoah to liberate the Israelites boomerangs. Not only does the Egyptian ruler refuse, but he instead greatly increases the workload of his Hebrew slaves so that they will be too exhausted to heed the call of Moses and Aaron to rebel.[46] The slaves angrily reproach the brothers for the extra burden placed upon them. When Moses next communicates with God, he demands, "Why have you done evil to this people, why have you sent me?"[47] The Master of the Universe responds, "You shall soon see what I shall do to Pharoah: he shall let them go because of a greater might; indeed, because of a greater might he shall drive them from his land."[48]

Although there appears to be nothing in the plain meaning of God's statement that implies any sort of rebuke, the Rabbis interpret it this way, as the Gemara judges that "[o]ne can infer: The war with Pharoah and his downfall you [Moses] shall see, but you will not see the war with the thirty-one kings in Eretz Yisrael, as you will not be privileged to conquer Eretz Yisrael for the Jewish people."[49] Rashi essentially echoes this conclusion

---

43. Rashi, *Commentary on the Torah* (Num), 13:2.
44. Deut 1:23.
45. See Shimon, "Shelach: Spy v. Spy," point 2.
46. See Exod 5:6–9.
47. Exod 5:22.
48. Exod 6:1.
49. b. Sanh. 111a.

without any further analysis.[50] However, other important medieval and later commentators offer competing interpretations that do not suggest that God is faulting Moses.

In this vein, Abraham Ibn Ezra (1089–1164), the great Spanish biblical commentator and polymath, reads this verse simply as one of comfort: "When I bring the plagues upon Egypt things will start getting better for Israel, as I will yet explain."[51] Nachmanides (or the "Ramban"), another great medieval Spanish commentator (1194–1270), also understands this verse not as criticism of Moses but simply as correcting his prophet's misapprehension about the timing of the liberation: "Soon shalt thou see what I will do to Pharaoh, for I will not prolong it for him to the extent that you thought, and his time is near to come, and his days shall not be prolonged."[52]

Similarly, Rabbi Meir Leibush ben Yehiel Michel Wisser ("Malbim," 1809–1879), a highly respected Eastern European rabbi and biblical exegete, interprets this and related verses simply as part of God's explanation to Moses of why he had not destroyed Pharoah and liberated the Hebrews until this time.[53] Accordingly, it may be that, as the moral sensitivities of the leading rabbis evolved, they could not accept that God would punish Moses for crying out against the greater suffering of the Hebrews, for which he is an unwilling instrument.[54]

This hypothesis appears to be bolstered by a medieval midrash that describes the Almighty as being *taught ethics by Moses*. Astonishingly, these authors assert that Moses corrects God on three occasions, and each time, the Almighty forthrightly acknowledges his error.[55] It seems that these narratives are serving to rewrite what these medieval rabbis regard as objectionable commandments.

The first instance, discussed further in chapter 3, occurs when God announces his intent to destroy the Israelites for the sin of the Golden Calf, and Moses intercedes on behalf of his people. According to this midrash, Moses offers two defenses: first, "Master of the Universe, from where do

50. See Rashi, *Commentary on the Torah* (Exod), 6:1.

51. *Ibn Ezra on Exodus*, quoted on Sefaria.org.

52. Nachmanides, *Commentary on the Torah*, quoted on Sefaria.org.

53. See *Malbim on Exodus*, quoted on Sefaria.org.

54. Special thanks to Ethan Borer-Newton, who alerted the author to these three references appearing to be at odds with Rashi's interpretation.

55. These three incidents are all recounted in Sefaria Community Translation, Midrash Rabbah (Num), 19:33. All midrashic quotations relating to these three episodes are from this source.

Israel know what they have done [was wrong]? Did they not grow up in Egypt, and all of Egypt are idolaters." Second, "You did not give [the Torah] to [the Israelites], and they were not standing there . . . You did not say: 'I am the Lord your God [plural],' but rather: 'I am the Lord your God [singular].' You said it to me. Did I, perhaps, sin?" According to this midrash, God then responds: "As you live, you have spoken well. You have taught Me. From now on, I will speak [in the plural form]."

The second case relates to God's pronouncement that he will "visit the sins of the father on the sons."[56] When Moses objects, "There are many righteous people whose parents are evildoers; will they pay for their parents' sins?" God relents, telling Moses, "You have taught Me. I shall nullify my policy and adopt yours."

The final instance is narrated by Moses himself as he recounts the Israelites' march to the eastern bank of the Jordan on their mission to conquer Eretz Israel. He recalls that God told him, "See, I give into your power Sihon the Amorite, king of Heshbon, and his land. Begin the occupation: engage him in battle."[57] Without explanation, the prophet then acknowledges that he ignored God's instructions: "Then I sent messengers from the wilderness of Kedemoth to King Sihon of Heshbon with an offer of peace, as follows, 'Let me pass through your country. I will keep strictly to the highway, turning off neither to the right nor to the left.'"[58] According to the midrash, God then endorses Moses' decision: "By your life, I will nullify My words and fulfill yours, as it says, 'When you approach a city to battle against it, extend an offer of peace.'"[59]

Rashi understands that Moses takes this bold step because "[he] learned to do so from that which was given to us in the Wilderness of Sinai, that is, from the Torah."[60] In the same commentary, Rashi then further elucidates that Moses is relying either on God's offer of the Torah to other nations before offering it to the Jewish people or his sending Moses and Aaron to plead with Pharoah for the release of the Hebrews, even though the Almighty knew that these offers would be in vain, as was Moses' to King Sihon. Either way, it seems that Moses elected to ignore a clearly unjust command because it conflicted with other overarching Torah values.

56. Exod 34:6–7.
57. Deut 2:24.
58. Deut 2:26–27.
59. Deut 20:10.
60. Rashi, *Commentary on the Torah* (Deut), 2:26.

What these three incidents have in common is the degree to which the commandments in question grossly violate basic moral values. God's announced intent to destroy the entire Jewish people for the sin of the limited number who constructed and worshipped the Golden Calf violates the fundamental principle of justice that God was at pains to affirm to Abraham before destroying Sodom and Gomorrah. By the same token, visiting the sins of the fathers on their sons is morally indefensible, as is fighting a war of annihilation without exploring the possibility of a peaceful resolution.

The theological novelty of this midrash is its portrayal of God's frank admission of his error in giving the now-overturned commandments. It is evident that the medieval rabbis who authored this midrash simply could not accept that their God would enforce them. They therefore found a creative way to rehabilitate God by wiping these mandates "off the books," as it were, using the Creator's beloved prophet as their proxy, a man he selected and tutored. It also appears that this seemingly heretical depiction of God being corrected by a mere human represents another case of a key Jewish text serving to model laudable conduct: Moses' exercise of his moral autonomy to uphold justice and God's open-mindedness in permitting him to do so.[61]

Orthodox rabbis generally either tactfully ignore this midrash, which one representative describes as "extremely daring and theologically problematic, to say the least,"[62] or they attempt to tame it as best they can. As Rav Chaim Navon, a respected Orthodox scholar, writes in analyzing the last of the three cases cited above, "we consider also the moral values to which God had already proven that He was devoted, we must interpret those words differently; God apparently meant that, first of all, we must send Sichon words of peace."[63] Rav Navon's position is that, despite its apparently clear import, God's commandment regarding Sihon was not actually immoral but merely appeared that way before Moses deciphered God's true intentions in light of the Torah's global values.

---

61. The Talmud also includes various aggadic tales that describe God being defied in halakhic matters by the Rabbis or deferring to them. One of these is Rabbi Yehoshua's and his colleagues' refusal to accept God's verdict regarding the purity of the Oven of Akhnai, with the battle cry, "It [the Law] is not in heaven." A second example is God's willingness to accept, without question, Rabbi Nahmani's opinion on the halakhah of leprosy. Both instances are discussed further in chapter 8.

62. M. Lichtenstein, "To Err is Human," part II.

63. Navon, "Halakha and Morality," para. 4.

In order to avoid the implication that people are *always* entitled to reinterpret God's commands when they conflict with one's own ethics, Navon says elsewhere in his essay that this "exegetical tool" is one of many and that "Those [other exegetical tools] may sometimes overwhelm the moral considerations . . . In such a situation, we must prefer the mitzva to our moral principles, on the assumption that God understands better than us what is good and what is fitting."[64] This seems a rather unsatisfying stance. First, it counsels that (at least in some circumstances) people should deliberately act contrary to their best moral judgment, which seems at odds with both God's words to Abraham vis-à-vis Sodom (discussed in the introduction) and the value assigned to moral autonomy throughout Scripture.

Secondly, it also forces Jews, it appears, to arbitrarily pick and choose when the Torah's overarching values align with the best secular ethics and when they do not. Finally, with respect to the specific matter of destroying Heshbon without offering peace to King Sihon, Rav Navon's apology seems an artificial and ad hoc effort to avoid the plain meaning of both the commandment at issue and this midrash's attitude towards it. His reading seems impossible to square with the just-quoted report that, upon being corrected by Moses, God states, "I will nullify My words and fulfill yours."

As argued above, a far more consistent and plausible way to reconcile the Torah's immoral mandates with the best secular ethics is to understand that God values autonomy above all else; and that he expects that humankind will employ it to advance far beyond the ethics of some 3,000 years ago. For reasons previously adduced, the Almighty allows humanity to proceed at its own pace in making moral progress. While many of his laws and commandments are manifestly unjust, Scripture offers the world a vision of the just and peaceful society to which persons can aspire, as well as the means of achieving it.

---

64. Navon, "Halakha and Morality," para. 5.

3

Liberalism and Critical Rationalism

KARL POPPER (1902–1994) is almost universally recognized as one of the last century's most important philosophers of science and one who also made a lasting impact on political theory. While both aspects of his work contribute to a more comprehensive understanding of liberalism and should be viewed as an integrated whole, in the interests of clarity, it is preferable to begin with a description of his broader epistemology and then move on to its application in political philosophy.

Critical Rationalism

Popper's system of thought, which he termed "critical rationalism," starts with the insight that there is a crucial asymmetry between investigators' efforts to verify or confirm a scientific theory on the one hand; and to discredit or falsify it on the other. This difference is readily illustrated by the famous example of the claim that "all swans are white," which apparently was, at one time, taken to be an established fact. As Popper observes, the truth of any proposition of this form can never be conclusively proven because, no matter how many white swans are spotted, it is never certain that a black swan will not turn up (as, indeed, one did).

Conversely, it is always possible to falsify such a hypothesis by finding a single counterexample. This idea, coupled with the realization that all scientific theories can be cast in the form "all As are Bs,"[1] led Popper to recommend that, rather than searching for bulletproof theories to serve as the foundation for further progress, investigators should concentrate on "solving" existing puzzles that arise when observations or experimental data do not align with an incumbent theory's predictions.

Thus, says Popper, when scientists encounter such puzzles, they should ideally formulate bold new theories that make far-reaching predictions that can readily be tested, and thereby either corroborated (but not "proven") or falsified.[2] If the new theory survives such testing without creating even more serious anomalies, it will displace the reigning theory. The process, which Popper terms "conjecture and refutation," would then begin anew.

With each cycle, researchers get closer to the truth,[3] and perhaps might even arrive at it, but due to the inescapable possibility of the unexpected "black swan," they can never be sure they have. This is Popper's concept of "fallibilism," by which he means that all ostensible knowledge—with the possible exception of "necessary truths"—is uncertain and potentially false.[4] However, Popper's acceptance of fallibilism should not be confused with any doubt about the existence of truth, as this assumption plays an essential part in his system. As Stefano Gattei, an academic admirer of Popper's work notes, for him:[5]

> critical rationalism is closely associated with the search for truth. As human beings, we should be aware of our fallibility and critical of our theories—but we can move from the awareness of our

---

1. See Steele, "Reply to Huemer," 205.
2. See Frederick, "A Regimented and Concise Exposition," 11–12.
3. This is Popper's controversial (among Popperians) notion of "verisimilitude," introduced later in his writings. See Popper, *The Open Society*, 492, where he writes that "a statement *a* gets nearer to the truth than a statement *b* if and only if its truth content has increased without an increase in its falsity content." This was a substantial modification of his earlier views, which held that one can only judge the merits of one theory relative to another, and this revision was (and continues to be) greeted with skepticism by some critical rationalists. See Gattei, *Karl Popper's Philosophy*, 42–46. For the reasons stated in Henderson, "The Problem of Induction," §6, it seems that Popper's more recent theory is preferable.
4. According to Byrne and Hall, a necessary truth is: "one that could not have been false, one that would have been true no matter how things had turned out. As Leibniz put it, a necessary truth is one that is 'true in all possible worlds.' Plausible examples include '17 is prime,' 'If Moore is a bachelor, he is unmarried,' and so on." Bryne and Hall, "Review of *Philosophical Analysis*," para. 15.
5. Gattei, *Karl Popper's Philosophy*, 3.

fallibility to the criticism of our theories only if we deliberately aim at the truth. That is why truth plays, for Popper—as opposed as [sic] for Kuhn and Wittgenstein, for instance—the role of the regulative idea of scientific research and rational discussion. (endnote omitted)

In Popper's worldview, the key to progress is open-mindedness, and its mortal enemy is a dogmatic mindset that clings to entrenched opinions. In short, it demands a psychology of humility, which Popper describes in this oft-quoted passage, as:[6]

> an attitude of readiness to listen to critical arguments and to learn from experience. It is fundamentally an attitude of admitting that *"I may be wrong and you may be right, and by an effort, we may get nearer to the truth."* It is an attitude which does not lightly give up hope that by such means as argument and careful observation, people may reach some kind of agreement on most problems of importance. In short, the rationalist attitude, or, as I may perhaps label it, the "attitude of reasonableness," is very similar to the scientific attitude, to the belief that in the search for truth we need co-operation, and that, with the help of argument, we can attain something like objectivity.

Popper's Liberalism

Popper's political theorizing is distinctive in that his epistemology is logically anterior to his politics. That is, rather than arguing for or simply assuming the correctness of a particular moral theory and then deriving the state's ideal institutional arrangements from it, he posits that the profound skepticism that characterizes the "open society" will produce the greatest possible material and moral progress, including in governance. As argued throughout the course of this study, because of the striking parallels between Popper's recommendations and the dialectics of core Jewish texts, it is illuminating to examine Judaism from this standpoint. As mentioned in the introduction, Menachem Fisch appears to have been the first to outline this connection in a systematic way.[7]

---

6. Popper, *The Open Society*, 431.

7. As noted below, Avi Sagi also explicitly draws connections between Popper's epistemology and the ideas of important talmudic and medieval Jewish thinkers. See Sagi, *The Open Canon*, 185–86.

As mentioned above, Popper's political philosophy and epistemology must be viewed as an integrated whole. Thus, Gattei observes:[8]

> Just as in science there is no absolutely true theory so, in politics, there is no perfect society; just as science may advance by appealing to ever better but never ultimate theories, so society may evolve by adopting ever better forms and political assets, but these are never final. Just as in science, so in society growth is neither necessary or predictable, but depends on the effectiveness of institutions designed by rulers. Just as in science the problem is not the elimination but the correction of errors, without appealing to ultimate foundations or undisputable authorities, so in the political arena the central problem becomes that of establishing institutional checks for political choices.

Popper describes his ideal polity as an "open society" because it would instantiate an uncompromising receptivity to new ideas and forms of living. As one might anticipate, Popper's concept of the "closed" society is one that is completely shut off from new theories and lifestyles. He describes it as a "primitive tribal" society that "lives in a charmed circle of unchanging taboos, of laws and customs which are felt to be as inevitable as the rising of the sun, or the cycle of the seasons, or similar obvious regularities of nature."[9] Sadly, many insular Orthodox communities much more closely resemble closed societies than open ones.[10]

Popper's primary work of political philosophy, *The Open Society and Its Enemies*, was written during World War II and published in 1945. Thus, it was written with the unspeakable horrors of this conflict fresh in his mind. Nevertheless, in his preface to the second edition (1950), while acknowledging the destructive forces unleashed by modern science, he speaks hopefully and in praise of Enlightenment values:[11]

> It is the longing of uncounted unknown men to free themselves and their minds from the tutelage of authority and prejudice. It is their attempt to build up an open society which rejects the absolute authority of the merely established and the merely traditional while trying to preserve, to develop, and to establish traditions, old

---

8. Gattei, *Karl Popper's Philosophy*, page 97, n77.
9. Popper, *The Open Society*, 55.
10. See the discussion in chapter 7 below, note 17.
11. Popper, *The Open Society*, 2nd ed., xl.

or new, that measure up to their standards of freedom, of humaneness, and of rational criticism.

Popper's commitment to fallibilism also shapes his approach to the amelioration of social problems. This principle counsels him against the adoption of far-reaching social or economic changes grounded in overconfidence about being on "the right side of history." Having experienced firsthand the horrors of Hitler's rise in his native Austria, Popper was acutely aware of the dangers posed by revolutionary movements, which in service to an untested ideology engage willy-nilly in what he derisively terms "utopian social engineering."[12]

In its stead, he favored small-scale, incremental reforms, which he terms "piecemeal social engineering," the consequences of which can be reevaluated before they become catastrophic.[13] He also thought that such programs should first be directed towards alleviating dire poverty, since this, if successful, would produce greater utilitarian gains than benefits conferred on society at large.[14] Somewhat confusingly, he dubs this concept "negative utilitarianism."

In the first edition of *The Open Society*, Popper seems surprisingly sanguine about the efficacy of central planning in alleviating poverty and other social ills without sacrificing freedom. Perhaps at that time he did not understand the "economic calculation problem" identified by Ludwig von Mises and F.A. Hayek. In any case, in subsequent editions of this work, he expressed greater respect for free markets and sensitivity to the threats to liberty posed by state control. Thus, in his 1965 "Addenda," he writes:[15]

> it is most important to realize that without a carefully protected free market, the whole economic system must cease to serve its only rational purpose, that is, *to serve the demands of the consumer* . . . the market must be controlled, but in such a way that the control does not impede the free choice of the consumer . . . Economic "planning" that does not plan for economic freedom in this sense will lead dangerously close to totalitarianism.

That Popper's thinking evolved in a more distinctly liberal direction may also be seen in his discussion of the meaning of "justice." In the first

12. Gorton, "Karl Popper: Political Philosophy," §1d.
13. Popper, *The Open Society*, 148–49.
14. See Popper, *The Open Society*, 548–49, n6.
15. Popper, *The Open Society*, 712–13, n26. Popper cites here Hayek's pamphlet *Freedom and the Economic System* (1939).

edition of *The Open Society* (1945), he speaks of it as "an equal distribution of the burden of citizenship."[16] However, in his 1965 "Addenda," he clarifies his conception in a manner that brings it squarely within the liberal worldview by quoting with approval Kant's "equal right" formulation, discussed in the previous chapter.[17] Accordingly, Professor William Gorton rightly says that:[18]

> Popper's political thought would seem to fit most comfortably within the liberal camp, broadly understood. Reason, toleration, nonviolence and individual freedom formed the core of his political values, and as we have seen, he identified modern liberal democracies as the best-to-date embodiment of an open society.

Popper's epistemology was highly controversial when first presented in the mid-1930s and certainly remains so. It is far more complex and elaborate than can be adequately described in a short summary of this sort, and has spawned a vast literature of criticism and defense that encompasses important interpretative disagreements, even among those in sympathy with Popper's general perspective. Nevertheless, what has been presented here appears sufficient as a description of liberalism and critical rationalism to enable a fair test of this book's thesis that Judaism's core values are liberal, and that this is most apparent when they are examined from the perspective of Kantian notions of autonomy in conjunction with Popper's worldview.

Examples of Critical Rationalism in Classic Texts

If it seems preposterous that foundational Jewish texts could anticipate Popper's epistemology, consider the following two examples in response. The first is taken from the Torah's account of the egregious incident of the Golden Calf, where God himself models the use of debate and dialogue as a means of getting closer to the truth. This catastrophe suddenly interrupts Moses' time with the Almighty on the mountaintop learning the details of the commandments—at which point God tells Moses to descend quickly to the encampment to see for himself,[19] observing that, "this is a stiffnecked

---

16. Popper, *The Open Society*, 86.
17. Popper, *The Open Society*, 562, n4.
18. Gorton, "Karl Popper: Political Philosophy," §2.d.
19. See Exod 32:7.

people."[20] He bids Moses to "let me be, that My anger shall blaze up against [the Israelites] and that I may destroy them."[21] He then proposes to start all over again with Moses as the new Abraham and to "make of you a great nation."[22] Moses is not interested and implores God to sheathe his sword. He offers the Almighty two brief arguments for mercy, and, remarkably, "the LORD renounced the punishment He planned to bring upon the people."[23]

While God is appeased for the moment, he has not fully forgiven. According to Chazal, after Moses restores order among the Israelites, he again ascends Sinai to make extended pleas and arguments on behalf of his people for a complete pardon.[24] The Torah concisely records that Moses acknowledges to God the gravity of the sin committed by his people but defiantly tells the Lord, "if you forgive their sin [well and good]; but if not, erase me from the record You have written."[25] God is thereby persuaded to eliminate only those who produced and worshipped the Calf, sparing those who failed to intervene in its creation.[26] Before the Hebrews continue their journey to the Promised Land, God twice more calls them "stiffnecked."[27] Rashi explains that, in this context, the meaning is, "They turn the hardness of the back of their necks toward those who admonish them and refuse to listen."[28]

It is difficult to make sense of this story without invoking something akin to critical rationalism. Initially, note that God's plea to Moses to "let me be" is understood by the midrashic rabbis, based on a close reading of the text, as a thinly disguised invitation for dialogue: "God at this moment was like a person who has a grievance in his heart against his friend, and

---

20. Exod 32:9.
21. Exod 32:10.
22. Exod 32:10.
23. Exod 32:14.
24. Many of the numerous midrashic stories describing the arguments between God and Moses about the punishment of the Israelites, both during Moses' initial appeasement and subsequent quest for complete forgiveness, are collected in Ginzburg, *Legends of the Jews*, 124–34. They include some clever argumentative jiujitsu by Moses, as when he first tells God that he "supposes" the Golden Calf will "send down the rain and . . . cause the wind to blow," and when God reminds him that this idol "is absolutely nothing," Moses then asks God why he is upset over "that which is nothing." Ginzberg, *Legends of the Jews*, 129.
25. See Exod 32:32.
26. Exod 32:33.
27. Exod 33:3, 33:5.
28. Rashi, *Commentary on the Torah* (Exod), 32:9.

yet wished to be reconciled with him, so he says to him, 'Tell me, what have I done to you.'"²⁹ In other words, God is offering Moses the opportunity to reason with him, a motif that recurs in chapter 8.

Moreover, an omniscient divinity must have foreseen (at least in general terms) what would transpire when Moses, at God's behest, left his people for a forty-day tutorial; therefore, the Almighty's anger is mysterious. It is also evident that God would know in advance all the possible considerations that would inveigh for mercy and would learn nothing from Moses' input. Thus, one should not understand from these verses that God actually changed his mind. Instead, it seems probable that the author has constructed this story to depict God as being open to disagreement and questioning; and thereby serve as a "how much more so" example for mere mortals.

Finally, it is also significant that God criticizes Israel three times in this pericope for being unreasonably stubborn, the exact opposite of the virtue God appears to be modeling. Accordingly, it seems that the most convincing interpretation of this narrative is that it is intended to exemplify the virtues of open-mindedness and Socratic dialogue, which are key values in Jewish theology. At the same time, one should recognize it as an example of the Torah's esteem for moral autonomy because, as just noted, God not only permits Moses to argue with him, but to actually persuade him.

The second example of the critical rationalist worldview embedded in Judaism's classical literature is the Talmud's story regarding God's endorsement of the legal rulings of the House of Hillel ("Beit Hillel") over the contrary arguments of Beit Shammai. Hillel and Shammai were two great Sages active in the decades prior to and at the start of the common era. According to Chazal, they were the last of the *zugot* ("pairs") of scholars who were authorized by God to rule on matters of Jewish law and practice prior to the destruction of the Second Temple. So great were their reputations that hundreds of students came to study under them, forming academies that survived for centuries. Over the years, many legal disagreements arose between these schools, apparently reflecting fundamentally different philosophies regarding the purpose of the mitzvot.

One prominent scholar understands the school of Hillel's perspective to be driven by the view that the commands present a means by which Jews can achieve "an intimacy with God, and easily incorporate everyday

29. MR (Exod), 42 §2. This midrash reasons that, while God's use of "Go, descend" [a traditional translation of Exodus 32:7], is harsh, this is followed by the gentler "the Lord further said to Moses" in Exod 32:9, thereby striking a conciliary tone. See MR (Exod), 42 §2 and n35.

experiences into a religious framework."[30] Accordingly, this philosophy tends towards leniency and accommodation. In contrast, the school of Shammai thought the law should induce a fear of God to deter transgressions, and thus its rulings sought to keep the faithful "in a state of awe mixed with guilt," which results in legal interpretations favoring greater stringency.[31]

The resolution of this theological controversy is recounted in the Talmud:[32]

> For three years Beit Shammai and Beit Hillel disagreed. These said: The *halakha* is in accordance with our opinion, and these said: The *halakha* is in accordance with our opinion. Ultimately, a Divine Voice emerged and proclaimed: Both these and those [the Hebrew here is more commonly translated as "these and these"] are the words of the living God. However, the *halakha* is in accordance with the opinion of Beit Hillel . . . The reason is that they were agreeable and forbearing, showing restraint when affronted, and when they taught the *halakha* they would teach both their own statements and the statements of Beit Shammai. Moreover, when they formulated their teachings and cited a dispute, they prioritized the statements of Beit Shammai to their own statements, in deference to Beit Shammai.

In other words, the students taught by Hillel and his intellectual descendants were epistemologically humble, open-minded, and willing to reverse course when confronted with new facts or superior arguments. In contrast, those taught in the tradition of Shammai were dogmatic and stubborn. God's preference for the rulings of the Hillelites is an unmistakable endorsement of the sort of intellectual modesty urged by critical rationalists.

It must be said, however, that God's verdict in the Hillel/Shammai dispute is deeply unsettling for the Rabbis and post-talmudic scholars since it seems to call into question the objective truth of *all* the laws and commandments. In other words, if Beit Hillel's understanding of the law is *only* correct because of its students' admirable personal characteristics, does this not undermine the existence of moral *facts*? Unsurprisingly, the "these and these" language of *Eruvin* 13b has been the subject of countless,

---

30. Knohl, *The Divine Symphony*, 141, and see generally 135–41.
31. Knohl, *The Divine Symphony*, 141.
32. b. Eruv. 13b.

diverse commentaries from talmudic times onward, which are masterfully categorized and analyzed by Avi Sagi in his 2007 book, *The Open Canon*.

Professor Sagi divides these opinions into two basic families: "monism" and "pluralism." The former holds that there is "only one correct solution for every normative dilemma," while the latter "acknowledges more than one option is possible,"[33] with numerous subvariants within each camp. Both schools of thought face significant theoretical challenges. As Professor Azzan Yadin expresses it, the monist "will have to grapple with the heavenly voice's willingness to recognize both Hillel's and Shammai's rulings as true; a pluralist thinker would need to establish limits for halakhic legitimacy, lest any and all positions be treated as equally legitimate."[34]

Accordingly, one approach taken by monists is to reconcile with the apparent plain meaning of God's pronouncement by asserting that it refers not to the substance of the opinions offered but to the epistemic virtue of controversy; so both sides are the "voice of the living God" because they have played an essential role in the discovery of the truth.[35] On the other hand, to avoid assenting to multiple halakhic truths, many pluralists embrace what Sagi labels "weak pluralism"; that is, the notion that there is only a single truth, but due to humans' cognitive limitations, we can never be sure of knowing it and must therefore act on our best understanding. Thus, multiple theories can have intrinsic value. Sagi expressly assimilates this option to the thinking of J.S. Mill and Popper.[36]

It would take this study too far afield to delve much deeper into Sagi's taxonomy, but it is undeniable that there is much in Chazal's interpretation of *Eruvin* 13b that anticipates critical rationalism, including—in addition to the value of open-mindedness mentioned above—truth as a regulative ideal; human fallibility; and the necessity of controversy. Thus, Rav Yitzchak Reines (1839–1915), a leading Russian Orthodox rabbi of the modernist school and early Religious Zionist, writes:[37]

> By giving the Torah in this way . . . leaving room for doubts and disputes, the Torah showed that the will of God, may He be blessed, was that everyone should endeavor to aim for the truth without assurance of actually finding it because the quest for truth

33. Sagi, *The Open Canon*, 13.
34. Yadin, "Review: *The Open Canon*," 291.
35. See Sagi, *The Open Canon*, 141–43.
36. See Sagi, *The Open Canon*, 185–86.
37. Sagi, *The Open Canon*, 132 (quoting Reines's *Orah ve-Simhah*, 1898).

is beloved by the Holy One, blessed be He, and it as dear as truth itself. Truth is not naturally or intrinsically limited, no man could grasp it entirely, and his mission in the world is only to seek the truth."

These words would fit comfortably into Karl Popper's mouth, and as argued in the remainder of this text, such values are an essential aspect of Jewish philosophy, embodied in the faith's key texts and their authoritative interpretations.

4

The Ten Commandments, the Oral Law, and the Decline of the Generations

REGARDLESS OF EXACTLY HOW this event is conceptualized, the history of the Jewish *people* begins "at Sinai" with the giving of the Torah ("Matan Torah") and the Israelites' acceptance of their eternal covenant with God. Observant Jews commemorate Matan Torah annually at Shavuot, which was one of the three great pilgrimage festivals of biblical times, and celebrated today in synagogue services. The centerpiece of the Torah's account of revelation is the Ten Commandments, and this chapter posits that they embody a liberal, open-minded ethos that supports the thesis advanced in this study.

However, Orthodox Judaism adheres to two conservative doctrines that are inconsistent with this understanding of the Commandments: first, the Oral Law from Sinai (*Torah shebeʿal peh*) and second, the Decline of the Generations (*yeridat hadorot*), both of which are critiqued in this chapter. Finally, because they tend to undermine these two regressive principles, the Rabbis' explanation for the end of prophecy and their famous declaration that "a sage is greater than a prophet" are also discussed below.

The Decalogue or Ten Commandments

As demonstrated by the Torah's minute attention to the Revelation and by the absolutely central place it occupies in Jewish theology (and one might even say "mythology"), there is clearly something unique and special about Matan Torah. Such is its importance that the Torah provides two distinct accounts, in Exodus and Deuteronomy. These narratives differ in many details, including the wording of some commandments, the timing of various events, and the extent to which Moses acts as an intermediary between God and the Jewish people.[1] Thus, it may be surmised that the final redactor of the Pentateuch thought the occasion held such meaning that they were unwilling to omit any information provided by the ancient traditions, even at the price of admitting some uncertainty regarding the particulars.

The Torah stresses the magnitude of Matan Torah in a variety of ways, including by recording God's mandate that the Israelites maintain a state of ritual purity for the three-day period up to and including the Revelation and that they not ascend the mountain upon pain of death.[2] Additionally, the Torah continually describes events in supernatural terms. Thus, as God prepares to "speak," there is "thunder, and lightning, and a dense cloud upon the mountain, and a very loud blast of the [ram's] horn, and all the people who were in the camp trembled" and "Mount Sinai was all in smoke . . . the whole mountain trembled violently. The blare of the horn grew louder and louder."[3]

In the same vein, according to the Bible, here—and only here—the entire Jewish community "heard" God speak.[4] Indeed, there is an ancient tradition that God's words were so overwhelming that they produced mass synesthesia; that is, the confusion of sensory pathways. The Rabbis holding this view translate Exodus 20:15 as "All the people could *see* the *sounds*" (emphasis added), which Rashi understands to mean "They were seeing that which is audible, which is impossible to see elsewhere."[5] In contrast, when the bulk of the laws are subsequently given, there is none of this high drama. The formulaic phrasing is simply "The LORD spoke to Moses saying: 'Speak to the Israelite people and say to them . . .'"

1. See Greenberg, "The Decalogue Tradition," 280–84.
2. See Exod 19:10–12.
3. Exod 19:16–19.
4. See Exod 20:1–14.
5. Rashi, *Commentary on the Torah* (Exod), 20:15.

The Ten Commandments, the Oral Law, and the Decline of the Generations

Finally, God evidently feels the Decalogue to be of such transcendent significance that he carves it in stone as an eternal record of his "treaty" with the Jewish people. When Moses descends from Sinai with these two tablets and witnesses the Israelites desecrating the covenant with the infamous Golden Calf, he casts down and shatters the stones. After he manages to salvage this relationship by means of his heroic intercession with the Almighty over the course of forty days, God inscribes a second set, symbolizing the renewal of the covenant.[6]

Accordingly, it seems clear that God carefully selects these laws from the 613 that the Rabbis have identified in the Torah. In fact, Tradition is unequivocal in holding that their broad and abstract character, and their bifurcation into equally numbered subsets defining one's obligations to God and to one's fellow humans, respectively, show that they symbolize and subsume *all* of the commandments.[7] As one scholar observes, citing a number of classic Jewish texts, "The Decalogue encompasses fundamental principles which contain the entire Mosaic teaching."[8]

Because these commandments speak only in apodictic terms—e.g., monotheism, respect for human life, the value of truth itself—they open up space for interpretations that reflect humanity's evolving moral consciousness. As Leon Kass, a polymath whose expertise encompasses Jewish theology, writes:[9]

> Like the preamble to the Constitution of the United States, [the Decalogue] enunciates the general principles on which the new covenant will be founded, principles that in this case connect—the relation both between man and God and between man and man. It is less a founding legal code, more an orienting aspirational guide for every Israelite and, perhaps, every human heart and mind.

One might plausibly analogize the open-ended character of these mandates to others, like the Eighth Amendment to the U.S. Constitution that prohibits the infliction of "cruel and unusual punishments." Rather than attempting to describe specific forms of punishment that would be forever banned, the framers opted for a general criterion that would

---

6. See Deut 4:12–13 and 10:1–4.

7. See Rashi, *Commentary on the Torah* (Exod), 24:12.

8. Kadosh, "Decalogue, In Rabbinic Literature," 526. See also Houston, "Exodus," 111.

9. Kass, "Why the Decalogue Matters," §1. See also Greenberg, "The Decalogue Tradition," 303–4.

necessarily have to be applied in light of future norms. What qualifies as "cruel and unusual" in the twenty-first century differs from that which met this test in the eighteenth. Indeed, as argued in chapter 6, the books constituting the Tanakh engage in many important intertextual disputes, and so for this and the other reasons adduced in this study, there is good cause to think that the Ten Commandments were themselves intended to be challenged, tested, and—when appropriate—reinterpreted in response to new social conditions and evolving moral knowledge.

The Oral Law from Sinai (*Torah Shebe'al Peh*)

Because the notion of *Torah shebe'al peh* appears to be the more influential of the two traditionalist doctrines, it will be examined first. The central idea here is that the keys for resolving all halakhic questions arising from the Pentateuch's written text were handed to Moses at Sinai. Of course, it is known as the "Oral Law" because Moses did not record these instructions. Nevertheless, this canon bestows divine sanction on the regnant halakhah on the assumption that it was passed down intact from God to his intended recipients in an unbroken chain of transmission until conveyed to the Rabbis and finally recorded in the Mishnah. Naturally, this perspective will tend to stifle innovations that are inconsistent with earlier traditions.

Absence of Scriptural Evidence for the Doctrine

As previously argued, the Pentateuch should not be understood as any sort of reliable *history*, and thus it cannot substantiate the existence of the Oral Law from Sinai. However, because this study is devoted to conceptualizing Judaism based on its primary sources, it is necessary to determine whether the notion of *Torah shebe'al peh* is something constituent in these traditions, or whether it has been grafted on. It is apparent that, since the Torah's written laws are rife with obvious lacunae and ambiguities, an interpretative framework must have evolved alongside them. Otherwise, the religion would simply be inert.[10]

One example of this, mentioned above, is the halakhah of Shabbat observance. Another obvious case is the laws governing *kashrut*. Here again, apart from outright prohibitions, like pork and shellfish, the Torah leaves a

---

10. See Herr, "Oral Law," 15:454–55.

great deal unsaid, such as the meaning of the repeated puzzling injunction to "not boil a kid in its mother's milk."[11] A voluminous corpus of rules has been promulgated over the centuries by the halakhic authorities interpreting this and other dietary commands. The doctrine of the Oral Law from Sinai rejects the theory that these norms simply evolved over the centuries in the way of folk customs, which were then adapted and enforced by the Rabbis; and instead holds that these rules were given by God to Moses.

Therefore, the question arises whether this interpretation is supported by the text of the Pentateuch or by the rabbinic arguments for *Torah shebe'al peh*. In fact, the Torah does not affirm this doctrine in any literal or direct fashion. Rather, the Orthodox base this dogma on very weak inferences, such as the purported redundant reference in Exodus 24:12 not only to the Torah but also to "the commandments," which is expediently understood as the Oral Law.[12] Moreover, the countervailing view has far more support in the Five Books, as there are at least four instances in which the Torah recounts that Moses and the other leaders are flummoxed by legal questions, which plainly seems anomalous if they are armed with the Oral Law.

The first of these is the complaint brought by certain men who are evidently prohibited under the existing custom from offering the Passover sacrifice at the appointed time because they were ritually impure due to contact with a corpse (perhaps they were tasked with burying the dead in the halakhic manner). When these men approach Moses and Aaron to see if there is not some remedy for this unfair outcome, Moses instructs them to "Stand by, and let me hear what instructions the LORD gives about you."[13] God then tells Moses to inform the petitioners that they are permitted to offer the Passover sacrifice and observe the related commandments one month after the established date, a holiday religious Jews now observe as *Pesach Sheni* (Second Passover).

Moses, Aaron, and the entire community are also unable, without God's intervention, to determine the proper method of execution for the Sabbath desecrator described in Numbers 15:32–35. Similarly, Moses defers to God on the legal question posed by the daughters of Zelophehad, who protest to him regarding their impending disinheritance. Without going into the details of this complaint, the Torah reports that "Moses brought their case before the LORD. And the LORD said to Moses as follows: 'The

---

11. Exod 23:19, 34:26 and Deut 14:21.
12. See, e.g., Silberberg, "What is the 'Oral Torah?'"
13. Num 9:6–12.

plea of Zelophehad's daughters is just,'" and they are granted the requested relief.[14] Note that God's judgment is explicitly grounded in the demands of justice and not on some dry legal analysis, although it seems the Sages saw very little distance between the two.

Finally, in Leviticus, Moses is baffled by the question of the punishment to be meted out to the blasphemer of the Holy Name. Here again, the Torah reports that, after being brought before Moses, the man "was placed in custody, until the decision of the LORD should be made clear to them," and subsequently God commands Moses to execute him.[15]

Moses is described in Deuteronomy 34:10 as God's greatest prophet, but Scripture does not depict prophets as jurists, deciding matters of contract law, criminal jurisprudence, nor the details of ritual observance. Rather, they are God's agents for upholding his ethical values and commandments by, when deserved, speaking out against Jewish leaders and even the entire community for its transgressions.[16] The disability of even Moses in the realm of halakhah is driven home in the talmudic narrative considered at the conclusion of this chapter.

The Rabbinic Assertion of the Oral Law from Sinai

The cornerstone of Chazal's commitment to *Torah shebe'al peh* is found in the Mishnah, tractate *Pirkei Avot* (Ethics of Our Fathers): "Moses received the Torah at Sinai and transmitted it to Joshua, Joshua to the elders, and the elders to the prophets, and the prophets to the Men of the Great Assembly."[17] This tractate then further traces the transmission from generation to generation, until the time of Hillel and Shammai in the last decades preceding the common era.[18] It is cited by proponents of *Torah shebe'al peh* as establishing that the Oral Law was given by God word-for-word to Moses and then handed down in an unbroken chain to the Sages.

However, this doctrine seems to be subverted by this same source, as *Pirkei Avot* reports for each generation the name(s) of the recipient(s) of this oral tradition and quotes at least one sapiential saying by each Sage. However, for those Sages listed after Hillel and Shammai, it omits the

14. Num 27:1–7.
15. Lev 24:10–14.
16. See Sacks, "A Sage is Greater."
17. *Pirkei Avot*, 1:1.
18. See *Pirkei Avot*, 1:12.

formulaic "[they] received [the oral tradition] from them." This implies that the author(s) of this tractate believed the chain of transmission had at this point been broken or, minimally, was less trustworthy than before.[19]

Of course, for those who reject Moses and Joshua as historical figures, the account in Pirkei Avot is a nonstarter. Regardless of its origin, the rabbinic claim for the Oral Law as an infallible guide to the application of the Torah's written commandments is highly problematic for two reasons. First, as the Talmud recognizes, there arose numerous intense controversies during the Mishnaic period:[20]

> From the time that the disciples of Shammai and Hillel grew in number, and they were disciples who did not attend to their masters to the requisite degree, dispute proliferated among the Jewish people and the Torah became like two Torahs. Two disparate systems of halakha developed, and there was no longer a halakhic consensus with regard to every matter.

The existence of important disagreements among the Tannaim seems inconsistent with an extant Oral Law that could have been invoked to settle them, and therefore constitutes evidence that authoritative oral traditions required to resolve such cases were unavailable to the Mishnah's redactors. Accordingly, the Rabbis were "forced" to resort to reasoned argument.

Second, there is no historical evidence of any widespread rabbinic commitment to the doctrine of *Torah shebe'al peh* prior to the Amoraic period. As just noted, according to *Pirkei Avot*, these interpretations were transmitted from the prophets to the Great Assembly (or Great Synagogue), which Tradition regards as an institution created by Ezra and comprised of outstanding leaders, scholars, and the last of the prophets. Little is known for certain about this body, but according to Chazal, it was formed in the mid-fifth century BCE and continued into the early third century BCE.[21] The Rabbis credit it with closing the biblical canon, formulating the structure and basic elements of organized prayer, and establishing the festival of Purim, among other accomplishments.[22] However, academic research does not suggest that the men of this institution regarded the oral traditions they possessed as being *from Sinai*.

---

19. See Halbertal, "History of Halakha," 2–6.
20. b. Sanh. 88b.
21. See Spiro, "History Crash Course #32."
22. See Sperber, "The Great Synagogue," 19:384.

Even more telling, the immediate predecessor to the Tannaim were the Pharisees, a loosely knit group of lay preachers that were ideological and political rivals to the Sadducees, the priestly class that controlled and administered Temple worship and sacrifice. They were prominent from around 150 BCE to the destruction of the Temple in 70 CE. It seems that, while the Pharisees accepted long-standing orally transmitted interpretations of the law as binding, the Sadducees hewed to what they saw as the plain meaning of the text; and while the latter held that the Temple cult was of paramount importance in religious life, the former emphasized the need to serve God in every place and at all times.[23]

Crucially, the Pharisees overlapped chronologically with—and ultimately gave way to—the Tannaim as the final authority on the oral traditions. As Professor Schiffman, one of the leading historians of this period, states, "Inherent in later traditions, and indeed, in most modern scholarly treatments, is the assumption that the Pharisees bequeathed their traditions to the tannaim." Further, he notes, "Pharisaism traced its nonbiblical legal and exegetical traditions to the 'traditions of the fathers' or 'unwritten laws.' Yet nowhere do we find the Pharisees asserting that these traditions came from Sinai."[24]

According to Schiffman, the doctrine of *Torah shebe'al peh* was only accepted as a fixed halakhic principle much later:[25]

> At some point between the late first century BCE and the first century CE the notion began to be expressed that the oral law, along with the written, had been given at Sinai ... In the difficult years after the revolt [of 66 CE], when the support of the people at large ... was so important, the rabbis, in order to guarantee the authority of their teachings, occasionally appealed to the divine origin and nature of the oral law. It was only in amoraic times,

---

23. See Mansoor, "Pharisees," 6:30–31; and Mansoor, "Sadducees," 17:654–55.
24. Schiffman, *From Text to Tradition*, 178. Louis Jacobs concurs:
   > there is no question, however, of a uniform *halakhah*, even at this early period [late Second Temple era], *handed down from generation to generation in the form the halakha assumes in the tannaitic period*. Apart from the great debates on legal matters between the Sadducees and the Pharisees, the *halakhah* in the books of the Apocrypha (and the writings of the Qumran sect) is not infrequently at variance with the *halakhah* as recorded in the Mishnah and other tannaitic sources ... Even in the Pharisaic party itself the schools of Hillel and Shammai at the beginning of the present era differed on hundreds of laws (emphasis added).

   Jacobs, "Halakhah, Development of Halakhah," 8:255.
25. Schiffman, *From Text to Tradition*, 179–81.

however, that the full midrashic basis for these ideas was worked out, with the rabbis asserting that the oral Torah and its authority were mentioned in the written law.

The late Professor David Weiss Halivni (1927–2022), one of the foremost authorities on talmudic history, agrees:[26]

> The founding Sages of the rabbinic movement, at least for the most part, did not conceive of *Torah Shebe'al Peh* as an independently revealed corpus, as was assumed in the Middle Ages. Such a notion of Oral Torah does not find convincing support in the *oeuvre* of the earliest Rabbis.

As detailed in the next chapter, a strong case can be made that, with respect to the Rabbis' actual legal decisions and ethical pronouncements, the notion of an immutable Oral Law was honored more in the breach than in the observance, which is an independent reason to regard this doctrine as a rabbinic construct.

The Historical Background to the Claim of *Torah Shebe'al peh*

In tracing the origin of this principle and Tradition's commitment to it, it is necessary to consider contemporaneous events. The Tannaim were active from approximately the start of the common era until about 220 CE, when the Mishnah is generally thought to have been redacted and the generations of the Amoraim commence.[27] This era witnessed not only the unsuccessful "great revolt" against Rome, resulting in an estimated loss of up to a million Jewish lives and the destruction of the Second Temple in 70 CE, but the almost equally catastrophic Bar Kochba revolt that began in 132 CE.

---

26. Halivni, "The Breaking of the Tablets," 144. See also Fraude, "Literary Composition and Oral Performance," 37, note 11: "the idea of a twofold revelation [written Torah and oral Torah] becomes more terminologically fixed and conceptually developed in later Rabbinic sources."

27. With respect to the timing of the Mishnah's final reduction to written form, all that can be said with some confidence is that, by the close of the second or the beginning of the third century CE, this orally transmitted corpus of law was recorded in what is known as the Mishnah. See Wald, "Mishnah," 14:319–20. It is not known what caused the Sages to cease their practice of transmitting this corpus orally from rabbinic masters to their disciples. It may have been spurred by the proliferation of arguments and rulings to a point that was beyond the powers of human memory; the desire for a written record that would facilitate uniformity; or the fear that this precious legacy would be lost due to political upheavals.

According to Berel Wein (an Orthodox historian who relies primarily on traditional sources), in response to the second rebellion, Emperor Hadrian (reigned 117 to 138) decided to attack the problem at its source:[28]

> Their plan was to eliminate the scholars and sages of Israel, who were, after all, the true leaders of the Jews, and to forbid the practice of Judaism, the lifeblood of Israel, thus guaranteeing the Jews' demise as a counterforce to Roman culture and hegemony. The Sabbath, circumcision, public study and teaching of Torah, as well as observances of all Jewish ritual and customs, were forbidden.

Although Rabbi Wein does not say so directly, it must have seemed to many Jews that God had, as during the Babylonian conquest and exile, abandoned his chosen people to a cruel fate. Accordingly, it is plausible that this demoralized population may have been susceptible to Roman coercion. Under such circumstances, it would have been natural for the Tannaim and the Amoraim to emphasize the paramount importance of the rituals and practices enshrined in Judaism's oral traditions by assigning them divine status.

This period also, of course, saw the emergence of Christianity in Eretz Israel. Initially just a rival sect to Rabbinic Judaism, Christianity was clearly attractive to a sizable number of Jews, and the Rabbis may have felt the need to draw a bright and unambiguous line between what were doctrinally acceptable beliefs and customs, and heretical ones.[29] During Hadrian's time, the rupture was just coming to the fore, but the threat to Judaism posed by this movement would continue for centuries.

Indeed, it reemerged, perhaps in an even more threatening form, at the beginning of the fifth century following the Church's acceptance of Jewish Scripture as part of its canon of sacred texts. This raised the possibility that Christianity might lay claim to *all* of the Sinaitic revelation, distinguishing itself from Judaism simply by more lenient cultic demands. As Professor Israel Yuval, an authority on ancient Jewish history, expresses it, "The study of Oral Torah, and not that of Written Torah, became the great religious principle from that point on until today, because it alone defined Jewish uniqueness in comparison to Christianity."[30]

Professor Yuval points to the Byzantine Emperor Justinian's decree of 553 "prohibiting Jews from reading their *deuterosis*" (according to him, the

---

28. Wein, *Echoes of Glory*, 217.
29. See Katz, "Separation of Judaism and Christianity," 74–76.
30. Yuval, "The Orality of Jewish Oral Law," 248.

precise meaning of this term is uncertain, but it refers to some form of oral exegesis, probably talmudic-style discourse) to support his thesis that "the Oral Torah and orality played an important role in the struggle with Christianity."[31] The apparent motive for this decree was Justinian's concern that the form of study in question was preventing Jews from being exposed to Christian doctrine.

Yuval therefore asserts that "the oral study of the Torah . . . was thus understood as a factor that supported Jewish uniqueness and their refusal to convert to Christianity."[32] He concludes that:[33]

> the very formation of the Oral Torah was in itself part of a profound religious transformation in which the study of Oral Torah and the fulfillment of its commandments were placed at the very center of Jewish religious life . . . Christianity questioned, first of all the validity of the Divine law, and it is natural to assume that the Jewish reaction would be the opposite: to place increasingly greater emphasis upon the law and the creation of a comprehensive system of halakhah, most of which was a new invention of the Sages of the Mishnah and Talmud.

A subsequent development likely strengthened the commitment of Jewish authorities to *Torah shebe'al peh*; namely, the Karaite heresy that followed the Babylonian Talmud's reduction to its final written form. According to Tradition, this occurred at the end of the fourth century CE, led by Rav Ashi and Ravina II (two of the great Amoraim), who, it is commonly thought, feared that political upheaval could lead to the loss of this critical intellectual heritage. Tradition acknowledges that very minor editing by the Savoroi ("Interpreters") continued through the middle of the fifth century.

However, as Professor Richard Hidary, an Orthodox rabbi who teaches Judaic Studies at Yeshiva University, notes, "Modern theories regarding the composition of the Bavli show that it was redacted by fifth to seventh-century anonymous rabbis."[34] Additionally, according to him, current scholarship attributes much greater importance to the final layer of editorial revisions fashioned by the Stammaim (the prevailing academic term for the Savoroi), including assigning to them substantial responsibility

---

31. Yuval, "The Orality of Jewish Oral Law," 249–50.
32. Yuval, "The Orality of Jewish Oral Law," 249–50.
33. Yuval, "The Orality of Jewish Oral Law," 248.
34. See Hidary, *Dispute for the Sake of Heaven*, 372; and Wald, "Talmud, Babylonian," 19:478.

for the much stronger theological pluralism expressed in the Babylonian Talmud relative to its Jerusalem counterpart.[35]

This timing aligns neatly with the theory that it was the closing of the Bavli that ignited the Karaite heresy. According to Professor Meira Polliack, an expert on this era of Jewish history:[36]

> As long as tradition remained an oral medium and rabbinic midrash was not elevated to the status of a sanctified interpretive system, the Jews were able to accept and mitigate the inherent tensions between literal and nonliteral interpretation. Once Oral Law was unified and canonized in the form of the Babylonian Talmud and disseminated and made binding through the authority of the geonim, the subterranean tensions erupted, and a sociopolitical split was inevitable.

This movement, initially known as the Ananites after its founder, Anan b. David (ca. 715–95), originated in Jewish communities in present-day Iraq and Iran in the eighth century. It presented a potent political/ideological threat to traditional Judaism by the middle of the ninth century, which persisted for hundreds of years, particularly in the Byzantine Empire.[37] According to Professor Polliack, the Karaites "simply did not accept that Oral Law embodied any kind of live or authentic tradition that could hail back to Moses, not even remnants of such a tradition."[38] In the first few centuries of their existence, the Karaites were aggressive proselytizers, which "forced the Rabbanites to take note of their existence and combat them."[39]

Karaite theology held that every educated Jew was free to interpret the Torah's text for themselves with respect to its laws and ritual practices. As Yefet ben 'Eli, one of the leading Karaite scholars (who lived in the second half of the tenth century) proudly proclaimed: "all the Karaite scholars used this method [independent reasoning] and established what appeared to them as the truth and encouraged people to search (themselves) so much that a man is entitled to disagree with his father."[40]

The Geonim and their rabbinic successors feared that the religious autonomy advocated by the Karaites would inevitably fragment Judaism

---

35. See Hidary, *Dispute for the Sake of Heaven*, 384–85.
36. Polliack, "Rethinking Karaism," 90.
37. See Heller and Nimoy, "Karaites," 11:786–87.
38. Polliack, "Rethinking Karaism," 82.
39. Heller and Nimoy, "Karaites," 11:789.
40. Quoted and discussed in Polliack, "Rethinking Karaism," 82–84.

The Ten Commandments, the Oral Law, and the Decline of the Generations

into innumerable different competing groups, ensuring deep divisions that would pose an existential threat. An example of this reaction is expressed by R. Yehuda Halevi (1075–1141), one of the greatest Rishonim, in his book *Sefer ha-Kuzari*:[41]

> Should Karaite methods prevail there would be as many different codes as opinions. Not one individual would remain constant to one code as everyday he forms new opinions, increases his knowledge, or meets with someone who refutes him with some argument and converts him to his views.

Therefore, it is reasonable to hypothesize that the emergence of Karaism exerted significant social pressure for a "counter-reformation" of sorts that sought to more deeply entrench the divine, immutable status of the oral traditions. Indeed, Moshe Halbertal, one of the leading historians of halakha, notes that the defense of *Torah shebe'al peh* by Abraham ibn Daud (ca. 1110–180), one of its most influential advocates, "is certainly connected to anti-Karaite polemics."[42]

The final development that likely contributed to medieval Judaism's elevation of the Oral Law to divine status was the vitriolic and hateful attack made against Jews, Christians, and their respective Scripture by the very prominent Islamic scholar Abu Muhammad Ali ibn Ahmad ibn Sa'id ibn Hazm al-Andalusi ("Abu" to his friends) (ca. 994–1064). In a book with a title even longer than the author's name, the first portion of which is *Treatise on the Obvious Contradictions and Evident Lies in the Book Which the Jews call the Torah . . . ,*" ibn Hazm accuses the Jews of all sorts of depravity and claims further that the sacred text delivered by God to Moses at Sinai was deliberately corrupted by the Sages and Rabbis to suppress its many (imaginary) references to the future prophet Muhammad (the Islamic doctrine of *tahrif*).[43]

The pressing need to rebut the pernicious effects of ibn Hazm's highly influential screed may well have prompted Maimonides to write his famous "Thirteen Fundamental Principles of Faith," found in the introduction to his first major book, *Commentary on the Mishnah* (written between 1158 and 1168).[44] For present purposes, the key principle is the eighth, where, in

---

41. Quoted and discussed in Eldar, "The Karaites and the Oral Law."
42. Halbertal, "History of Halakhah," 3.
43. See Berman, *Ani Maamin: Biblical Criticism*, 196–98.
44. See Shapiro, *Limits of Orthodox Theology*, 120–21; and Berman, *Ani Maamin*, 201–3.

his elucidation, Rambam avers that *all* of the written Torah and much (but importantly, *not* all) of the Oral Law were revealed to Moses at Sinai and faithfully preserved, which leaves little room for subsequent manipulation or forgery, thus answering ibn Hazm's allegations.[45]

Although the epistemological challenges faced by historians and the crude tools they have available to surmount them make it impossible to say this with any certainty, it seems probable that the historical developments just identified had a dramatic effect on traditional Judaism that is felt to this day, including the notion of *Torah shebe'ah peh*. As Halivni expresses it:[46]

> The medieval notion that virtually all received rabbinic law was not only revealed to Moses on Mount Sinai, but was also transmitted by him to the generations gave rise to an untenable theological generalization regarding the Oral Law, eventually extending revelatory authority to every authoritative dictum found in a revered tome ... An essential and healthy acknowledgement of any sage's humanity and fallibility is missing in the zeal of the pious, and that lack, which leads to intolerance and rigidity, is a legacy of the medieval elevation of the entire Oral Law to the level of revelation.

Resistance to *Torah Shebe'al Peh* by Maimonides and Later Rishonim

As exemplified in the writings of Sherira ben Hanina (also called Sherira Gaon, 906–1006) and Saadia Gaon (892–942), both heads of important Persian academies, the Geonim generally accepted the notion of Oral Law from Sinai.[47] The undeniable existence of numerous legal controversies recorded in the Mishnah and Gemara were understood to be unfortunate breaks in the chain of transmission.[48] Accordingly, as explained by Professor Blidstein (1938–2020), one of the preeminent authorities on halakhic philosophy, the Geonim regarded much of the related discourse recorded in the Gemara, not as plowing new ground, but simply as "an attempt to recover aspects of the tradition lost by forgetfulness or error."[49]

---

45. See the discussion in Berman, *Ani Maamin: Biblical Criticism*, 201–2.
46. Halivni, "The Breaking of the Tablets," 162; see also Jaffe, "Oral Traditions," 11.
47. See the discussion and citations in Blidstein, "Oral Law as Institution," 171.
48. See Halbertal, "The History of Halakhah," 2–6.
49. Blidstein, "Oral Law as Institution," 171.

The Ten Commandments, the Oral Law, and the Decline of the Generations

However, as Blidstein persuasively argues, Maimonides' writings are inconsistent with the doctrine of *Torah shebe'al peh* because "the very structure of halakhic decision-making is reared on the distinction between the Scriptural and the rabbinic . . . Maimonides found it impossible, I believe, to silence this testimony."[50] Instead, according to Blidstein, Maimonides reads the commandment in Deuteronomy 17:11: "to act in accordance with the instructions given you and the ruling handed down to you [by the levitical priests or the magistrates mentioned in 17:9]," as an *institutional* authorization, starting with the Great Sanhedrin and including the Rabbis and their successors, to answer unresolved questions by their own lights.[51]

A number of Rishonim active in the second half of this era would reject the doctrine of Oral Law from Sinai in an even more profound way. The "both these and these" language of the heavenly voice that resolved the long-simmering Hillel/Shammai disputes is given a provocative interpretative twist in the writings of two important Catalonian talmudic commentators, Yom Tov Ishbili ("Ritba," ca. 1260–320) and Nissim Gerondi ("Ran," 1320–376). In his commentary to this aggadah, Ritba writes:[52]

> The French Rabbis of blessed memory asked how it were possible that both positions could be the words of the living God when one prohibits and the other permits, and they answered: When Moses ascended to heaven to receive that Torah they have shown him forty-nine reasons for prohibition and forty nine reasons for permission concerning each rule. He asked God about this and God answered that the matter will be given to the sages of Israel in each generation and the ruling will be as they decide.

Ran adopted a similar position, as did certain other late medieval rabbis.[53] This interpretation goes beyond Maimonides' view in regarding the Oral Law as open-ended *from its inception*, such that God invested Moses, Joshua, and all the successors mentioned in *Pirkei Avot*, and the Amorim, etc., with the authority to decide the law by majority rule.[54] Of course,

---

50. Blidstein, "Oral Law as Institution," 176.

51. See Blidstein, "Oral Law as Institution," 176–77. Halbertal agrees: "[Maimonides] was the first to claim that alongside the received tradition from Moses, the sages introduced new interpretations of the Torah of their own invention." "The History of Halakhah," 6. See also Berman, *Ani Maamin: Biblical Criticism*, 203.

52. Quoted and discussed in Halbertal, "History of Halakhah," 7.

53. See Halbertal, "History of Halakhah," 11–12 and n12.

54. See Halbertal, "The History of Halakhah," 12–13.

this licenses more liberal interpretations of halakha that reflect humanity's evolving moral sensibility.

The Decline of the Generations (*Yeridat Hadorot*)

The central idea of this doctrine is that the Sinaitic revelation is the absolute fountainhead of spiritual consciousness, inspiration, and piety; and that the wisdom and understanding conveyed by this awesome, otherworldly experience inevitably degrades with each passing generation.[55] Accordingly, later *posekim* should not overturn decisions of those who came before. However, there is no support in Scripture for the idea that God created the world in such a way as to ensure the unending regression of his chosen people nor, as argued below, is there any talmudic evidence for it as a coherent ideology. Accordingly, like the claim of Oral Law from Sinai, which was adopted by the Amoraim and enshrined by the Geonim to defend the theological status quo against perceived external threats, the notion of *yeridat hadorot* was created by them for this same purpose.

The textual evidence cited for the Decline of the Generations is a limited number of self-deprecating remarks by the Rabbis. As noted by Menachem Kellner, who has written the most comprehensive treatment of this subject, "there are about a dozen passages in which Tannaim or Amoraim give expression to the idea that they are inferior to their predecessors or that their generation is inferior to that of their predecessors."[56] Perhaps the most famous example of this is: "Rabbi Zeira said that Rava bar Zimuna said: If the early generations are characterized as sons of angels, we are the sons of men. And if the early generations are characterized as the sons of men, we are akin to donkeys."[57]

As Kellner notes, however, there are several talmudic counterexamples to this extraordinary modesty, such as this story praising Hillel: "The Sages taught: Hillel the Elder had eighty students. Thirty of them were sufficiently worthy that the Divine Presence should rest upon them as it did

---

55. See Spiro, "History Crash Course #32."

56. Kellner, "Maimonides on the Decline of the Generations," 156.

57. b. Shabb. 112b. R. Zimuna, apparently wishing to be precise, is said to have continued, "And I do not mean that we are akin to either the donkey of Rabbi Ḥanina ben Dosa or the donkey of Rabbi Pinḥas ben Yair, who were both extraordinarily intelligent donkeys; rather, we are akin to other typical donkeys." b. Shabb 112b. See Kellner, "Maimonides on the Decline of the Generations," 166, for Professor Kellner's discussion of this *sugya* and his compilation of similar instances.

upon Moses our teacher . . .".[58] A second would certainly be the aggadah involving Moses and R. Akiva that will be analyzed at the end of this chapter.

Further, Kellner points out that the talmudic examples of the Rabbis' professed inferiority do not establish that they viewed themselves as less adept in their legal reasoning nor more callous in their ethics.[59] Perhaps they saw themselves as lacking the supreme piety of their predecessors or were simply paying tribute to them for preserving the oral traditions during the chaotic, cataclysmic times that followed the destruction of the Second Temple in 70 CE. If this is so, it would not necessitate a slavish adherence to earlier legal decisions.

It is of paramount importance in examining the Decline of the Generations theory to recognize that its earliest known expression as a halakhic principle is in the tenth century, when Sherira Gaon used it as "an explanation for the fact that Amoraim did not dispute Tannaim and that Geonim do not dispute Amoraim."[60] However, the intervention of several centuries between the self-effacing rabbinic remarks discussed above and the declaration of this precept discredits the idea that it shaped the Rabbis' jurisprudence or ethics. As Kellner cautions, "[t]here does not appear to be any textual or logical connection, however, between that *practice* [upholding the Tannaim's precedents] and the idea that the generations must necessarily decline."[61]

It is true that, after R. Sherira formulated this concept, it was widely accepted by the Geonim, although Kellner has identified several respected Orthodox holdouts in more recent eras, including R. Yom Tov Lippmann Heller (ca. 1579-1654) and, more recently, R. Zadok ha-Cohen (1823-1900), whose views are discussed below; Yaakov Dovid Wilovsky ("Ridbaz") (1845-1913); and R. Abraham Isaac Kook (1865-1935). Without doubt, however, according to Kellner, the most conspicuous dissenter is Maimonides.

While he was apparently unaware of R. Sherira's specific pronouncement, Maimonides never articulated anything remotely sympathetic to this idea. Moreover, after reviewing a variety of the Rambam's writings, Kellner convincingly argues that he could not have done so without contradicting

---

58. b. Sukkah 28a, quoted and discussed in Kellner, "Maimonides on the Decline of the Generations, 168-70.

59. See Kellner, "Maimonides on the Decline of the Generations," 168.

60. Kellner, "Maimonides on the Decline of the Generations," 171.

61. Kellner, "Maimonides on the Decline of the Generations," 167.

his entire rationalist theology.[62] As such, according to Kellner, Maimonides was committed to the stability of nature over time:[63]

> In sum, [for Maimonides] the world is created but everlasting, and all the types of creatures in it will exist forever in the state in which they were created. There is no possibility that they might undergo a change of essential nature. Were this to occur, it would be an indication that God's original creation was defective and had to be repaired."

Accordingly, the notion that the character of Jewish leaders permanently changed for the worse after Sinai, plainly violates the Rambam's entire system of thought.[64]

Further, it appears that support by Maimonides for *yeridat hadorot* would be inconsistent with his forthright rejection in his Thirteen Principles (see above) of the claim that *all* of the Oral Law was given to Moses at Sinai. Accordingly, if the Amoraim and subsequent generations felt themselves free to resolve new questions without relying on ancient oral traditions, then they would, it seems, believe themselves at liberty to modify the rulings of earlier generations of *posekim*.[65] Deference to the earliest Sages would also be at odds with the Rambam's supreme commitment to the truth above all else and his faith that philosophical inquiry was, even above Torah study, the surest path to the knowledge of God, which he saw as the religious Jew's ultimate goal.[66]

This topic should not be left without mentioning the views of the late Rabbi Norman Lamm (1927–2020), a widely published scholar and longtime chancellor of Yeshiva University. After reviewing in some detail the talmudic origins of *yeridat hadorot*; its theological application in various contexts; the reservations expressed by important Rishonim and

---

62. See Kellner, "Maimonides on the Decline of the Generations," 174–85.

63. Kellner, "Maimonides on the Decline of the Generations," 175.

64. Nor, says Kellner, is it possible that the Decline of the Generations might be understood by Maimonides as some sort of "negative miracle," because in his thought even miracles are temporary. Thus, Kellner quotes Maimonides' *Guide of the Perplexed* III.50 (p.616): "It is well known that it is impossible and inconceivable that a miracle lasts permanently throughout the succession of generations so that all men can see it." Kellner, "Maimonides on the Decline of the Generations," 184.

65. See Kaplan, "Daas Torah," 38–41

66. See Guttmann, *Philosophies of Judaism*, 155–56, 180–81; and Seeskin, "Maimonides," §§ 2, 3.

The Ten Commandments, the Oral Law, and the Decline of the Generations

subsequent authorities; and other evidence,[67] Rabbi Lamm concludes that, while the judgments of the earliest rabbinic generations should be respected, they cannot be decisive for modern rabbis and jurists:[68]

> For all these reasons, the *nitkatnu ha-dorot* or degeneration-of-the-generations argument cannot be employed uncritically.
>
> Not all questions have been resolved for all time. "Our ancestors left us space to grow."
>
> Not only is there space for *hiddush* [innovation within the Tradition], but intellectual, scientific, halakhic, and philosophical creativity are positive goods, part of the unending search for truth, a search that—as we have seen—is characteristic of striving for holiness.

A Sage is Greater than a Prophet

The Rabbis report that, according to the annals of the Tanakh,[69]

> Forty-eight prophets and seven prophetesses prophesied on behalf of the Jewish people, and they neither subtracted from nor added onto what is written in the Torah, *introducing no changes or additions to the mitzvot* except for the reading of the Megillah, which they added as an obligation for all future generations (emphasis added).

However, this calculation only accounts for the oracles named in Scripture. Astonishingly, in response to a question by an anonymous Rabbi regarding the completeness of this list, the Gemara answers that, in biblical times, there was double the number of prophets as the number of (adult male) Israelites who left Egypt (meaning twice 600,000, or 1.2 million!). However, neither their names nor prophecies were recorded "because only prophecy that was needed for future generations was written down in the Bible for posterity, but that which was not needed, as it was not pertinent to later generations, was not written."[70]

According to Tradition, Malachi, who by his words appears to have been active in Jerusalem after the Second Temple was inaugurated, was

---

67. See Lamm, *Torah Umadda*, 75–89.
68. Lamm, *Torah Umadda*, 89.
69. b. Meg. 14a.
70. b. Meg. 14a.

the last of the biblical prophets, and prophecy then ceased until messianic times.[71] However, the Rabbis evidently did not view this termination as a grave threat, as they boldly declared that:[72]

> And a Sage is greater than a prophet, as it is stated: "And a prophet has a heart of wisdom" (Psalms 90:12), i.e., he is wise. When comparisons are drawn, who is compared to whom? You must say that the lesser is compared to the greater. Here too, prophecy is compared to wisdom, thus indicating that wisdom is greater than prophecy.

At first blush, this assertion reeks of arrogance. How can the Rabbis so casually conclude that a prophet like Moses, handpicked by God to lead the Jewish people, is inferior in wisdom to the Sages, who possess no such credential?

The most logically satisfying explanation of the Rabbis' assertion appears to be that offered by the above-referenced Chassidic master, R. Zadok of Lublin. He was a disciple and successor of R. Mordecai Yosef Leiner (1801–1854), founder of the Izhbitza-Radzin rabbinical dynasty of Eastern Poland.

As elucidated by Professor Elman,[73] R. Zadok's holds that, "For Moses and, by extension, his generation, Torah was still 'in Heaven,' and the human intellect was irrelevant to understanding. Those who had received the Torah were not destined to be its cultivators."[74] Therefore, because "the biblical period had prophesy, in the main human reason could not come into its own until the cessation of prophesy, after the Babylonian Exile."[75] In other words, as Orthodox Rabbi and scholar Hayyim Angel notes:

> the end of prophecy facilitated a flourishing of the development of the Oral Law, a step impossible as long as people could turn to the prophets for absolute religious guidance and knowledge of God's Will. Sages needed to interpret texts and traditions to arrive at rulings, enabling them to develop axioms that could keep the eternal Torah relevant as society changed.

71. See Angel, "End of Prophecy"; and Sommer, "Did Prophecy Cease?"
72. b. B. Bat. 12b.
73. My discussion of R. Zadok's views on the history of halakhah and related matters relies on the above-cited paper by Professor Elman, a respected talmudic authority. Given the depth and detail Elman devotes to elucidating R. Zadok's important theory, my presentation necessarily involves some simplification.
74. See Elman, "R. Zadok HaKohen," 8. Recall the four cases cited above in which Moses needed God's intercession to answer halakhic questions.
75. Elman, "R. Zadok HaKohen," 12, summarizing R. Zadok.

The Ten Commandments, the Oral Law, and the Decline of the Generations

But what of the two deeply conservative doctrines discussed above? With respect to *Torah shebe'ah peh*, R. Zadok answers that while Moses and the subsequent prophets *had* received the Oral Law, they understood it only in the way of messengers and not intellectually. This depth of understanding does not come quickly or easily. To this point, R. Zadok cites the talmudic dictum that "A person does not understand statements of Torah unless he stumbles in them."[76] Rashi, in his commentary on this *sugya*, explains that the use of "stumbling" conveys that "a person does not have a firm standing on their truth unless he stumbles on them, to teach mistakes and be humiliated by them, and then one pays attention and understands."[77]

Thus, says R. Zodok, the revelation of the inner wisdom encoded in the Torah would have to wait indefinitely because "only in the course of the generations do they see the light of day through the sages of each generation and through each individual soul which reveals innovations in Torah which have been prepared for it."[78] This, of course, is exactly the ongoing epistemological process envisioned by critical rationalists.

Nor does R. Zadok accept that *yeridat hadorot* implies that more recent generations of rabbis may not innovate, because knowledge is cumulative:[79]

> [O]nce these lights [of knowledge] are made available to every generation by the great ones among the sages of Israel, they are not sealed up; they remain open forever and become fixed laws for all Israel. Therefore, even though later generations are inferior [to earlier ones], they nevertheless maintain their awareness of [knowledge] as dwarfs [on the shoulders of] giants . . . and they themselves continue the process of opening new Gates. Even though they themselves are greatly inferior [in comparison to their forebears, their insights] are *more profound* for they have already passed through the Gates opened for the earlier generations."

Thus, any *spiritual* inferiority of later generations to their predecessors does not impugn their legal and moral reasoning.

R. Zadok's epistemology and the ontological distinction he makes between prophecy and jurisprudence, informs his analysis of the famous talmudic story that depicts Moses, upon arriving in Heaven, finding God

---

76. b. Git. 43a. See Elman, "R. Zadok HaKohen," 15 and n55.
77. Rashi, *Commentary on Talmud*, Git. 43a.
78. R. Zadok quoted in Elman, "R. Zadok HaKohen," 8–9.
79. Elman, "R. Zadok HaKohen," 6, quoting R. Zadok.

"sitting and tying crowns on the letters of the Torah."[80] Moses is puzzled, but the Master of the Universe explains to him that a future genius, Akiva ben Yosef, will one day be able "to derive from each and every thorn of these crowns mounds upon mounds of *halakhot*. It is for his sake that the crowns must be added to the letters of the Torah."[81] This story rests on R. Akiva's fame for ascertaining laws in arcane ways, including, by legend, from the decorative marks placed above letters in the Torah scroll.[82]

Moses is duly impressed and requests to see this maven in action, whereupon God miraculously transports him to the eighth row (the beginners' section) of Rabbi Akiva's future study hall. Moses is troubled that he cannot understand R. Akiva's teaching, but when the Sage responds to his students questioning the source for a certain law by telling them, "It is a *halakha* transmitted to Moses from Sinai," Moses is put at ease.[83]

While this narrative appears intended to defend the doctrine of *Torah shebe'al peh* by depicting even R. Akiva's esoteric halakhic interpretations as firmly anchored in the Revelation,[84] it fails to do so because, as noted by R. Zadok, Moses' grasp of these laws is of an entirely different nature than Akiva's. Thus, the latter was *not* simply acting as a clerk mechanically decoding the crowns God attached to the Torah's letters, but was finding *new* meanings. Moreover, this tale seems plainly inconsistent with the notion of *yeridat hadorot*, since R. Akiva is portrayed as every bit the equal of Moses. Finally, because knowledge is cumulative, this process will continue beyond Akiva as future rabbis adapt the law to the needs of their time, unhindered by the two constrictive doctrines described above.[85]

80. b. Menah. 29b.

81. b. Menah. 29b

82. See Kahana, "Midreshi Halakhah," 14:196–99, for a detailed analysis of his exegetical methods.

83. Elman, "R. Zadok HaKohen," 8.

84. There can be little doubt that, when necessary, the Rabbis felt free to interpret the Pentateuch's commandments in their best judgment without considering themselves rigidly bound by either precedent or the literal text. For example, their transformation of the mandate in Leviticus of "an eye for an eye, a tooth for a tooth" (24:19–20) into the requirement of monetary compensation. This idea will be revisited in the next chapter and in chapter 8, where the "Oven of Akhnai" story is examined.

85. Judaism's universal adoption of the more liberal and pluralistic Bavli over the Yerushalmi as the authoritative expression of the Rabbis' legal and ethical thought might also reasonably be seen to undermine the claims of the two arch-conservative doctrines considered in this chapter. The Bavli is clearly the more recent of the two Talmuds, thus risking more errors in the chain of transmission of the Oral Law, and since it was written

The Ten Commandments, the Oral Law, and the Decline of the Generations

Haggadah versus Aggadah

Because this study employs aggadah as an important tool for characterizing rabbinic ethics, a few words regarding its history and significance are required before proceeding further. In their hyper-focus on understanding, then rigorously observing halakhah down to the minutest detail, the ultra-Orthodox tend to greatly downplay the significance of the important but more abstract, qualitative norms conveyed by aggadah. Thus, one authority writes that:[86]

> In the world of yeshivot, especially those in Lithuania, central Europe, and Eastern Europe, in the past, and in Israel and the United States over the last few generations, an almost categorical distinction is made between *lamdanut* (traditional casuistic study), focusing exclusively on halakhic matters, and *aggadta* (i.e., aggadah, primarily of the Babylonian Talmud). The latter is not, and has never been, included in the classical yeshiva curriculum.

In explaining this emphasis, Orthodox thought-leaders typically cite pronouncements by the Geonim, such as the one by R. Saadya Gaon (c.882–942), head of the Sura Academy, that "one does not rely on aggadah [for biblical exegesis]," and the subsequent concurring opinion of R. Hai Gaon (939–1038), head of the Pumbedita Academy: "It should be known that the words of aggadah do not have the status of oral tradition ... And these *midrashot* are not tradition (*shemu'ah*) and not halakhah but were only stated by way of conjecture."[87] However, just as in the case of the doctrines of Oral Law from Sinai and the Decline of the Generations, it is evident that this dichotomy is not encoded in Judaism's core texts, but most likely is the product of historical developments in the Geonic era; namely, the previously-referenced threats posed by the Karaite heresy and Islam. As one prominent scholar notes,[88]

> Starting in the 8th century, Karaites challenged the legitimacy of the Talmud and the tradition of Oral Law that it represented. For

---

by Rabbis more distant from Sinai, there was arguably a "decline" in these authors' spirituality and wisdom. Accordingly, the Bavli's superior status seems plainly inconsistent with these two theories.

86. Lorberbaum, Reflections on Aggadah, 37–38. See also Harris, "Yeshiva."

87. The statements of these two Geonim are quoted and discussed in Lorberbaum, "Reflections on Aggadah," 33.

88. Simon-Shoshan, "World of Talmudic Aggada," Lecture 2.

the first time, rabbis were forced to become self-conscious about the nature and meaning of aggada in order to defend it from these attacks. At the same time, rabbis came face to face with the tradition of rational philosophy which was first developed by the Greeks and then embraced by early Muslims. Many important rabbis saw great value in this approach to theology. They had to figure out how to reconcile this systematic rationalism with the apparently ad hoc and highly figurative approach to theology found in the aggada.

Under such circumstances, the Geonim were understandably embarrassed by such "wild" talmudic stories as Moses dueling with angels (b. Sabb. 88a—89b); a Rabbi training animals to perform mitzvot (b. Hul. 7a–7b); and a Rabbi monster-slayer (b. Kid. 29b).[89] Therefore, as described by Professor Simon-Shoshan, they "demot[ed] Aggadah to informed opinion at best."[90] However, the Geonim's approach appears sharply at odds with the viewpoint of the Tannaim and Amoraim.

Indeed, there is persuasive evidence that the former understood there to be no meaningful distinction in the authority of the two sources. Not only does the Mishnah include an entire tractate (*Pirkei Avot*) devoted to defining ethical conduct in all aspects of social life and divine worship, but other tractates not only include midrashic stories, but seamlessly integrate aggadic elements with halakhic rulings.

For example, the Mishnah, tractate Sanhedrin, chapter four, describes how in a capital case the high court takes great care to ensure that witnesses testify truthfully, including warnings that their testimony will be examined carefully by the judges, "and if you are lying, your lie will be discovered." Furthermore, they admonish witnesses not to repeat rumor or hearsay (even from a trusted source).

The court underscores the gravity of the witness's responsibility in this matter by introducing the novel idea that:[91]

> Adam the first man was created alone, to teach you that with regard to anyone who destroys one soul from the Jewish people,[92]

---

89. The stories are identified and described in "10 Wild Talmud Stories."
90. Simon-Shoshan, "World of Talmudic Aggadah," Lecture 2.
91. m. Sanh. 4.
92. The language just quoted is, by scholarly consensus, *not* the original language of the Mishnah and Babylonian Talmud, which referred to "one life," but was subsequently changed in the Middle Ages to "saves an Israelite [or Jewish] life," probably because of the severe persecution suffered by Jewish communities at the hands of Christians. As Professor Marc Shapiro, a highly respected Modern Orthodox scholar, explains: "It is almost

i.e., kills one Jew, the verse ascribes him blame as if he destroyed an entire world, as Adam was one person, from whom the population of an entire world came forth. And conversely, anyone who sustains one soul from the Jewish people, the verse ascribes him credit as if he sustained an entire world.

In other words, saving a life by truthful testimony is like saving an entire world, while false testimony that convicts the innocent is like destroying an whole world.

The Mishnah then proceeds to give three additional reasons why Adam was created alone: (i) to promote peace by preventing any person from asserting that they are inherently superior to any other; (ii) to preclude any heretic from saying that there are many gods, each creating different people; and (iii) to teach that because God purposefully created all people from a common ancestor, and yet made every individual unique, each is a part of God's creation, with a personal contribution to make. Accordingly, every person must recognize the significance of their actions, especially when testifying in a capital case.

Obviously, the teaching regarding the supreme importance of "one life" not only has legal implications but also ethical and philosophical consequences that extend far beyond "blackletter" law. For one thing, it seems to plainly cut against utilitarianism, or the idea that we should act to promote "the greatest good for the greatest number." Under the Mishnah's principle, "saving one life" may oblige other people to make great sacrifices in their own happiness or welfare.

Accordingly, Stephen Wald, Ph.D., a prolific independent scholar, seems justified in writing that in the Mishnah:[93]

> Aggadah . . . investigates and interprets the *meaning*, the *values*, and the *ideas* which underlie the concrete forms of religious life. . . . Continuing the tendency to define aggadah as "that which is not halakhah," we could say that the relation between aggadah and halakhah is similar in many ways to the relations between theory and practice, between idea and application, and in the area of ethics between character and behavior.

In support of this view he quotes *Sifre Deuteronomy* 49 (an ancient halakhic midrash, recorded contemporaneously with the Mishnah): "If you desire to

---

certain that the addition of 'Jewish' was ideologically based, designed to limit the universalist message found in the original." See Shapiro, *Limits of Orthodox Theology*, 213.

93. Wald, "Mishnah," 14:322. See also, Schiffman, *From Text to Tradition*, 187–88.

know the One who spoke and the world came to be, then you should study aggadah, for in this way you will come to know the One who spoke and the world came to be, and *you will cleave to his ways*."[94]

It does appear that by Amoraic times the Rabbis had begun to differentiate halakhah and aggadah, and at least the talmudic Rabbis (but not their midrashic counterparts) had begun to assert the superiority of the former for determining the law; however, they did not exclude aggadah for purposes of legal interpretation nor denigrate its importance as an ethical guide. Thus, Simon-Shoshan writes: "What is the relationship between halakha and aggada in these [Tannaitic and Amoraic] sources? They are certainly distinct categories, and quite possibly contrasting. However, there is nothing in these texts to suggest that they are either mutually exclusive or antithetical."[95]

Judah Goldin (1914–1998), a distinguished scholar of the Talmud, has a similar view, seeing halakhah and aggadah as two irreducible, competing ways of appreciating God's will. His investigation of this controversy from Tannaitic times through the Geonic era reveals a constant struggle to reconcile these perspectives, both of which are essential elements of the faith:[96]

> There are three parts of the Oral Law, [legal] midrash, halakhot, and aggadot, and I wish to submit that already in the early talmudic centuries there had developed a tension between the first two parts and the third. Keep to the four ells of the halakhah means bluntly, haggadah is not important. Study haggadah if you wish to recognize the Creator and cleave to His ways means bluntly, It's not from halakhot that you'll learn this momentous lesson. We are in the presence of the permanent human agon between restraint and freedom. . . . They are an articulation of the fundamental, universal, interminable combat of obedience and individual conceit.

Moreover, any effort to disparage the theological importance of aggadah would have to explain why the Almighty devoted most of the Pentateuch to superb, meaning-infused stories, rather than a dry recitation of

---

94. Quoted by Wald, "Mishnah," 14:322.

95. Simon-Shoshan, "Talmudic Aggada, Lecture 1."

96. Goldin, "Halakah and Aggadah," 69 (endnote omitted). Heschel writes something in this same vein: "To maintain that the essence of Judaism consists exclusively of halakhah is as erroneous as to maintain that the essence of Judaism consists exclusively of agadah. The interrelationship between halakhah and agadah is the very heart of Judaism. Halakhah without agadah is dead, agadah without halakhah is wild." "Halakhah and Agadah," 175–76.

the 613 laws,[97] and why the books of the Prophets and Writings consist almost entirely of non-legal materials. Further, the Rabbis not only devote minute attention to these narratives, but also compose their own, including (in addition to the "wild" stories cited above) God's arbitration of the Hillel/Shammai dispute (chapter three); Moses visiting Akiva's academy, discussed above; and the Oven of Akhnai controversy, examined in chapter eight. It is evident they understood full well the power of narrative to convey deep truths in a manner beyond the power of formal argument.[98]

Although he does not use this terminology, Professor Robert Cover's (1943–1986) interpretation of the ancient Greek word "nomos" as describing a society's "normative universe" provides valuable insight into the relationship between aggadah and halakhah.[99] Cover asserts that "No set of legal institutions or prescriptions exist apart from the narratives that locate it and give it meaning."[100] He enlists the Torah as a classic example by juxtaposing the traditional law of birthright—giving the elder son the right to head the household and receive a double inheritance upon the death of the father[101]—with "all the stories of the patriarchs [that] revolve around the overturning of the 'normal' order of succession."[102]

---

97. If the Almighty distains narrative as a vehicle for conveying his will, it would be well-neigh impossible to account for the presence in the Five Books of the tale of King Balak and Balam, the gentile prophet (Num chs. 22–23), whom the former hires to defeat the Israelites by cursing them. God not only demonstrates the futility of such a project by literally substituting words of praise for curses in Balaam's mouth, but also humiliates the prophet by causing him to be justly berated by the magically talking she-ass he has been riding.

98. Indeed, stories are an essential aspect of human consciousness, the means by which order is imposed on a chaotic, impersonal world. The essayist Joan Didion beautifully expresses this idea in her essay "The White Album":

> We tell ourselves stories in order to live . . . The naked woman on the ledge outside the window on the sixteenth floor is a victim of acidie, or the naked woman is an exhibitionist, and it would be "interesting" to know which . . . We look for the sermon in the suicide, for the social or moral lesson in the murder of five. We interpret what we see, select the most workable of the multiple choices. We live entirely, especially if we are writers, by the imposition of a narrative line upon disparate images, by the "ideas" with which we have learned to freeze the shifting phantasmagoria which is our actual experience.

99. Didion, *The White Album*, 11.

100. Cover, "Nomos and Narrative," 4 (footnote omitted).

101. See Deut 21:15–17.

102. Cover, "Nomos and Narrative," 20–21 (footnote omitted).

The consequence of this dualism is that:[103]

> in every instance in the Bible where the issue of succession is contested, there is a layer of meaning added to the event by virtue of the fact that the mythos of this people has associated the divine hand of destiny with the typology of reversal of this particular rule . . . To be an inhabitant of the biblical normative world is to understand first, that the rule of succession can be overturned; second, that it takes a conviction of divine destiny to overturn it; and third that divine destiny is likely to manifest itself precisely in overturning this specific rule.

Accordingly, it would be highly misleading to interpret the laws promulgated by the Rabbis apart from the narratives that envelope them or to impugn the authority of aggadah in the realm of Jewish ethics.

Summary

To sum up the arguments presented in this chapter: accepting the scholarly consensus that the final redaction of the Pentateuch occurred around the late sixth century BCE[104] and that the full rabbinic commitment to *Torah shebe'al peh* did not occur until the Amoraic period, there is an approximately seven-century gap between the Torah's finalized text and the adoption of this doctrine. An even longer interval intrudes before the idea of *yeridat hadorot* is expounded in any systematic way. This alone strongly suggests that neither of these regressive doctrines, nor the values they represent, are intrinsic to Judaism. Rather, they were the product of the respective Amoraim's and Geonim's perception that Judaism was threatened by exigent external forces that justified extraordinary countermeasures.

Furthermore, as the centuries passed, traditionalist scholars had second thoughts about both doctrines, as there are prominent Rishonim and subsequent commentators that reject both principles. Moreover, it seems that the Rabbis' declaration that the age of prophecy had ended and that they would now assume sole responsibility for determining the Oral Law ("a sage is greater than a prophet") is best explained by invoking the notions of moral autonomy and epistemic humility.

---

103. Cover, "Nomos and Narrative," 22.
104. See Schmid, "Who Wrote the Torah?"; and Davies, "Introduction to the Pentateuch," 26–27, 50–51.

The Ten Commandments, the Oral Law, and the Decline of the Generations

Finally, the reactionary impulse embodied in these two creeds is contrary to the liberal, open-minded ideals of the Ten Commandments; and with the great weight accorded moral agency, pluralism, controversy, and tolerance in the Torah and rabbinic literature. Accordingly, these doctrines should be regarded as unfortunate and illiberal missteps that do not constitute or define authentic Judaism.

5

Rabbinic Innovation and Pluralism

A LIBERAL SOCIETY WILL be sensitive and responsive to changes in social norms and conditions, and its members will continuously explore new ideas and forms of living. In this chapter, rabbinic Judaism will be evaluated in terms of its allegiance to the values that facilitate such innovation. The historical evidence reveals the Rabbis' remarkably strong commitment to the tolerance and open-mindedness recommended by Popper and liberal thinkers generally.

The Embrace of Controversy

Given the diversity of ideologies and worldviews held by its members, a society governed by liberal values will, by definition, be rife with disagreement, much of it fundamental. Ideally, it will facilitate and defend an unfettered marketplace of ideas within which all such views may be contested. This is necessary both because persons have the moral right to express themselves, even in an ignorant or hateful manner, and because, as Popper emphasized, only by recognizing the fallibility of all human theories and beliefs will humanity make progress in its social and intellectual endeavors. Perhaps the most eloquent defense of this idea remains John Stuart Mill's *On Liberty*.[1]

---

1. Mill, *On Liberty*.

Rabbinic Innovation and Pluralism

To a degree that seems to be far in advance of the norms of their era, the Rabbis embrace robust debate, disagreement, and dissent. In fact, this idea is directly endorsed by the Mishnah, the earliest and thus, in the eyes of Chazal, the most authoritative stratum of the Talmud:[2]

> Every dispute that is for the sake of Heaven, will in the end endure; But one that is not for the sake of Heaven, will not endure. Which is the controversy that is for the sake of Heaven? Such was the controversy of Hillel and Shammai. And which is the controversy that is not for the sake of Heaven? Such was the controversy of Korah and all his congregation.

As seen in chapter 3, Tradition holds that the disputes between the Houses of Shammai and Hillel advanced the cause of truth, and so, the Talmud holds, "will endure."[3]

A second well-known talmudic *sugya* similarly illustrates a controversy that is for the sake of heaven. When the famous Rabbi Shimon ben Lakish (third century CE) died, his dear friend and longtime study partner Rabbi Yohanan was disconsolate. His fellow rabbis sought to ease his suffering by designating a new partner, Rabbi Eleazar, to learn with him. However, this evidently was a bad match, for the Talmud records that R. Yohanan complained that, when he studied with R. Lakish, he "would raise twenty-four separate objections, to which I gave twenty-four answers, which led to a fuller understanding of the law. And [all] you say is: There is a baraita that supports you. Do I not know that my opinions are well-grounded."[4]

In stark contrast, the controversy instigated by Korach in the Wilderness is chosen to illustrate a dispute that was not "for the sake of heaven," and was therefore terminated in sudden, dramatic fashion. Korach (a member of the elite priestly class), in the eponymous Torah *parshat*, leads

---

2. *Pirkei Avot*, 5:17.

3. As mentioned above, the academies of Beit Hillel and Beit Shammai existed for hundreds of years, extending deep into the period of the Amoraim. The Talmud includes accounts of harmony between members of the two academies, including a report that, despite their intense legal disagreements, they permitted their children to intermarry. See b. Yevam. 14a–b. This happy picture is marred by stories of conflict and even murderous violence perpetrated by Beit Shammai against members of Beit Hillel. See m. Shabb. 1:4. The most natural interpretation of the Mishnah's statement that the disputes between these two schools was "for the sake of heaven" is that this refers to the generally friendly relationship that existed, rather than the episodic outbreaks of violence.

4. b. B. Metz. 84a. Quoted and discussed in Ben-Menahem, "Controversy and Dialogue," 5–6.

an open mutiny against Moses.[5] According to Tradition, this insurrection was motivated by Korach's anger that Elitzafan, one of his cousins, was granted leadership over their branch of the tribe of Levi, even though Korach's father was the older brother of Elitzafan's father, which customarily would have made the position Korach's.[6] The text in Numbers makes it patent that the controversy Korach initiates is driven by his lust for power and his stubborn refusal to recognize that Moses' leadership is ordained by God. The rebellion ends when the Earth opens up and swallows Korach, his inner circle, and all their possessions, while his 250 followers are consumed by fire.

Intriguingly, according to this midrash, Korach sought to advance his revolution by subverting Moses' authority with insincere halakhic arguments designed to make it appear that Moses was not faithfully conveying God's will, including his appointment of his brother Aaron as High Priest. It is noteworthy that Moses patiently answers Korach's devious objections, preferring persuasion to force. Only when all attempts to peacefully dissuade Korach fail do he and his co-conspirators meet their fate.[7]

To be sure, there were Rabbis who deeply distrusted controversy because, among other reasons, they believed (i) that the Torah provided clear answers to all halakhic disputes, discoverable by proper study, and that multiple acceptable "answers" would confuse people into believing that they could follow the most "convenient" interpretation, even aberrant ones; and (ii) that competing interpretations would weaken social cohesion, potentially endangering the community in the face of external threats.[8]

Nevertheless, in addressing the Rabbis' attitude towards controversy, Professor Ben-Menahem concludes that:[9]

> The halakhic acceptance of controversy, properly conducted, as a positive phenomenon ... reaches fruition in the idea that not only is ongoing controversy not harmful, but it is actually beneficial and desirable inasmuch as it fosters harmonious intellectual creativity ... The conception that peace is achieved through controversy is also grounded in the notion that that one is duty-bound to engage in controversy if doing so is conducive to arriving at the truth.

---

5. See Num 16:1–35.
6. See *Midrash Tanchuma*, Korach, siman (chapter) 1
7. See *Midrash Tanchuma*. Korach, siman 2.
8. See Ben-Menahem, "Controversy and Dialogue," 20–21; and chapter 3 above.
9. Ben-Menahem, "Controversy and Dialogue," 32–33.

Ben-Menahem goes on to observe that, as discussed in the previous chapter, opposition to controversy was much more intense in the Geonic period as a response to the Karaite heresy.[10]

The Bavli's positive view of controversy is echoed in modern times by Rabbi Naftali Zvi Yehuda Berlin, commonly known as the "Netziv" (1816–1893), for several decades the head of the legendary Volozhin Yeshiva in Lithuania. He interprets the first sentence in Genesis, chapter 11, that introduces the Tower of Babel story—"Everyone on earth had the same language and the same words"[11]—as a harbinger of doom, revealing that community's unholy quest to enforce uniformity of thought:[12]

> They feared that since not all human thoughts are identical, if some would leave they might adopt different thoughts. And so they saw to it that no one left their enclave. Anyone who deviated from *devarim ahadim*, the "one speech" that was among them would be sentenced to burning, as was done to our forefather Abraham. What emerges [from this text] is . . . they decided to kill anyone who did not think as they did.

According to the Netziv, God could not abide this project, and so the "LORD scattered them from there over the face of the whole earth; and they stopped building the city."[13]

Respect for Minority Opinions

A community that values controversy will necessarily respect and preserve minority opinions, both within its legal system and more broadly. The wholehearted acceptance of dissent and dissenters is a hallmark of the liberal state, both because people have a right to their opinions and because of the fallible nature of human beings. What appears indubitable today will often seem, with equal certainty, false at some future time.

This is characteristic of the American judicial system, where dissenting opinions are published alongside the majority's. There are numerous examples of Supreme Court decisions that were subsequently understood to

---

10. See Ben-Menahem, "Controversy and Dialogue," 34.
11. Gen 11:1–9.
12. Quoted and discussed in Klitsner, *Subversive Sequels in the Bible*, 39–40.
13. Gen 11:8.

be egregiously wrong both as a matter of constitutional law and morality.[14] Limiting this discussion to a single infamous case, in *Plessy v. Ferguson*, 163 U.S. 537 (1896), the Court, by a seven-to-one majority (one Justice being unable to participate), upheld a Louisiana law mandating segregated railroad cars for white and non-white passengers and imposing criminal punishment on passengers who dared to sit in cars not designated for their race.

The constitutional challenge to this statute was based on the Thirteenth Amendment's abolition of slavery and the Fourteenth Amendment's equal protection clause. While the court could not deny that the text of the latter Amendment expressly prohibits the denial to any citizen of "the equal protection of the laws," it held—based on existing social practices—that "it could not have been intended to abolish distinctions based upon color, or to enforce social, as distinguished from political, equality, or a commingling of the two races upon terms unsatisfactory to either."[15] Accordingly, the majority was satisfied by the law's formal requirement that the railroad service provided to whites and non-whites be of equal quality (the so-called "separate but equal" doctrine).

Justice Harlan, who came to be known as the Great Dissenter, strongly objected. He argues that, among other reasons, the "equal accommodation" provision of the law was an obvious pretext for racial discrimination, and that its real intent was clearly to keep black people from mixing with white people: "The fundamental objection, therefore, to the statute, is that it interferes with the personal freedom of citizens."[16] Harlan correctly predicted that "the judgment this day rendered will, in time, prove to be quite as pernicious as the decision made by this tribunal in the *Dred Scott case* [*Dred Scott v. Sandford*, 60 U.S. 393 (1857)]."[17] And yet, this decision remained good law for almost six decades until *Brown v. Board of Education of Topeka*, 347 U.S. 483 (1954) overruled it, at least in the context of public education. Unsurprisingly, the future Supreme Court Justice Thurgood Marshall, in his capacity as attorney for plaintiffs in *Brown*, cites Harlan's dissent in his successful arguments to the Court.[18]

---

14. A list and brief description of thirteen important Supreme Court decisions that were overturned either by subsequent rulings of the court or by acts of Congress may be found in Grabianowski and McManus, "13 Overturned Supreme Court Cases."

15. *Plessy v. Ferguson*, 163 U.S. at 544.

16. *Plessy v. Ferguson*, 163 U.S. at 557 (Harlan, J., dissenting).

17. *Plessy v. Ferguson*, 163 U.S. at 559 (Harlan, J., dissenting). .

18. See Thompson, "Plessy v. Ferguson." It is virtually beyond question that the opposite outcomes in *Plessy* and *Brown* cannot be attributed to the superior reasoning

Rabbinic Innovation and Pluralism

Like the United States Supreme Court, the House of Hillel demonstrated the willingness to change its opinion,[19] and this plausibly explains God's preference for its rulings. As Noam Zion, a respected Jewish philosopher, argues:[20]

> Humility and teaching the opponent's view means in the future that the decision can be reconsidered while preferring Shammai is the end of debate. Shammai will suppress the dissenting view. Decisions made by Hillel, even if mistaken, are subject therefore to reconsideration. So there is less risk in choosing Hillel's view since it is open to a self-corrective process unlike that of Shammai.

It seems that the Sages keenly appreciated that, in order to avoid potentially disastrous consequences, some means *must* exist to reverse legal rulings that were wrongly decided. Accordingly, this problem is explicitly addressed in the well-known Mishnaic tractate *Eduyot* 1:5. Here, it is asked: "And why do they record the opinion of a single person among the many, when the halakhah must be according to the opinion of the many?"[21]

The Mishnah then answers:[22]

> So that if a court prefers the opinion of the single person it may depend on him. For no court may set aside the decision of another court unless it is greater than it in wisdom and in number. If it was greater than it in wisdom but not in number, in number but not in wisdom, it may not set aside its decision, unless it is greater than it in wisdom and in number.

---

ability of the justices in the latter case (decided unanimously), but rather to the evolution of social attitudes, reflecting moral progress. The *Plessy* court knew that an overwhelming majority of white Southerners strongly desired segregated rail cars, schools, housing, and all forms of public accommodation. Attitudes in the North would no doubt have been somewhat more tolerant, but even there, legally enforced segregation would have likely garnered strong minority or even majority support. Had the *Plessy* court overruled Louisiana's law, the justices would have been personally vilified, and riots may well have ensued. By the time of *Brown*, there was probably much less of a chance for widespread violence, even in the South, and likely a solid majority support for the ruling outside of it. It seems reasonable to suppose that the Rabbis also felt the force of public opinion.

19. Kimelman, "Judaism and Pluralism," 138 ("The Mishnah reports quite a few instances in which Beit Hillel reversed their position in favor of Beit Shammai, while there is only a single ambiguous instance of the latter following suit.")

20. Zion, "Elu v'Elu," 25.

21. m. Ed. 1:5.

22. m. Ed. 1:5.

The logical connection between the "depend on him" phrase in the first sentence quoted above and "set aside" procedure in what follows is somewhat obscure. One common understanding is that, while the basic rule is that a later court can reverse the decision of a prior court only if it is greater both in "wisdom and number," an "inferior" court may nevertheless overrule it if it relies on a dissenting view expressed at the time of the original ruling.[23]

Moreover, while the exact latitude of this power is widely contested, in a number of circumstances the Rabbis explicitly authorize a *beit din* (religious court) to rely on minority opinions in cases where the majority-backed rule would impose great financial loss or other hardships.[24] Additionally, there are a number of categories of halakhic decision-making where the Talmud expressly authorizes use of the more lenient legal interpretation, even if (as is often the case) it is the minority view. These include matters of mourning[25]; *eruvim* (ritual enclosures)[26]; and the application outside the Land of Israel of laws originally intended to be observed there.[27] For a discussion of these and other examples, see Helfgot's "Minority Opinions and their Role in Hora'ah"[28] and the section immediately below regarding halakhic innovations.

In light of the postulated affinity described in chapter 3 between rabbinic methodology and critical rationalism, it is interesting that one theological basis advanced by medieval Jewish commentators for the study and retention of minority opinions is the idea of multiple truths, articulated by the *bat kol* (heavenly voice) when opting for the rulings of Beit Hillel. Rashi writes:[29]

---

23. See Helfgot, "Minority Opinions," 41–43; see also Riskin, "The Importance of Dissenting Views."

24. b. Ber. 9a, discussed in Helfgot, "Minority Opinions, 43–48.

25. b. Mo'ed Qat. 18a.

26. b. Eruv. 46a. The concept of the *eruv* was developed to mitigate the hardships imposed by strict religious observance. One of the thirty-nine categories of activities prohibited on the Sabbath (and other holy days) by Jewish law is the carrying of items from private space into a public one. This stringency would impose great inconvenience on Jews needing to leave their homes for various reasons, including attending religious services. In response, a largely symbolic or notional "private" space may be created by joining together a number of private properties, known as an *eruv*. See Kaplan, Eruv, 6:484–85).

27. b. Ber. 36a.

28. Helfgot, "Minority Opinions," 52–54.

29. Rashi's commentary on b. Ketub. 57a, quoted and discussed in Rosensweig, "Elu va-Elu." See also the discussion in chapter 3.

> When a debate revolves around the attribution of a doctrine to a particular individual, there is only room for one truth. However, when two Amoraim enter into a halakhic dispute, each arguing the halakhic merits of his view, each drawing upon comparisons to establish the authenticity of his perspective, there is no absolute truth and falsehood. About such issues one can declare that both represent the view of the living God. On some occasions one perspective will prove more authentic, and under other circumstances the other view will appear to be more compelling.

This perspective might reasonably be regarded as a precursor to Popper's epistemology, which, as previously noted, holds that, while there is a single objective reality, and thus at least the possibility of reaching the ultimate truth about it, due to the fallible nature of human reason, one can never be certain. Thus, for purposes of scientific praxis, it may be said that there is no "absolute truth and falsehood." In this, both talmudic logic and critical rationalism seem to lead to the same place with respect to minority views.

Halakhic Innovation

As discussed in chapter 3, a liberal society is inherently dynamic because its vibrant marketplace of ideas will give rise to new modes of thinking and behavior in all realms—cultural, commercial, legal, scientific, economic, philosophical, political, and so on. Inevitably, some of these theories and experiments in living will prove attractive and become widely adopted. In the comparison of the legal codes of Exodus and Deuteronomy offered in chapter 6, it will become evident that the more progressive norms in the latter text seem to have been spurred by important social changes.

This dynamism is reflected in the Talmud's legal discourse and aggadah. Despite the doctrines described in the previous chapter favoring stasis, when existing laws were deemed harmful or unjust, the Rabbis innovated, even radically. Leon Roth (1896–1963), a prominent Jewish philosopher, terms this the "moralization" of Jewish law. As he writes, when confronted by unjust laws, the Rabbis "limited, extended, broadened, narrowed, ignored, blandly changed, even in some striking cases perverted the plain sense, in order to achieve their aim [of reforming it]."[30] Roth notes that this phenomenon continued into the Middle Ages and beyond.

---

30. Roth, "Moralization and Demoralization," 298.

One prominent example is the Rabbis' extreme reluctance to enforce the death penalty prescribed in the Torah for a wide variety of crimes, evidenced by their imposition of seemingly insurmountable procedural and evidentiary hurdles. Thus, in the Talmud it is stated, "The mishna teaches: A Sanhedrin [High Court] that executes a transgressor once in seven years is characterized as a destructive [often translated as 'murderous'] tribunal."[31] Another Sage then volunteers that this would be true even if the court were to execute "a transgressor once in seventy years." This bid is then raised by Rabbi Tarfon and Rabbi Akiva, who say: "If we had been members of the Sanhedrin, we would have conducted trials in a manner whereby no person would have ever been executed." This example shows that the Talmud—the fountainhead of the halakhic rules observed by Orthodox Jews—can express a quite daring and imaginative exegetical spirit that often dramatically departs from the Torah's literal words.

In this same spirit, Eliezer Berkovits argues that the Torah is animated by humanistic values that shaped the Rabbis' understanding of the "dry" law in three fundamental ways:[32]

> (i) as guided by common sense or *sevara*; (ii) as the wisdom of the feasible, according to which the law must maintain its applicability in practice; and (iii) the priority of the ethical, according to which it is understood as furthering the larger moral principles embodied in the Tora.

R. Berkovits provides many examples within each category.

The first principle may be expected of any reasonably just legal system, and since it does not imply much in the way of ethics, it will not be discussed further. However, the "feasibility" criterion referenced in Berkovits' second category encompasses a variety of pragmatic considerations that have substantive moral consequences. These include the need to accommodate certain intrinsic aspects of human nature, the prevention of unnecessary hardship (especially for the poor), and economic waste. Here it is impossible to separate the ethical from the financial because, as Berkovits puts it, "Concern for the material welfare of society is not materialism, but an expression of moral responsibility for the life of the people."[33]

His examples include exempting those employed as agricultural guards from observing the biblical commandment to dwell in a sukkah during the

---

31. b. Mak. 2:7a.
32. Berkovits, "The Nature and Function," 41.
33. Berkovits, "The Nature and Function," 58.

festival of Sukkot because, given what is required to "dwell" and the nature of their duties, "It would put them to too much trouble."[34] Similarly, to avert unnecessary economic hardship, the Rabbis avoided adding a leap month to the calendar during a sabbatical (seventh) year, as "the period during which the land had to lie fallow would have been lengthened."[35]

No doubt the most famous of these concessions to "feasibility" is Rabbi Hillel's creation of the *prozbul*, probably in the late first century BCE. Without going into its legal mechanics, this was a halakhic "workaround" created out of whole cloth that gave creditors a means of avoiding the cancellation of their loans, pursuant to Deuteronomy 15:9, at the start of every seventh (Sabbatical) year.[36] In the absence of such relief, lenders would not make long-term loans in the sixth year, only to see the debt automatically forgiven the following year. By means of this new legal procedure, Hillel permitted intracommunal lending to continue, so that, as Berkovits explains, "The rich did not lose their money; the poor, in need of a loan, were able to find people who were willing to lend it to them."[37]

In discussing his third category, the "priority of the ethical," Berkovits starts with the Torah's own dictate to "do what is right and good in the sight of the LORD, so that it may go well with you."[38] He cites, as well, the admonition of Proverbs (2:20–22):[39]

> So follow the ways of the good
> And keep to the paths of the just.
> For the upright will inhabit the earth,
> The blameless will remain in it.
> While the wicked will vanish from the land
> And the treacherous will be rooted out of it.

According to Berkovits, the Rabbis understood that one of the Torah's foremost values is "the way of peace," and this prompted them to construe halakhah so as to preserve the dignity of persons, and to avoid unjust or overly harsh outcomes.[40] As examples, he cites the reinterpretation of the literal demand of "an eye for an eye" (Exodus 21:23) as requiring only

---

34. Berkovits, "The Nature and Function," 53, citing b. Sukkah 26a.
35. Berkovits, "The Nature and Function," 54, citing b. Sanh. 12a.
36. See Rothkoff, "Prosbul," 16:586–87.
37. Berkovits, "The Nature and Function," 53–54, summarizing b. Git. 36a–b.
38. Berkovits, "The Nature and Function," 59, quoting Deut 6:18.
39. Berkovits, "The Nature and Function," 59, quoting Prov. 2:20–22.
40. Berkovits, "The Nature and Function," 60–73.

monetary compensation; the creative interpretation of the laws of flogging to lessen the severity of the punishment; the reforming of various rituals so as not to expose the illiteracy or ignorance of uneducated Jews, or their poverty (when certain costly items are required for performance); overturning the conventional law regarding property damage if it would unfairly harm workers; relaxing various legal requirements that might otherwise obstruct a wife from obtaining a divorce from her husband, among many others.[41]

Although not mentioned by Berkovits in the text discussed above, it is difficult to imagine a more audacious nullification of an unjust law than Rabbi Yohanan ben Zakkai's (one of the most influential of the Tannaim, sometimes transliterated as "Johanan") abolishment of the trial by ordeal prescribed in Numbers 5:11–31. This procedure (the "bitter waters") was invoked by a husband who suspected his wife of adultery. According to the Gemara's account, R. Yohanan took this drastic step because he had concluded that the purpose of this ordeal—the preservation of spiritually pure monogamous marriages, a key element of the covenant—could not be realized because the husbands themselves had become morally corrupt:[42]

> From the time when adulterers proliferated, the performance of the ritual of the bitter waters was nullified; they would not administer the bitter waters to the sota. And it was Rabbi Yohanan ben Zakkai who nullified it, as it is stated: "I will not punish your daughters when they commit harlotry, nor your daughters-in-law when they commit adultery; for they [the husbands] consort with lewd women" [quoting Hosea 4:14], meaning that, when the husbands are adulterers, the wives are not punished for their own adultery.

Because there is no mention of the test of bitter waters in Deuteronomy, it may be that this primitive ritual had already fallen out of favor with the Sages long before R. Yohanan's time. Nevertheless, the Rabbis' authorship of this story, even if fanciful, certainly attests to their willingness to modify or suspend the enforcement of laws when required by emerging ethical norms or social conditions.

---

41. See Berkovits, "The Nature and Function," 83–87. It is clear, however, that, while these innovations may have been helpful at the margin, they fall well short of solving this problem, which arises from the structural power dichotomy between husband and wife in matters of divorce. See Weiss, "5 Misconceptions."

42. b. Sotah 47a.

Pluralism

It seems reasonable to regard pluralism, understood here as a community's acceptance of diverse forms of ritual observance and practice, as the acid test of its liberalism or "openness." It is one thing for a society to tolerate differences of opinion but a more demanding test to have what the majority views as perverse or immoral customs "rubbed in its face." One obvious example of this laissez-faire within Tradition is the acceptance of different ritual practices between Ashkenazim and Sephardim. These communities worship with different prayer books; permit different foods to be consumed during Passover; vary in the details of wedding ceremonies; and diverge in many other halakhic matters. Yet, neither community holds that the other is consequently less "Jewish."[43]

However, there are practical limits to this lenience. A particular shul either permits mixed seating or not; allows only kosher food to be served there or not; conducts services in Hebrew using a siddur based on centuries-old antecedents or in English, using one that incorporates secular prose and poetry; and so forth. These differences and many others are obviously not merely matters of taste or trivial preferences but reflect deeply held beliefs about God's will. Such commitments in turn affect the willingness of those affected to intermarry or even to form friendships with those holding radically different views, which is why there are three main "streams" of Judaism and many currents within each stream.

Nevertheless, while the Rabbis argue over the permissible scope of such tolerance, as discussed below, it seems fair to say that the debates recorded in the Bavli exhibit a marked preference for pluralism. Thus, while Rabbi Yohanan rules in the Jerusalem Talmud that the conflicting legal interpretations promulgated by the schools of Hillel and Shammai must all be resolved so that the Jewish people follow a single set of laws, the Babylonian Rabbis are much more permissive. Some hold that uniformity of legal opinions is only required within a single town, while the court of a neighboring town is free to disagree. Others are more tolerant still, permitting inconsistent rulings by different courts, even within the same town.[44]

---

43. One authority attributes this mutual acceptance to the decision by R. Moses Isserles (1530–572), a leading Ashkenazic halakhist of his day, to append his commentary to the (Sephardic) *Shulkan Aruch*, rather than publish a separate compilation of Ashkenazi legal rulings. See Kimelman, "Judaism and Pluralism," 132.

44. See Kimelman, "Judaism and Pluralism," 141–42, discussing b. Yevam. 14a.

In fact, the just cited *sugya* is a classic proof text for ancient Judaism's real-world pluralism:[45]

> In the locale of Rabbi Eliezer, where his ruling was followed, they would cut down trees on Shabbat to prepare charcoal from them to fashion iron tools with which to circumcise a child on Shabbat. In Rabbi Eliezer's opinion, not only does the mitzva of circumcision override Shabbat, but also any action required for the preparation of the tools necessary for the circumcision likewise overrides Shabbat . . .
>
> The Gemara infers: In the locale of Rabbi Eliezer, yes, they would act in this manner, whereas in the locale of Rabbi Akiva, for instance, no, they would not do so, as it is taught in a *baraita* that a principle was stated by Rabbi Akiva: Any prohibited labor that can be performed on Shabbat eve does not override Shabbat even if it involves a mitzva. A mitzva whose proper time is on Shabbat overrides Shabbat only if its performance was impossible earlier, e.g., the act of circumcision itself, which cannot be performed earlier . . .
>
> In other words, one might have thought that the permission to tolerate diverse customs in different places applies only to other prohibitions, whereas the prohibition of Shabbat is so severe that it is unacceptable to allow different customs, as this might lead people to disrespect Shabbat. Therefore, the baraita teaches us that even in the case of Shabbat there can be different customs in various locales.

Indeed, the weight of scholarly opinion holds that, on balance, pluralism, rather than monism, is the dominant position voiced in the Bavli, uniformly regarded as the more authoritative of the two Talmuds. Thus, Richard Hidary, a Professor of Judaic Studies at Yeshiva University, writes:[46]

> Texts supporting positive and universal pluralism are also mostly found in the Bavli, which encourages theoretical debate more than earlier Palestinian texts. Although, as noted above, no rabbinic text invalidates multiplicity of opinion, the Bavli goes beyond previous texts in its positive view of multiplicity of opinions. This also informs its nonnegative, and sometimes even positive, attitude toward pluralism of practice . . . The motivation directing attitudes of pluralism is peace, that is communal unity through acceptance of diversity.

---

45. b. Yevam. 14a.
46. Hidary, *Dispute for the Sake of Heaven*, 393 (footnote omitted).

Professor David Kraemer, another widely recognized authority on the Talmud, is even more emphatic in this regard. He argues for a pluralistic reading by analyzing in depth the just-refenced *sugya* regarding the R. Eliezer/R. Akiva disagreement. Initially, note that this dispute is discussed within the broader context of whether or not the House of Shammai did, in fact, maintain its different customs even *after* the heavenly voice pronounced that the law is according to the House of Hillel.[47] If it did, this would be another very powerful example in the Bavli affirming the permissibility of pluralistic observance.[48]

The most probative evidence *against* the claim that the House of Shammai was allowed to act on its opinions is the acknowledged fact that the two communities intermarried, despite holding conflicting views regarding the definition of a *mamzer* (illegitimate child). Given their disagreement on this point, if the Shammaites had intermarried with Hillelites, this would appear to imply that the former *were* obliged to compromise their beliefs, rather than acting on them, lest they unknowingly marry Hillelites they held to be *mamzers*.

However, the Bavli resolves this apparent contradiction by noting that the Shammaites informed the Hillelites of problematic cases, and they avoided such marriages.[49] Therefore, Professor Kraemer concludes that, taken together, all the elements of this *sugya*:[50]

> serve to create a surprisingly forceful statement on behalf of the legitimacy of different practices in different rabbinic communities. Given the care with which this argument was formulated, there can be little doubt that this was the author's purpose from the very beginning.

Professor (and President of the Schechter Institutes, Jerusalem) David Golinkin concurs. His insightful 2015 essay, "Is Judaism Really in Favor of Pluralism and Tolerance?" argues that an in-depth analysis of Judaism's classic sources shows that, "Judaism is in favor of *unity* but opposed to *uniformity*."[51]

---

47. See Kraemer, "Composition and Meaning," 275–81.

48. As noted above, the Yerushalmi is much more oriented towards monism and thus unsurprisingly concludes with little discussion that the House of Shammai followed the opinions of the House of Hillel. See Kraemer, "Composition and Meaning," 278.

49. See b. Yevam. 14a.

50. Kraemer, "Composition and Meaning," 281.

51. Golinkin, "Is Judaism Really in Favor."

Codification and Liberalism

Professor Berkovits, having reviewed in detail the Rabbis' willingness to shape halakha to address the needs of the community and the demands of morality, bemoans the codification of the Oral Law as being incompatible with the Rabbis' bold and innovative spirit:[52]

> It was an unavoidable violation of the essence of halacha when the spoken word was forced into the straitjacket of a written mold . . . it was a spiritual calamity of the first magnitude. Orthodoxy is in a sense halacha in a straitjacket . . . It was part of the spiritual tragedy of exile that exactly what halacha in its original vitality and wisdom intended to protect us from has happened. In a sense, we have become Karaites. God can no longer rejoice over his "defeat" by his children.

What Berkovits describes above as the Bavli's "vitality and wisdom" is likely attributable in major part to the far-flung, decentralized nature of communal life in Babylonia. As Professor Hidary explains,[53]

> This gave each local authority a great degree of autonomy to teach and practice as he saw fit without intervention from colleagues in neighboring towns When one rabbi did go and visit the town of a colleague, the visitor maintained respect for the rulings of the local rabbi. This social reality is most explicitly stated in b. Ketub. 54a, which actually maps out the jurisdictions belonging to Rav and Shmuel.

In such an environment, the Rabbis' approach to halakha would embody many of the characteristics associated with the United States' federal system, under which state courts independently decide cases presenting the same legal issues, with their rulings constituting binding precedent only within that jurisdiction.[54] Similarly, the Rabbis would interpret the Torah's written laws regarding, for example, Sabbath observance, criminal matters, and the dietary laws, based on widely shared, but inchoate, community

---

52. Berkovits, "The Nature and Function," 101; see also chapter 8 below.
53. Hidary, *Dispute for the Sake of Heaven*, 378 (footnote omitted).
54. This analogy would no doubt be even more apt in the era preceding the New Deal, at which point the Supreme Court's expansive interpretation of the General Welfare and Commerce Clauses extended the reach and authority of federal law at the expense of the states. See Barnett, *Restoring the Lost Constitution*.

norms. They did so without knowing what their peers had decided in other communities with respect to like cases.

In this way, different rules and practices might evolve, and their virtues and flaws tested over many years in the crucible of experience. If a particular norm proved to have unexpected negative consequences, it might, over time, be superseded by contrary rulings. Legal codes, while ensuring greater predictability and uniformity of outcomes, and enhancing efficiency in the administration of justice, are less adaptable and thus less likely to produce useful innovations, since judicial creativity is limited by the plain meaning of a code's provisions. It seems that it is this trade-off that underlies Berkovits' lament regarding codification, and he is certainly not the first prominent rabbi to raise this concern; in fact, it is an argument that resounds through Jewish history.

As described above, in about the late sixth or early seventh century CE, the Babylonian Talmud was "closed" and then circulated among scholars in manuscript form. It may be said that this redaction marked the start of the process by which halakha was transformed from a common-law system of jurisprudence to an essentially statutory one.[55] There were earlier, less influential efforts, but Maimonides completed the first widely accepted codification with his monumental *Mishneh Torah* ("Review of the Torah") in 1180. He intended this lengthy work to organize and condense the encyclopedia-sized, sprawling, haphazardly arranged, and often inconclusive Talmud into a user-friendly, straight-to-the-point legal guide.

Naturally, not all Jewish thought-leaders agreed with Maimonides' methodology nor all his halakhic decisions. More than this, the Rambam appears to speak *ex cathedra*, that is, without citing his sources or authorities, and without discussing alternative opinions. One prominent contemporary scholar, Abraham b. David of Posquieres, criticized the absence of sources because, he said, without such information, he did not know how much weight to give any particular ruling. He also objected that "there are matters to which the *geonim* disagree and the author has selected the opinion of one ... Why should I rely on his choice ... It can only be one that an overbearing spirit is in him."[56] The last point highlights the stifling effect of a legal code, since, as noted by Professor Dienstag, it threatens to dry up "the source and wellspring of dynamic halakhic creativity."[57]

55. See Berman, *Ani Maamin*, 157–60.
56. Quoted and discussed in Dienstag, "Moses Maimonides, as Halakhist," 13:387.
57. Dienstag, "Moses Maimonides, as Halakhist," 13:387.

Similar criticism followed the publication of the last great halakhic code, the *Shulchan Aruch* (literally, "Set Table," often referred to as the *Code of Jewish Law* in English) authored by Rabbi Joseph Karo (1475–1588) in 1563. R. Karo was the leader of the Safed's (in present-day northern Israel) illustrious rabbinic community, known for its revival of Jewish mysticism, and his scholarly reputation rivaled that of Maimonides. While the *Mishneh Torah* was an effort to synthesize Jewish law into a uniform code—that is, without regard to the varying customs and practices of different ethnographic communities—the *Shulchan Aruch* reflects the Sephardic perspective. As mentioned above, when R. Moses Isserles, a leading Ashkenazic halakhist, elected to append his commentary to the *Shulchan Aruch*, it secured this work's status as the most authoritative codification of Jewish law to this day.

Nevertheless, the leading Polish and German rabbis vehemently objected that this code would, in effect, induce intellectual sloth and distract from the deep study of Talmud, the ultimate source of knowledge. They feared it would produce robotic decision-making without an adequate understanding of the legal and moral logic undergirding the code's provisions. In their view, the uniformity of judgment brought on by codification is not a virtue but a vice, ignoring the previously discussed verdict of the *bat kol* that "these and those are the words of the living God."[58] Menachem Elon (1923–2013), an internationally recognized halakhic authority and longtime member of the Israeli Supreme Court, writes that, for these critics, "dispute was vital to the substance of *halakhah* and offered increased possibilities for deciding the law according to the *dayyan's* [judge's] own lights and existing circumstances."[59] Here again, Judaism's intellectual elite embraces controversy as the royal road to truth.

One final comment is in order before leaving this subject. In a liberal democracy, the overall benefits of detailed legal codes may well outweigh their costs because the citizenry can rely on the political process to revise them, even radically, in light of its experience. However, from the time of the destruction of the Second Temple until the formation of the state of Israel, the Jewish people were in exile, living as a minority at the mercy of the dominant ethnic/religious population and their rulers, and thereby denied full self-governance. Thus, Maimonides' code and its successors were accepted by default as authoritative summaries of halakhah until Jewish

---

58. See Elon, "Codification of Law," 4:778.
59. Elon, "Codification of Law," 4:778.

emancipation, including the repeal of discriminatory laws, starting in the late eighteenth century, when other streams of Judaism were born. These movements provoked a regressive "counter-reformation," reaffirming biblical dogmatism.[60]

Berkovits, in a 1943 text, explains that he regards Zionism, if it were to bring into existence a Jewish state, as the last best chance to revitalize halakha by forcing it to grapple with all the juridical and moral questions, profound and mundane, posed by modernity. He hoped that this engagement would produce legal and political institutions reflecting the Jewish people's distinctive values and history: "The creation of an autonomous Jewish body corporate is the *sine que non* for the regeneration of Jewish religion and culture. Without it, further development of Judaism is impossible; without it, Judaism can hardly be saved in the present circumstances."[61]

In a 1979 essay, he does not try to hide his disappointment with the outcome:[62]

> How far removed we are from a proper understanding of what Tora and halacha are about cannot be more strikingly illustrated than by the one-sided educational ideal of the yeshivot in Israel. Most of them frown on what is called *limudei hol*, "secular studies.". . . If the Tora desires a Jewish people living in its own land, it must also desire soldiers, physicians, scientists, architects, engineers, policemen and social workers. In a Jewish state, halacha cannot refuse responsibility for the effective functioning of the entire polity. This requires, however, a new educational philosophy, which would lead, in turn, to new ways of learning Tora and Talmud, and new ways of teaching both.

Surely his frustration only deepened with time.

---

60. See Berman, *Ani Maamin*, 279–80, on the renewed interest in and use of Maimonides' Thirteen Principles as a "boundary marker" to identify and defend what was perceived as authentic Judaism against the "Reform heresy." See also Silber, "Orthodoxy," on the reaction of Eastern European Jewry to the Haskalah (Jewish Enlightenment).

61. Berkovits, "Return to Jewish National Life," 164.

62. Berkovits, "Spiritual Crisis in Israel," 209–10.

6

The Fractious Canon

THIS BOOK'S THESIS IS that Judaism, understood in terms of its classic sources and their rabbinic interpretations, has liberal values at its very core. As discussed above, this ethos is manifested in the paramount importance these texts ascribe to moral autonomy, controversy, pluralism, and halakhic innovation. This chapter argues that these ideals animate Scripture, as well, in its endorsement of norms that evolve over time and its intertextual debates regarding vexing philosophical questions. The positive view of controversy expressed in these texts prods the reader to contemplate and resolve such questions for oneself while discouraging pat or dogmatic conclusions about what Judaism "says" or "means." As critical rationalism anticipates, this process will yield an endless series of further inquiries.[1]

Biblical Controversy

The Tanakh is rife with famous narratives that lend themselves to a multiplicity of interpretations. Examples include the suffering of Job (discussed below); the *Akedah*; and God's refusal to permit Moses to enter the Promised Land for the seemingly trivial sin of striking the water-bearing rock instead of speaking to it.[2] The elucidation of these and many other stories

---

1. See Brettler, *How to Read the Jewish Bible*, 272.
2. See Num 20:9–12.

The Fractious Canon

has been the subject of endless discussion and debate from ancient times onward. However, while all great literature lends itself to a wide variety of possible readings, the Bible seems to intentionally challenge us to choose between or reconcile the seemingly incompatible viewpoints expressed in different texts. The former invites controversy, while the latter models it.

Accordingly, this chapter will focus on intertextual conflicts, as they represent a striking display of Judaism's fruitful use of disagreement. It will pursue this project across three distinct dimensions of Tanakh: (i) conflicts within the Pentateuchal texts regarding (a) halakhah and (b) gender roles; (ii) disagreements between the views of the literary prophets and the Pentateuch regarding the relative importance of ritual and ethics; and (iii) the Writings and Prophets' many revisionary challenges articulated to Judaism's longstanding principles regarding the nature of divine justice, particularism, Jewish identity, and other matters.[3]

Before proceeding further, it is necessary to briefly address the notion of a holy "canon." The eminent biblical scholar Brevard S. Childs (1923–2007) persuasively argues for this construct as the most fruitful heuristic for identifying the key values and commitments of Jewish and Christian theology.[4] Accordingly, the Jewish canon should not be viewed as twenty-four distinct books that just happen to be bound together by historical accident but rather as an integrated and fundamental theological unit. As Frank Kermode (1919–2010) the famous literary critic puts it:[5]

> Mythologies are clusters of stories which seem to make sense themselves but often contradict one another. Considered as parts of a corpus, they have a different import, which is sought precisely at the junctions between them. These joins and conflicting versions have real religious significance . . . It is as if the parapraxes of the canonical texts give us access to their deepest meaning.

---

3. The book of Jonah, discussed in some depth below, is found in *Nevi'im* (Prophets) as one of the twelve so-called Minor Prophets. However, as Prof. Alter notes, "in fact it is not like the [other books in *Nevi'im*], a book of prophesies but rather a fable about prophesy featuring a fictitious prophet, and as such it really should have been placed in Ketuvim, the miscellaneous writings." See Alter, *The Hebrew Bible (Prophets)*, 1201.

4. Childs, *Biblical Theology in Crisis*, 99–107. While Childs was speaking more specifically about the Christian canon, the logic of his argument appears to apply equally to the Tanakh.

5. Kermode, "Canons."

Intra-Pentateuchal Controversy

The Law Codes

One obvious conflict within the Pentateuch is between the legal codes of Deuteronomy and Exodus. There is a consensus among scholars "that the Deuteronomic law represents a later stage in the history of Israelite law."[6] This conclusion reflects not only what is generally understood to be the actual chronology of composition but, more importantly, is consistent with the Torah's narrative structure.[7] Exodus depicts events earlier in this "history," beginning ominously with a new Pharoah "who did not know Joseph"; and ending with the Israelites recently liberated from their excruciating bondage, building their portable Tabernacle in the Wilderness. Deuteronomy is set some forty years later and records Moses' valedictory address to his people as they are poised to conquer the Promised Land.

Accordingly, the laws of Exodus were given in the immediate aftermath of the Jewish people's liberation from what, according to that text, was a 430-year[8] exile in what Chazal views as a profoundly immoral and corrupt society: one that would reasonably be expected to make them callous and unfeeling. The freed Israelites were, then, in a real sense, a newly created entity, a people in their moral infancy. As will be shown, Exodus offers little in the way of what would be recognized today as moral reasoning; but rather promises lavish rewards for obedience to the commandments and threatens severe punishment for disobedience. Perhaps this was the only ethics appropriate under the prevailing circumstances.

In contrast, the commandments in Deuteronomy were given to a new generation that had not spent their adulthood as slaves and that had

---

6. Bultmann, "Deuteronomy," 189; see also Nelson, "Deuteronomy," 211.

7. As is characteristic of the Pentateuchal books, Deuteronomy almost certainly draws on popular oral traditions and folklore that predate the initial "Ur-manuscript" (or manuscripts) by several centuries, and there can be little doubt that the first manuscript(s) went through many iterations, spanning centuries, before the received text was standardized during the exile or shortly thereafter. Thus, many scholars believe that the "Book of the Law" (Torah) purportedly "discovered" by King Josiah in 622 BCE (as recorded in 2 Kings ch. 22) was an early version of the present text. See Weinfeld and Sperling, "Deuteronomy," 5:619; and Nelson, "Deuteronomy," 211.

8. Exod 12:40. Tradition holds that, due to the incompatibility of the 430-year figure with the recorded lifespans of Moses and other biblical personalities involved in the Exodus narrative, the actual duration of the Egyptian exile was only 210 years, with the 430 years marking the time from when God revealed himself to Abraham until liberation. See Rashi, *Commentary on the Torah* (Exod), 12:40.

experienced God's protective beneficence in the Wilderness while also surviving numerous crises, disasters, and tests of faith. The former would include protection by the "clouds of glory," manna from Heaven, and Miriam's miraculous portable well, while the latter would encompass the cowardice of the Spies, bitter complaints regarding the manna, and Korach's rebellion. As Rabbi Ismar Schorsch, a professor of Jewish history and now chancellor emeritus of the Jewish Theological Seminary (JTS) has written:[9]

> The wilderness provided a spartan setting without distractions to concentrate on the meaning of Torah. Setbacks and suffering were an indispensable part of the process. In the words of Maimonides: "It is known that but for their misery and weariness in the desert, they would not have been able to conquer the land and to fight ... For prosperity does away with courage, whereas a hard life and fatigue necessarily produce courage ..." Raised sternly and simply, the next generation would command the inner resources to conquer the land and create a just society.

Theologically, then, the commandments in Deuteronomy represent a more mature and well-developed statement of the Torah's worldview.

Because this study's primary concern is the Torah's moral values, it will skip over the differences in the two books regarding ritual obligations. There is widespread scholarly agreement that Deuteronomy, in Alter's words, is characterized by a "humanitarian social ethos."[10] This verdict is based on this book's broad reformulation of the laws of Exodus, enhancing the protection offered to the weak and marginalized elements of society, including women. Although not part of Exodus's legal code but introduced in Numbers,[11] the humiliating and overtly sexist trial by "bitter waters" of a wife suspected by her husband of adultery is not found in Deuteronomy, apparently abandoned because it was by then considered unjust (see chapter 5).

It seems highly probable that these emendations were not simply the product of abstract philosophical theorizing but rather were, as argued by Professor Nelson, a response to the profound social changes then occurring in Judea, both in the cultic and civil spheres.[12] According to him, this progress was, as a reaction to the circumstance that the nation had "shift[ed]

---

9. Schorsch, "Our Journey in the Wilderness," final para.

10. Alter, *The Hebrew Bible (Torah)*, 670; See also Brettler, *How to Read the Jewish Bible*, 90; Weinfeld and Sperling, "Deuteronomy," 5:618; Nelson, "Deuteronomy," 211.

11. Num 5:11–31.

12. See Nelson, "Deuteronomy," 209–10.

from a purely agricultural barter economy to a money economy in which wealth could be accumulated and lent at interest . . . The gap between the rich and poor was widening."[13] Probably as a result of this rising inequality, "The judicial system was corrupted by bribery and had become unfair to those most in need of justice."[14]

To address the plight of the needy, a seven-year cycle of tithing and remission of all debt is instituted.[15] Of similar purpose is the command that "in the case of sacrifices that can be eaten by the person bringing the offering, the meat is to be shared with 'foreigners, orphans, and widows.'"[16] To remediate corruption in the administration of justice, the qualification for jurists is modified. Whereas in Exodus, Moses accepts Jethro's counsel to select "capable men who fear God, trustworthy men who spurn ill-gotten gain,"[17] in Deuteronomy, Moses instructs his people to "Pick from each of your tribes men who are wise, discerning, and experienced."[18] In staffing this critical social function, wisdom now trumps holiness.

As Professor Kugel and others have noted, in this context, "wisdom" is akin to a term of art, as it was an "international pursuit in the ancient Near East . . . almost a code word . . . like 'scientist,' 'wise' meant someone who pursued a certain way of knowledge."[19] Deuteronomy's emphasis on wisdom represents a philosophical shift from the spirit of Exodus. Professor Bultmann, in commenting on Deuteronomy 25:13–16—the mandate for honest weights and measures—notes that these laws are "permeated by a sapiential spirit of humanism typical of many sections of Deuteronomy . . . It appeals to a common sense of what is just in order to keep the human being from doing 'unrighteousness.'"[20]

As noted above, Exodus explicitly counsels obedience to the law on the promise of reward and threat of punishment. Thus, the people are warned not to mistreat the widow or orphan because "[God's] anger shall blaze forth, and [he] will put you to the sword, and your own wives shall

---

13. Nelson, "Deuteronomy," 209–10.
14. Nelson, "Deuteronomy," 210.
15. See Deut 15:1–2, 26:12–13.
16. Kugel, *How to Read the Bible*, 313, quoting Deut 16:11, 14.
17. Exod 18:21.
18. Deut 1:13.
19. Weinfeld and Sperling, "Deuteronomy," 5:617.
20. Bultmann, "Deuteronomy," 209.

become widows and your children orphans."²¹ Conversely, if the Israelites shun foreign gods, God says, "I will remove sickness from your midst. No woman in your land shall miscarry or be barren."²²

In contrast, Deuteronomy employs, in addition to the reward/punishment paradigm, moral suasion; that is, appealing to the people's natural sympathy for their fellow human beings and basic notions of fairness. For example, Deuteronomy provides that with respect to a Jew taken into bondage by a fellow Jew to work off a debt, the slave must be freed after six years of labor, and the master is enjoined to "not let him go empty-handed: Furnish him out of the flock, threshing floor, and vat, with which the LORD your God has blessed you."²³ Exodus has no such mandate.²⁴

Deuteronomy also reminds the former master not to regret the slave's liberation, because "you were slaves in the land of Egypt, and the LORD your God redeemed you."²⁵ In other words, "emulate the beneficence God showed you." Further, if that is not sufficient reason, Moses reminds the master that "in the six years he has given you double the service of a hired man."²⁶ As Professor Brettler puts it, "the slave was already a good buy, so do not be tempted to take further advantage of the situation. The argument to release the slave here is secular and logical rather than religious and symbolic."²⁷

Similarly, Deuteronomy provides that, with respect to workers—Jews or foreigners—"You must pay him his wages on the same day, before the sun sets, for he is needy and urgently depends on it."²⁸ In the same spirit, Deuteronomy protects the welfare of the seduced maiden. As Weinberg and Sperling note, while Exodus²⁹ is concerned with the potential loss suffered by the girl's father, i.e., the loss of the bride price,³⁰

> Deuteronomy is concerned with the humiliation or moral degradation of the virgin and therefore does not deal explicitly with the

21. Exod 22:23.
22. Exod 23:25–26.
23. Deut 15:13–14.
24. See Exod 21:1–11.
25. Deut 15:15.
26. Deut 15:18.
27. Brettler, *How to Read the Jewish Bible*, 90.
28. Deut 24:14–15.
29. See Exod 22:15–16.
30. See Weinfeld and Sperling, "Deuteronomy," 5:617 (referencing Deut 22:28–29).

bride price and does not grant the man who violated the virgin the right to refuse to marry her, but compels him to marry her forever.

It may be that this mandate was intended to discourage rape, since marriage would impose financial responsibilities on the perpetrator and limit his options for a more "desirable" spouse. With respect to this and other laws, "Deuteronomy actually deprived [them] of their civil-financial character and turned them into purely moral-social laws."[31]

Deuteronomy also, without fanfare, rolls back some of the harsh theology present in Exodus. For example, in the latter, when Moses finally succeeds in winning God's forgiveness for the egregious sin of the Golden Calf, the Almighty proclaims his famous Thirteen Attributes of Mercy. Here, he emphasizes how dramatically his attribute of kindness outweighs that of strict justice: "extending kindness to the thousandth generation . . . yet He does not remit all punishment, but visits the iniquity of parents upon children and children's children, upon the third and fourth generation."[32] While Deuteronomy reiterates the Thirteen Attributes in a formulaic way, it expressly holds that "a person shall be put to death only for his own crime."[33]

It seems indisputable that Deuteronomy's legal code represents substantial moral advancement relative to its counterpart in Exodus. Interestingly, the commands in Exodus, although revised and supplemented by Deuteronomy's more humane counterparts, are not repudiated or erased but are left "on the books" in the same manner as are analogous decisions in common-law jurisdictions. One virtue of this approach is that experience may demonstrate that the earlier ruling was, in fact, better reasoned; or that the internal logic of both precedents can be complementary in resolving new cases. The analogy to common-law jurisprudence emphasizes the

---

31. Weinfeld and Sperling, "Deuteronomy," 5:617.

32. Exod 34:6–7.

33. Deut 5:9, 24:16; see also Brettler, *How to Read the Jewish Bible*, 66–67. Perhaps this apparent contradiction between the severity of God's punishment and the relative leniency of the criminal code may be resolved by understanding the restriction of punishment in Deuteronomy solely to the offender as a recognition of the unbridgeable difference between divine and human justice. A wicked father will transmit corrupt values to his children, who will in turn pass them on to their offspring. Accordingly, God may exact punishment for the father's sin to the "third or fourth generation" simply by permitting the consequences of immorality to take their natural course. In contrast, the administration of capital punishment by human judges is inherently fallible, and so, if it is to be used at all, must be limited solely to the guilty party.

dynamic, open-ended nature of halakha, where longstanding precedent may always be questioned and even overturned.

Gender Roles

There is also unmistakable tension in the Pentateuch's narratives regarding gender roles. These rigid norms are inherited from the wider social/cultural milieu of the ancient Near East and therefore are blatantly patriarchal. Accordingly, the creation myth of Genesis (chapters 1–11) plainly assigns Adam the dominant role in the husband/wife relationship.[34] Not only does God appear to create Eve solely for Adam's benefit ("It is not good for man to be alone; I will make a fitting helper for him"),[35] but God also decrees to Eve that, as punishment for her part in the Tree of Knowledge episode: "In pain shall you bear children. Yet your urge shall be for your husband, And he shall rule over you."[36]

Because Adam and Eve are evidently the archetypes for all future human beings, the Sages regard the afflictions meted out to them and the gender dynamics established by God's decree as applying generically to all future men and women, and not just to these two individuals. See, for example, PRE 49:13 ("for thus the Torah says that the man shall rule his wife, as it is said, 'And he shall rule over thee.'")[37]

By biblical law and custom, husbands control most aspects of their wives' and (until marriage) daughters' lives, and social norms require that the leaders and tribal chieftains be men. Thus, God appears and announces himself to Abraham, and then (early in Exodus) to Moses, his greatest prophet, who will throughout the remainder of the Five Books lead the Israelites to the Promised Land. Some critics have observed that it is possible to regard all the post-Genesis books of the Pentateuch as essentially Moses' biography.

Similarly, only men are involved in any material way in the pivotal story of Joseph and his brothers, and many potentially interesting female

---

34. See Klitsner, *Subversive Sequels in the Bible*, 99.

35. Gen 2:18.

36. Gen 3:16.

37. This Midrash is attributed to the great Tanna Eliezer ben Hyrkanus; while it may incorporate earlier material associated with this Sage, its final compilation probably dates to the late eighth or early ninth century, many centuries after his death. See Herr, "Pirkei De-Rabbi Eliezer," 16:182.

biblical characters are ignored and go unnamed, such as Noah's wife, the wives of his sons, and Jacob's many daughters-in-law. However, after the *Mabul* (the Great Flood), which, among human beings, spares only Noah (who alone "walked with God") and his family,[38] the Pentateuch introduces the matriarchs, all of whom are active agents in shaping the destiny of the Jewish people, subverting the dominant patriarchal worldview.[39] There are, of course, great Jewish heroines depicted in Scripture outside of the Pentateuch, including Deborah, the great prophet and military leader whose deeds are depicted in the book of Judges (chs. 4 and 5); Queen Esther (heroine of the story of Purim); Ruth; and others. However, because the Pentateuch seems to be the origin of Tradition's patriarchal worldview, it is important to show the internal tensions present even within this text.

Turning then first to the matriarch Sarah, Genesis describes her as having been barren for many years and then deciding on her own initiative to give her maidservant Hagar to Abraham as a concubine. She hopes, "perhaps I shall have a son through her,"[40] thereby enabling her husband to accomplish his divine mission. A son, Ishmael, is indeed born of this union,[41] which lays the groundwork for a profound disagreement between the couple that comes to a head some thirteen years later.

At this time, God performs a miracle so that the 100-year-old Abraham fathers and the 90-year-old Sarah gives birth to Isaac.[42] Soon, however, a conflict between the spouses erupts. On the day Isaac is weaned, Sarah observes Ishmael "playing" and tells Abraham, "Cast out that slave woman and her son, for the son of that slave shall not share in the inheritance of my son Isaac."[43] Rashi, drawing on various rabbinic texts, interprets "playing" as

---

38. See Gen 6:11–13.

39. Sarah's and Rebekah's (Hebrew, "Rivka") critical roles in Jewish history are discussed in this section, while Rachel's contribution is discussed above in chapter 2. According to Tradition, Leah also altered Judaism's trajectory by persuading God, by means of her intense, tearful prayers, to annul the plan of Rebekah and Laban to marry her to the wicked Esau. According to MR (Gen), 70:16, the explanation for Leah's "weak (literally "soft") eyes" mentioned in Gen 29:17 is that they resulted from these anguished prayers. See Kadari, "Leah: Midrash and Aggadah."

40. Gen 16:2.

41. See Gen 16:15.

42. See Gen 21:1–5.

43. Gen 21:10.

idolatry or various other grave sins.[44] Regardless, the Torah makes clear that Sarah's demand "distressed Abraham greatly, as it concerned a son of his."[45]

Nevertheless, God comes down firmly on Sarah's side: "whatever Sarah tells you, do as she says, for it is through Isaac that offspring shall be continued for you."[46] The Almighty then reassures Abraham regarding Ishmael, telling him that "I will make a nation of him, too." Rashi infers from this verse "that Abraham was secondary to Sarah in matters of prophecy."[47] Thus, in this case, the husband does not "rule over" his wife; in fact, his wife overrules him.

As recounted in Genesis, Isaac marries Rebekah, who also plays a momentous role in Jewish history. Here again, the couple has two sons, the fraternal twins Esau and Jacob, with the former born just moments before the latter. While Rebekah was pregnant, the twins "struggled in her womb," and on account of this, she is moved to prayer ("to inquire of the LORD"). In response, God informs Rebekah: "Two nations are in your womb . . . And the older shall serve the younger."[48]

The Torah reports that, "When the boys grew up, Esau became a skillful hunter, a man of the outdoors; but Jacob was a mild man who stayed in camp."[49] Their father "favored Esau because, he had a taste for game, but Rebekah favored Jacob."[50] Rashi understands these verses as subtly telling the reader that, although Esau presents himself to his father as a righteous man, this is a deliberate deception, concealing a thoroughly wicked nature.[51]

When Isaac is near death and "his eyes too dim to see," he asks Esau to hunt game for him and "prepare a dish for me such that I like . . . so that I may give you my innermost blessing before I die."[52] This blessing is intended to bestow the responsibility and honor of carrying on Isaac's covenantal relationship with God. Rebekah overhears this dialogue and, knowing that

---

44. See Rashi, *Commentary on the Torah* (Gen), 21:9.
45. Gen 21:11.
46. Gen 21:12.
47. Rashi, *Commentary on the Torah* (Gen), 21:12.
48. Gen 25:19–23.
49. Gen 25:27.
50. Gen 25:28.
51. Rashi, *Commentary on the Torah* (Gen), 25:27 ("Once they turned thirteen years old, this one [Jacob] set out for the houses of Torah study, and the other one [Esau] set out for idolatry. He [Esau] knew how to ensnare and deceive his father with his mouth."
52. Gen 27:3–4.

God intends Jacob to be Isaac's spiritual heir, springs into action, devising an elaborate plot to exploit her husband's blindness and deceive him into giving his primary blessing to her younger son.[53] Rebekah persuades the reluctant Jacob to carry out her scheme, it is successfully executed, and he receives the desired blessing.

This narrative poses profound questions regarding the reasons for Rebekah's apparent failure to communicate God's intentions to Isaac; whether and to what extent he is really fooled by Rebekah's switch; Isaac's actual intentions in giving his respective blessings; the ethics of Rebekah's deception; and related matters.[54] Fortunately, we need not wade into these deep waters, as for our purposes it is sufficient that Rebekah took bold and decisive action that had a pivotal, positive impact on Judaism's character.

Tamar, the daughter-in-law of Jacob's son Judah, is another woman depicted in the Pentateuch as acting intrepidly under trying circumstances. After she is twice widowed and left childless by the early deaths of Judah's sons Er and Onan, a fearful Judah refuses to honor his ancient legal obligation (known as "levirate marriage") to give his youngest son, Shelah, to Tamar in marriage. Genesis devotes all of chapter 38 to Tamar's successful effort to vindicate her rights under Jewish law and to fulfill what, by virtue of prophecy, she knows to be her divinely ordained role in Jewish history.[55]

Like the Matriarch Rebekah before her, Tamar devises a devious yet virtuous plot that involves her posing as a prostitute to trick Judah into having intercourse with her. She cleverly obtains personal items from Judah that exonerate her from the charge of harlotry when she is later accused of it. From this union come the twins Perez and Zerah, with the former listed in the genealogy found in the Book of Ruth, as the great-great-great-great-grandfather of Boaz, making him a direct ancestor of both King David and thereby, according to Tradition, the Messiah.[56]

This survey of Pentateuchal heroines would be incomplete without any mention of the prophetess Miriam,[57] Moses' and Aaron's older sister, who is credited in the Five Books and by Tradition with a number of crucial

---

53. See Gen 27:5–13.
54. See, for example, Sacks, "Was Jacob Right?"
55. See Gen, ch. 38.
56. See Ginsberg, "Tamar," 19:493.
57. Exod 15:20 refers to "Miriam, the prophetess, Aaron's sister" who leads the Israelites in a song of praise to God after Pharoah's troops are drowned in the Sea of Reeds.

good deeds.[58] For example, Exodus 2:4–10 describes how she saves Moses' life when his mother, in response to Pharoah's decree to kill all Israelite male newborns, desperately casts her baby into the Nile. According to the Bible, on her merit God provides the Israelites with a miraculous well that sustains them as they wander in the Wilderness (see Num 21:1–2).

Not only individual women but Israelite women, collectively, are portrayed in Exodus as independent minded and righteous. When the Jewish people miscalculate the forty days Moses is to spend learning the divine commandments from God, and rashly conclude that Moses has abandoned them, they aggressively demand the construction of the Golden Calf.[59] Stalling for time, Aaron tells the men to "take off the gold rings that are on the ears of your wives, your sons, and your daughters."[60] As Rashi explains, Aaron reasons that, "the women and children are protective of their jewelry, perhaps they will object and the matter will be delayed, and in the meantime Moses will come."[61]

While Exodus next reports that "all the people took off the gold rings that were in their ears and brought them to Aaron," Rashi elucidates (relying on a midrash and grammatical hints) that "all" refers only to the men, who "did not wait for the women and children to surrender their jewelry; instead, they—the men—removed their own jewelry from themselves."[62] The women never gave theirs. The plain implication of Rashi's commentary is that, while the men were all gung-ho to build this idol, the women were either reluctant or refused altogether.

This reading is confirmed in PRE 45:4:

> The women heard [this], but they were unwilling to give their earrings to their husbands; but they said to them: Ye desire to make a graven image and a molten image without any power in it to deliver. The Holy One, blessed be He, gave the women their reward in this world and in the world to come.

The point of these examples is not to argue that the world of the Torah comports with modern feminist ideals, but to note that rabbis and scholars are able to cite these precedents in arguing for a more egalitarian Judaism that has, outside of insular Orthodox communities, largely prevailed.

58. See Coopersmith, "Miriam, Instiller of Faith."
59. See Exod 32:1–4.
60. Exod 32:3.
61. Rashi, *Commentary on the Torah* (Exod), 32:2.
62. Rashi, *Commentary on The Torah* (Exod), 32:2.

The Literary Prophets and Ritual Observance

At the very conclusion of Deuteronomy, it is said: "Never again did there arise in Israel a prophet like Moses."[63] This is a bit perplexing because, according to the Bible's chronology, this benediction takes place *before* the Israelites cross Jordan, thereby opening an entirely new era of Jewish history. It might be thought that this praise intends to immunize Deuteronomy's laws and teachings against all future innovations and revisions.

However, as argued in chapter 1, all the canonical books convey the divine word filtered through human consciousness, and no text enjoys any ontological privilege, although some have more obvious theological importance than others. Accordingly, the books of the literary prophets may rightly be understood to modify the values articulated in the Pentateuch. Moreover, the idea that Judaism froze in place with Moses' final words in Deuteronomy is gainsaid by the evidence adduced throughout this study establishing the faith's openness to new ideas. Finally, Moses' uniqueness may not lie in his greater wisdom but in his character; that is, his humility, qualities of leadership, love of the Jewish people, and so on.

Even if inferior to Moses in some sense, the classical prophets had much to say regarding the relative importance of ritual and ethical behavior.[64] They appear to have preached to a society in which cultic observance played the dominant theological role. Perhaps this was because, in Judaism's early stages, it was animated (like all other ancient religions) by the urgent quest to find a mechanism to tame and appease the God(s) that were thought to control the awesome and unpredictable forces of nature, including storms, floods, earthquakes, and the like; as well as to mitigate such human afflictions as disease, suffering, and death. This drive for self- and

---

63. Deut 34:10.

64. There exists a variety of terms to differentiate the prophets depicted in the texts collectively known as the Former Prophets (the books of Judges, Samuel, and Kings), such as Samuel, Elijah, Elisa, Nathan, etc.; and those later oracles whose warnings and rebukes are recorded in books bearing their names: Isaiah, Jeremiah, Ezekiel, and the twelve so-called Minor Prophets. This book adopts what is common terminology and refers to the first group as the "non-classical prophets"; and the second as the "classical" or "literary" prophets. The two groups differ in a number of important ways. For the purposes of this study, the major distinctions are that the former mainly focused their criticism on the Israelites' flirtation with alien gods and practices, while the latter emphasized deviations from justice; and while the former called out ethical failures by individual monarchs and leaders, the latter decried societal values generally, especially those of elite groups. See Brettler, *How to Read the Jewish Bible*, 142–47, for an excellent summary of these and other differences; see also Kaufmann, *The Religion of Israel*, 159–60, 345.

group preservation must have led to primitive forms of worship and communal sacrifice designed to curry divine favor.

It seems likely that, over the course of time, this impulse was combined with powerful norms that regulated and reduced intracommunal violence, thus enhancing social cohesion and improving the group's prospects for survival and flourishing. Exodus may represent an early form of this hybrid belief system, combining a rigid commitment to ritual observance with the simple reward/punishment ethics that is evident throughout.

As has been discussed, the book of Deuteronomy marks an important theological shift. While it continues to acknowledge the need for strict compliance with the demands of the cult, it places greater emphasis on both the moral aspects of the law and on the value of human wisdom in its administration. However, Judaism's prophetic literature, which seems to have developed largely independently of the Pentateuch,[65] presents a more fundamental challenge to Tradition, as the classical prophets subordinate the value of ritual observance to the demands of morality. For these oracles, ceremonial practices are worthless if offered with "unclean hands."

It seems that underlying this verdict was the realization that a supreme, all-powerful being gains nothing from animal sacrifice, prayers, fasting, and the like. The Jewish God is not, like Zeus and other members of the Pantheon, essentially a comic-book superhero with human appetites and superhuman powers. While the literary prophets at various times decry both the worship of alien gods and laxity in ritual observance on the one hand and the violation of ethical duties on the other, it seems they understood that God would scorn even the most rigorously perfect observance unless accompanied by kindness towards one's fellows.

Thus, the classical prophets repeatedly condemn and chastise those who offer sacrifices while simultaneously abusing the poor and vulnerable, with (First) Isaiah declaring in God's name: "What need have I of all your sacrifices? . . . Who asked that of you? . . . Learn to do good. Devote yourself to justice; Aid the wronged. Uphold the rights of the orphan; Defend the cause of the widow."[66] Similarly, Amos says on God's behalf: "I hate, I spurn

---

65. The qualification "largely" is required because there is strong linguistic evidence that the final editors of the book of Jeremiah and those of Deuteronomy were part of the same circle of scribes or priests and shared common concerns and doctrines. However, it is also true that there are no overt references to the classical prophets in the Pentateuch, and very few references in the books of the classical prophets to the Pentateuchal texts. See Kaufmann, *The Religion of Israel*, 165–66; and Holm, "Moses in the Prophets," 37–46.

66. Isa 1:10–17.

your festivals and smell no fragrance in your convocations ... But let justice well up like water and righteousness like a steady stream."[67]

Perhaps the most poetic expression of this theme is by Micah,[68] unambiguously subordinating cultic obligations to ethical duties:

> Would the LORD be pleased with thousands of rams,
> With myriads of streams of oil?
> Shall I give my first-born for my transgression,
> The fruit of my body for my sins?
>
> He has told you, O man, what is good,
> And what the LORD requires of you:
> Only to do justice,
> And to love goodness,
> And to walk modestly with your God;
> Then will your name achieve wisdom.

Note the absence of any reference to the dietary laws, Sabbath observance, sexual immorality, etc.

In sum, the literary prophets' ethical demands far exceed anything that had preceded them. As Yehezkel Kaufmann (1889–1963), a highly influential biblical scholar, observes when speaking of the classical prophets: "The great new doctrine of prophesy was the primacy of morality over the cult. Whether or not the prophets objected to sacrifice on principle, it is plain that they considered morality the essence of religion and valued it over the cult."[69] It is reasonable to see the theology of the literary prophets as a continuation of the humanistic trend found in Deuteronomy.

Having said this, it is essential to pause here and note that none of the prophets called for the elimination of worship and sacrifice. Indeed, they could not do so within the bounds of Judaism, as it did not acknowledge until modern times any fundamental distinction between ethical and ritual

---

67. Amos 5:21–27.

68. Mic 6:7–9.

69. Kaufmann, *The Religion of Israel*, 160. See also Paul and Sperling, "Prophets and Prophecy," 16:579: ("The prophets, however, devalued the intrinsic significance of ritual, and stressed God's ultimate concern with correct behavior. Justice, righteousness, kindness, integrity and faithfulness were among God's chief demands.") and Unterman, *Justice for All*, 94–108: ("Now, however, the prophets articulate a radical criterion: in the eyes of God, the destiny of the people is determined first and foremost by their ethical behavior.").

obligations.[70] Traditionally, all of them are of divine origin, and God desires that they all be obeyed.

When read in the context of the entire canon and its related rabbinic discourse, it is most sensible to interpret the literary prophets as holding that ritual observance, when offered from the heart in gratitude or supplication and *not* as a substitute for good deeds, pleases God; further, that Judaism's ethical and ritual elements are two strands that must be woven together to create the most durable and vibrant theological fabric. Accordingly, ritual observance in some substantial form, with the specifics determined by the values and psychology of each individual Jew, is an essential aspect of Judaism. As observed in chapter 1, without offering believers a means of connecting with the ineffable, religion becomes merely a dressed-up social philosophy.

The Canon's Internal Debates

While most of the books comprising the Writings and Prophets do not challenge traditional doctrines, a substantial minority not only introduce new genres into Scripture but clearly dissent from then-accepted dogmas regarding divine justice, Jewish particularism, gender roles, the efficacy of human agency absent divine intervention, the authority of reason independent of faith, and other matters.[71] The values defended in these disparate texts often seem in deep conflict with established beliefs. The books of Jonah and Job are classic examples of such intertextual disputes and will be analyzed in depth, but before getting to them, certain of the other "troubling" texts within the Writings and Prophets will be briefly discussed.

Most scholars hold that the final decision regarding the Jewish roster of holy books was made no earlier than the first century of the common era; and that, because of their discordant tropes, intense controversy surrounded the inclusion of several. While Jonah and Job certainly question long-held commitments, it appears that they were welcomed into the canon without serious objection. As argued below, it is likely that this was the result of their having been interpreted by the Rabbis in such a way as to effectively bowdlerize them. On the other hand, Ecclesiastes (alternatively, Kohelet or Qohelet), Song of Songs, Proverbs, the book of Esther, and Ezekiel were all evidently on the chopping block.

70. See Levenson, *Sinai and Zion*, 31.
71. See Alter, *The Hebrew Bible*, (*Writings*), xliv–xlv.

It is easy to understand why certain Sages looked askance at Ecclesiastes.[72] It is an overtly philosophical work that often questions the received pieties and folk wisdom expressed, for instance, in Proverbs and Psalms. As two prominent Jewish theologians describe it, the author attempts "to determine the good by application of human reason alone, without appeal to tradition of revelation. Kohelet, alone of the Bible, follows this path."[73] Kohelet, the nominal author, is deeply troubled by the obvious fact that, at least in this world, the virtuous often suffer profound hardship and loss, while evil men prosper, live long, and die peacefully in bed, a disquietude he is unable to dispel within the confines of prevailing doctrines. Professor James Crenshaw notes that "Qohelet's radical views have branded his teachings an alien body within the Hebrew Bible" and conjectures that it was only the addition of a pious-sounding epilogue by a later editor that prevented its exclusion.[74]

Alter offers a different perspective, suggesting that this postscript would likely have led few readers to overlook the author's cynicism regarding the ways of God's world, and opines that:[75]

> There must have been many Hebrew readers . . . who were not willing to let go of Qohelet, who felt that it somehow belonged in the anthology of texts—not quite yet a canon—that constituted the literary legacy of the nation. They may have felt this attraction to Qohelet despite the fact that it challenged long-cherished notions about human destiny and the nature of reality. It is even possible that they embraced the book precisely because of the challenges it posed, for there is not a great deal of doctrinal consistency in the whole body of incipient texts, and the so-called biblical worldview, which is really a construct of later interpreters, was at this early moment far from a settled issue.

---

72. See b. Meg. 7a.
73. Ginsberg and Fox, "Ecclesiastes," 6:89.
74. See Crenshaw, "Ecclesiastes," 520. Kohelet, like the book of Job, expresses deep skepticism regarding the pietism expressed in such texts as Psalms and Proverbs, and these overlapping concerns have led one prominent scholar to write that, "it is my impression that Ecclesiastes not only had the Book of Job in mind when he wrote his book, but also wrote for readers who knew the Book of Job fairly well and were able to associate texts, ideas and discussions from the Book of Job with what they read in Ecclesiastes." Kruger, "And They Have No Comforter," 104.
75. See Alter, *The Hebrew Bible (Writings)*, 678. Alter is surely not in need of my approbation, but in my book, he is one of the few scholars of the humanities for which no word other than "genius" will suffice.

The Mishnah reports that certain Sages questioned both Kohelet and the Song of Songs (also called, Song of Solomon), but on the great authority of Rabbi Akiva, it was held that only Kohelet may have been distrusted by earlier authorities.[76] Notwithstanding R. Akiva's assurances, that he had to offer them at all is evidence that the inclusion of the Song of Songs in the canon was problematic for the Sages, not only for its unabashed eroticism and unmistakable sexual allusions but because, as Alter observes, it is "without reference to God, or covenant or Torah."[77] This anthology of ancient love poetry was "sanitized" by interpreting it as a metaphorical love story between God and the Jewish people, and the Rabbis apparently "anointed" it both on this basis and its attribution to King Solomon.[78]

In light of the discussion above regarding gender roles, it is worth recognizing that the Song of Songs has plausibly been read as a proto-feminist text, as there:[79]

> Women speak as assertively as men, initiating action as least as often . . . Men and women similarly praise each other for their sensuality and beauty, and identical phrases are sometimes used to describe lovers of both genders. Domination and subordination between the sexes, or, for that matter, sexual stereotyping of any kind, have no place in the Song. Remarkably, the Song seems to describe a nonsexist world, and thus it can act for us as an antidote to some of the themes of biblical patriarchy.

Even the holy status of the seemingly anodyne book of Proverbs was doubted because it (like Ecclesiastes) apparently includes internally inconsistent positions. However, it was held that these could be reconciled.[80] Perhaps the same spirit that led the Rabbis to accept that "these and these are the words of the living God," as described in chapter 3, explains its final acceptance. This hypothesis dovetails nicely with the theory that Judaism's sacred texts are not intended to enforce intellectual conformity but to dispel it.

It is also evident from commentary by the Rabbis that there was substantial resistance to the canonization of the book of Esther,[81] probably

---

76. m. Yad. 3.
77. Alter, *The Hebrew Bible (Prophets)*, 583.
78. Schoville and Sperling, "Song of Songs," 19:16.
79. Falk, "Song of Songs," 528.
80. See b. Shabb. 30b.
81. See m. Yad. 3.

written towards the very end of the fifth century BCE.[82] As Alter notes, the book was somewhat scandalous, "not merely because it never mentions the name of God but also because its narrative world is fundamentally secular."[83] Notably, as far as this story lets on, Mordechai and Esther save the entire community of Persian Jews on their own, without divine intervention. He judges that, "Of the several biblical books that test the limits of the canon, Esther may well be the most anomalous."[84]

Although presented as history, the overwhelming weight of scholarly opinion holds (contra Tradition) that, in the words of Professor Brettler, the book of Esther is "not a historical account. Rather, it is more like a comedy, burlesque, or farce."[85] Even so, the Rabbis concluded that the text contains evidence of divine inspiration, and therefore it belonged.[86]

Finally, the Talmud is quite explicit that the Rabbis were deeply troubled by the oracles of Ezekiel, a book that scholars generally hold to have been written in the early decades of the Babylonian exile. The text was disturbing because "by the first century CE the many conflicts between the Torah and laws in Ezekiel's program had become so worrisome that withdrawal of the book from circulation was being considered."[87] Nevertheless, as recorded in the Talmud, the Sage Hananiah ben Hezekiah heroically "sat isolated in the upper story and did not move from there until he homiletically interpreted all of those verses in the book of Ezekiel that seemed contradictory, and resolved the contradictions."[88]

Moreover, this prophet's exuberant and elaborate vision of a "divine chariot" threatened to open avenues of radical, dangerous theological speculation that could lead many astray. However, here again, R. Hananiah intervened to preserve Ezekiel within the canon by arguing that this danger was overblown.[89]

---

82. See Alter, *The Hebrew Bible (Writings)*, 713; and Baumgarten and Sperling, "Scroll of Esther," 18:218.

83. Alter, *The Hebrew Bible (Writings)*, 713.

84. Alter, *The Hebrew Bible (Writings)*, 713.

85. Brettler, *How to Read the Jewish Bible*, 269.

86. See b. Meg. 7a. For a thorough analysis of the sociological and cultural forces that may have persuaded the Rabbis to include it, see Segal, *The Book of Esther*, 103–14.

87. Greenberg, "Ezekiel," 6:644.

88. b. Shabb. 13b.

89. See Greenberg, "Ezekiel," 6:644, citing b. Hag. 13a.

The Book of Jonah

Judaism honors the short book of Jonah by reading it aloud in its entirety as the *haftarah* (the excerpt from Prophets always read in conjunction with the Torah portion for a particular week or holiday) for the afternoon service on Yom Kippur, the faith's holiest day. It will soon become clear why Jonah was an obvious and natural selection for this distinction. However, the inner meaning of this text is far more complicated and controversial.

This brief yet highly provocative book is a classic example of a text that appears consciously designed to controvert and undermine received doctrines. The consensus of scholarly opinion is that it is a post-exilic work, although Tradition dates it to the eighth century BCE.[90] As discussed below, the date of authorship necessarily impacts one's understanding of the plot, thus narrowing the range of plausible interpretations.

The title character, "Jonah son of Amittai"[91] bears the name of a prophet active in the eighth century, who has a walk-on role in 2 Kings 14:25, although there is no other information in the book that identifies, or even suggests, that the titular Jonah is the same individual mentioned in Kings. In fact, as scholars have hypothesized, one may reasonably suppose that the author chose to use an earlier prophet's name simply "to give a later book more authority."[92] Although Chazal affirms this identification, the available linguistic evidence is inconsistent with composition in the eighth century BCE. As two respected scholars aver, "The presence of many Aramaisms . . . suggests a relatively late date."[93] Alter concurs: "there are quite a few turns of phrase that indicate this is Late Biblical prose, a kind of Hebrew not written until after the return from the Babylonian exile in the fifth century BCE."[94]

In any case, Jonah, probably residing in Jerusalem, is commanded by the Almighty to "Go at once to Nineveh [present-day Mosul, Iraq], that great city, and proclaim judgment upon it, for their wickedness has come

---

90. See Cohn and Sperling, "Jonah, Book of," 11:389.
91. Jonah 1:1.
92. Cohn and Sperling, "Jonah, Book of," 11:389.
93. Cohn and Sperling, "Jonah, Book of," 11:390.

94. Alter, *The Hebrew Bible (Prophets)*, 1285. See also Fretheim, "Jonah," 728: "The Book of Jonah probably dates from the fifth century B.C. when continuing hardships, foreign subjugation, and the nonfulfillment of exilic promises raised the issue of God's justice for Israel."

before Me."[95] In Jonah, son of Amittai's time, Nineveh was the capital of the mighty Assyrian Empire. Until it was defeated by the Babylonians in 612 BCE, Assyria was an aggressive war-like nation that conquered the Northern Kingdom (Israel) in 722 and was known for its brutal treatment of subjugated peoples.

Shockingly, Jonah neither accepts this mission nor attempts, a la Moses, to argue his way out of it. Rather, he runs for the border, paying passage on a ship bound for Tarshish (exact location uncertain, but to the west, far from Nineveh) "away from the service of the Lord."[96] It may seem peculiar that Jonah thought he could run away from God, but as will be seen, it may be that he was simply unable to comprehend why the Almighty would desire to send a prophet to this gentile nation.

"Not so fast," says God, as Jonah's ship is buffeted by a mighty storm, causing the sailors to fear for their lives. It is soon determined that Jonah is the cause of the mortal danger. Indeed, he informs them of this fact and suggests heaving him overboard in order to calm the raging sea.[97] The text is quite clear that the ship's captain and crew treat the prophet with scrupulous justice and dignity, reluctantly throwing him overboard only to save their lives after they have exhausted every possible alternative.[98] Moreover, these pagans show great respect for Jonah's God, as the text reports: "The men feared the Lord greatly, they offered a sacrifice to the Lord and they made vows."[99] Inadvertently, Jonah makes known the glory of God.

After being swallowed and then vomited onto dry land by a "huge fish," God repeats his command to his recalcitrant prophet, and this time Jonah obeys. He proceeds to "Nineveh, that great city" and simply proclaims, "Forty days more and Nineveh shall be overthrown."[100] As on board the ship, the king and the people of Nineveh "believed God" and repent their evil and unjust ways. The king orders a fast to be observed by man *and* beast. Additionally, he orders that, "They shall be covered in sackcloth—man *and*

---

95. Jonah 1:2.
96. Jonah 1:3.
97. See Jonah 1:12.
98. See Angel, "The Meaning of Jonah"
99. Jonah 1:16.
100. Jonah 3:4.

beast—and shall cry mightily to God" (emphasis added).[101] In response, "God renounced the punishment He had planned to bring upon them."[102]

This prime example of the Almighty's merciful forgiveness of sin, even the egregious wickedness of the (eighth century) Assyrians, is one of the common reasons Tradition gives for Jonah's prominent placement in the Yom Kippur liturgy. The idea is that If God will pardon even *them*, surely there is hope for all who sincerely repent. It is apparent, however, that this motif hardly exhausts the range of credible interpretations.

Rather than be delighted by God's mercy, "This displeased Jonah greatly, and he was grieved."[103] The reluctant prophet then explains that his knowledge of God's kindness was the reason he fled to begin with: "For I know that you are a compassionate and gracious God, slow to anger, abounding in kindness, renouncing punishment."[104] In other words, Jonah fervently wishes the idolaters of Nineveh to be destroyed, and so intense is his disappointment that he pleads for death and constructs a booth outside the city where he can sulk "until he should see what happened to the city."[105] Faced with this rather unbecoming reaction by his chosen spokesman, God decides to teach him (and the readers) a valuable object lesson.

First, God causes a "ricinus" plant [exact reference unclear; perhaps a gourd] to grow over Jonah, providing much-needed shade, and he "was very happy about the plant."[106] Then, God sends a worm to destroy the plant and "provided a sultry east wind; the sun beat down on Jonah's head, and he became faint."[107] God then asks the prophet if he grieves the loss of this plant, and Jonah avers that, yes, "so deeply that I want to die."[108] Then, the Almighty delivers his riposte, pointing out that Jonah did nothing to create the shade plant that "appeared overnight and perished overnight," and if so: "should I not care about Nineveh, that great city, in which there are more than one hundred and twenty thousand persons, who did not yet know their right hand from their left, and many beasts as well!"[109]

101. Jonah 3:7-8.
102. Jonah 3:10.
103. Jonah 4:1.
104. Jonah 4:2.
105. Jonah 4:5.
106. Jonah 4:6.
107. Jonah 4:8.
108. Jonah 4:9.
109. Jonah 4:11. It may be that God is making a joke: "Well, if the beasts are going

Premised on an eighth-century backdrop, the traditional explanation for Jonah's initial refusal to accept God's mission is that he is simply unable to accept that God's mercy could extend to pagans, especially the nemesis of the Jewish people. However, such a setting seems unlikely for a number of reasons. First, consider that the text's relatively benign portrayal of the Assyrians is inconsistent with their real-life barbarity prior to the collapse of their Empire, as it does not suggest the sort of malice and cruelty that characterized their wars. In fact, dressing their cattle in sackcloth smacks of genuine clownishness, a judgment that appears to be confirmed when, at the conclusion of this tale, God describes the Ninevites as not "know[ing] their right hand from their left," seemingly in the manner of young children. Jonah's insolent disapproval of God's mercy on this eager-to-repent community earns him the rebuke delivered via the shade plant.

Second, placing this tale in the eighth century seems to render the whole story rather nihilistic and pointless. The infamously brutal Assyrians sincerely and immediately repent after hearing a single sentence of warning from some unknown foreigner and, according to Tradition, their reward from Heaven is obliteration within a few decades by the Babylonians and Medes.[110] As will become evident below, the story is far more coherent when Nineveh is understood as a purely literary construct employed by a late fifth century author to represent the capital of an empire that had disappeared from Jewish historical consciousness after its destruction some two centuries earlier. In effect, it functions as a legendary "land far, far away."

Further, the book's account of righteous conduct by the gentile captain and polyglot crew of the Tarshish-bound vessel becomes anomalous if set in the eighth century because the author would not view and describe the neighboring (idolatrous) peoples as moral exemplars; quite the contrary. This is demonstrated by the routine curses on the nations scattered throughout the books of the early literary prophets.[111] As argued below, the

---

to repent like humans, how can I not extend *to them* the same courtesy that I show their owners!"

110. Chazal understands that the residents of Nineveh soon returned to their evil ways and were then severely punished: "For forty years was the Holy One, blessed be He, slow to anger with them, corresponding to the forty days during which He had sent Jonah. After forty years they returned to their many evil deeds, more so than their former ones, and they were swallowed up like the dead, in the lowest Sheol, as it is said, 'Out of the city of the dead they groan.'" PRE, 43:8, quoting Job 24:12.

111. See Kugel, *How to Read the Bible,* 566–68.

flattering portrait of the gentiles in the book of Jonah only makes sense if written after the exile, which, again, is where most scholars place it.

Returning to the question of Jonah's motivation in first refusing God's mission, the Rabbis offer an account of the prophet's motive that opens the way to a deeper interpretation of this narrative than as a simple illustration of God's compassion for even the worst of sinners. Namely, that Jonah feared that Nineveh *would* repent. As Rabbi Hayyim Angel explains, "One midrashic line suggests that unrepentant Israel would look bad by comparison were non-Israelites to repent."[112] Assuming a fifth century setting, such a scenario would then present an unflattering comparison between the Israelites, whose failure to heed their prophets' warnings, caused the Temple to be destroyed and the sinners of Nineveh who heeded Jonah's oracle, feared God, and were saved. It presents an equally unfavorable contrast between the Jewish people and the Tarshish-bound mariners, who exhibited exemplary kindness to a fleeing stranger and honored his God.

Accordingly, the book implicitly critiques the notion that the Jewish people's relationship with God is an *exclusive* one, or that their covenant with him implies any superior national character. As articulated by Alter:[113]

> [The book of Jonah] aims to recast traditional Israelite notions of prophesy in a radically universalist framework. The prophets of Israel all work in an emphatically nationalist context . . . The God with whom [Jonah] has such difficulties because of his Israelite nationalist mindset is not chiefly the God of Israel but the God of the whole world, of all creatures great and small. He is not a God you can pin down to national settings.

Alter's interpretation seems to be an almost perfect fit with a post-exilic date of composition. To see this, a brief historical review is helpful. The Temple was destroyed by the Babylonians in 586 BCE. Cyrus II (ruled 559–30 BCE) of Persia conquered Babylonia in 539, and in the following year, he permitted the return of a cadre of Jews to Jerusalem to rebuild the Temple.[114] Although the historical evidence is scant, "In all probability the initial return from Babylon was a rather limited matter."[115] Only over

---

112. Angel, "Meaning of Jonah," 1 and the sources cited in note 2. Angel accepts Tradition's view of an eighth century authorship of Jonah.

113. Alter, *The Hebrew Bible*, vol. 2 (Prophets), 1287; see also Magonet, *Form and Meaning*, 94–99.

114. See Miller and Hayes, *A History of Ancient Israel*, 508–10.

115. Miller and Hayes, *A History of Ancient Israel*, 511.

the course of some two decades, as conditions improved in Jerusalem and worsened in Babylon, did this trickle of returning exiles turn into a steady stream.[116] The rebuilt Temple was dedicated in either 516 or 515 BCE.[117]

Little is known of events and developments in Judea between the time of the Second Temple's dedication and the arrival on scene many decades later of the two biblical figures Ezra and Nehemiah, each the putative author of an eponymous canonical text. The weight of historical evidence suggests that Nehemiah, an official in the court of the Persian King Artaxerxes I (ruled 465–24), arrived first, probably in 445 BCE, with the goal of enhancing Jerusalem's security by refortifying its walls. Ezra, who served as the community's religious leader, came somewhat later, likely in 428 BCE, or even 397 BCE.[118]

For present purposes, the key point is that these sacred texts and the available independent evidence suggest that Nehemiah's arrival caused great tension between the returning exiles, on the one hand; and the descendants of the Jews that escaped exile and gentiles, on the other. Nehemiah's mission was apparently opposed by the leaders of both the satraps Samaria and Ammon[119] and by elements within the Jewish community who feared loss of power and prestige.[120] Nehemiah subscribed to a strict "Yawist" version of Judaism, requiring stringent obedience to the Deuteronomistic laws and, to promote this observance, prohibited marriages between Jews and non-Jews, including neighboring Samaritans.[121]

---

116. See Miller and Hayes, *A History of Ancient Israel*, 511–12.

117. See Miller and Hayes, *A History of Ancient Israel*, 522.

118. See Marcus, "Ezra," 6:652.

119. See Neh. 2:9–11.

120. See Matassa, "Samaritans," 17:720–21; and Miller and Hayes, *A History of Ancient Israel*, 531.

121. See Miller and Hayes, *A History of Ancient Israel*, 533–35. Samaria was the principal city of the Northern Kingdom of Israel (also called the Kingdom of Samaria), which, as described in 1 Kings ch. 12, broke away from the United Monarchy following King Solomon's death (which Tradition dates to the ninth century BCE). As mentioned, this kingdom was destroyed by the Assyrians in 722 BCE, and most of its population was killed or exiled. The origin, ethnic identity, and religious practices of the Samaritans at the time of Nehemiah and Ezra, some three centuries later, is a matter of opinion and debate. In their own self-conception, the Samarians were either descendants of those Jews living in the Northern Kingdom at the time of its downfall or Jews that split with their brethren even prior to the construction of the First Temple. See Matassa, "Samaritans," 17:719–21.

The Fractious Canon

Ezra took this a giant step further, attempting to compel Jews who wished to remain in good standing within the community to divorce their foreign wives and separate from them and their children. The extent to which Ezra was able to actually enforce this decree is unclear.[122] It is plausible that the halakhic doctrine of matrilineal descent has its origin in Nehemiah and Ezra's rejection of Jewish intermarriage with non-Jewish women.[123]

Alter sums up the situation as follows:[124]

> The community of returned exiles found itself in sharp conflict with other groups in the country, and the ideology promoted by both Ezra and Nehemiah was stringently separatist. Those who remained in the land and claimed to be part of the people of Israel—in particular, the Samaritans—were regarded as inauthentic claimants to membership in the nation and were to have no role in the project of rebuilding.

He notes, however, as discussed below, that "there was a strong antithetical view on this issue within the community of returned exiles that is reflected in the Book of Ruth."[125]

If Alter's interpretation is correct, the book of Jonah is almost certainly intended as a condemnation of the separatist policy implemented by Nehemiah and Ezra in their quest to achieve theological purity by means of ethnic segregation. As he suggests, this links Jonah thematically with the book of Ruth. The latter has as its central focus the love story and marriage between the title character, a Moabite widow (the Moabites constituting an especially disfavored out-group), and Boaz, an older Jewish man of noble descent. It casts both partners in this mixed marriage as exemplars of virtue.

To drive home its universalist message, Ruth includes a genealogy that positions Boaz as the great-grandfather of King David, from whose house will come the Messiah. Obviously, this makes Ruth, a convert, David's great-grandmother. Thus, both Ruth and Jonah invite the reader to weigh the importance in God's eyes of good character relative to genetic heritage. They may together represent the opening salvo in the "who is a Jew?" debate that burns as intensely today in Israel as it did some two-and-a-half millennia ago.

---

122. See Miller and Hayes, *A History of Ancient Israel*, 537–38.
123. See Marcus, "Ezra," 6:652.
124. Alter, *The Hebrew Bible* (*Writings*), 804.
125. Alter, *The Hebrew Bible* (*Writings*), 804; and see Kugel, *Reading the Bible*, 403.

The Book of Job

Perhaps the most radical challenge to the biblical picture of a just world that rewards virtue and punishes inequity is the book of Job. It far more closely resembles a bizarre thought experiment than any conventional drama portraying aspects of the human condition. The tale provides little information regarding the protagonist and includes obviously fantastical elements that clearly indicate that one is not supposed to imagine Job as a historical figure; but rather to understand this story as a fable or legend designed to make an important theological point.[126]

As a result, the plot may be briefly summarized. The title character is a righteous, God-fearing man who has been amply rewarded for his piety. Job has it all: immense wealth; honor; a well-earned reputation for charity; the respect of his community; and a loving, close-knit family consisting of a wife and ten children. However, unbeknownst to him, his world is about to be shattered after God's boasts to "the Adversary" (a.k.a., the Satan, i.e., an officeholder, not a particular individual) about Job's unique merits. This is met by the reply that this "saint" is worthy only because he has never faced adversity. In response, the Adversary is given permission to test Job's faith by whatever grotesque and cruel means he can devise short of death.[127]

There then ensues a rapid-fire series of catastrophes in which human aggressors and natural calamities kill all Job's children and destroy all his wealth. Nevertheless, Job toes the party line by conducting the prescribed mourning rituals and pronouncing that "the Lord has given, and the Lord has taken away; blessed be the name of the Lord."[128] But the Satan is not done, afflicting Job with an excruciating skin disease from head to toe.[129] Nevertheless, Job perseveres . . . at least for a time.

Eventually, perhaps because of the pain inflicted by his disease, Job ever-more forcefully questions God's justice and moral order. While the friends who have arrived to comfort him are initially sympathetic, they affirm the teachings of the ancient wisdom literature, as recorded in Proverbs.[130] As Professor Kugel puts it, "the heart of the book thus consists of a series of learned exchanges between these exponents of orthodox wisdom

---

126. See Alter, *The Hebrew Bible, (Writings)*, 465, n1; and Good, "Job," 407.
127. See Job 1:8–12.
128. Job 1:20–21.
129. See Job 2:4–7.
130. See, e.g., Prov 22:5.

and Job who, in 'refusing to be comforted,' ultimately calls into question the most hallowed doctrines of the wisdom outlook."[131]

However, since Job knows he is innocent of all wrongdoing, his anger and frustration with both his friends and the Almighty grow exponentially. He does not curse God, but his complaint is both bitter and logically unassailable: I am virtuous; God is all-knowing and all-powerful; therefore, He is intentionally allowing a righteous man to suffer unbearably.[132] With ever-greater intensity, Job demands an accounting from the Master of the Universe.[133]

After Job has affirmed his innocence for the final time, he gets the confrontation or "trial" he has been demanding. God speaks to him at length "from the whirlwind" with unsurpassed eloquence and grandeur.[134] The exact meaning of these two long speeches is a matter of great controversy, but it seems fair to say that at least part of the message is that workings of the world are fine-tuned in a way far beyond human understanding. Accordingly, God asks rhetorically:[135]

> Where were you when I laid the earth's foundations?
> Speak if you have understanding.
> Do you know who fixed its dimensions
> Or who measured it with a line?
> Onto what were its bases sunk?
> Who set its cornerstone
> When the morning stars sang together
> And all the divine beings shouted for joy?

The Almighty then suggests that his handiwork has established a perfect balance of birth and death, rain and drought, light and darkness, ensuring the survival of life, great and small, predators and prey:[136]

---

131. Kugel, *How to Read the Bible*, 639. As Prof. Kugel explains, "refusing to be comforted" was a prescribed ritual in the ancient Near East for those suffering a severe loss.

132. See Job 30:20–31.

133. See Job 31:35–40.

134. Thomas Carlyle, the great Victorian historian, wrote: "I call that [book of Job], apart from all theories about it, one of the grandest things ever written with the pen." Carlyle, *On Heroes*, 59.

135. Job 38:4–7.

136. Job 38:39–41.

> Can you hunt prey for the lion,
> And satisfy the appetite of the king of beasts?
> They crouch in their dens,
> Lie in ambush in their lairs,
> Who provides food for the raven
> When his young cry out to God
> And wander about without food?

As many commentators have noted, it is not clear exactly how God's finely wrought poetry constitutes a defense to Job's claims of moral anarchy, but whatever Job understands to be God's defense, he is cowed into silence: "Indeed, I spoke without understanding, Of things beyond me which I did not know ... Therefore, I recant and relent, Being but dust and ashes."[137] Surprisingly, despite Job's earlier-expressed deep skepticism regarding the quality of God's justice, the Almighty unambiguously takes his side in his dispute with his friends, saying to their leader, "I am incensed at you and your two friends, for you have not *spoken the truth about me as did my servant Job*" (emphasis added).[138] He demands that they beg Job to intercede for them lest they face divine wrath. Finally, "the LORD restored Job's fortunes when he prayed on behalf of his friends, and the LORD gave Job twice what he had before."[139]

The traditional interpretation is straightforward: God's speeches reassure Job that that he is not indifferent to his suffering and that of other innocents. The Almighty remains deeply engaged in the world, but one must accept that there are things simply beyond human comprehension. Abraham Twerski (1930–2021), the famed Hassidic rabbi and psychiatrist, articulates this view when he interprets the underlying meaning of God's question to Job, "And where were you when I created the world?" as follows:[140]

> In other words, there is a master plan knowable to only a Being who has infinite knowledge of time and space. We may think of a jigsaw puzzle of a thousand pieces. One who has only one piece of the puzzle may say, "This piece doesn't make any sense." Of course,

---

137. Job 42:3–6.

138. Job 42:7.

139. Job 42:10. This includes ten "new" children. It seems that the reader is intended to ignore the impossibility of "replacing" Job's murdered children and simply accept this as a formulistic ending to fairy tales in which the protagonist "lives happily ever after." It is worth noting that there is no intimation in this book that God "balances accounts" in an afterlife or World-to-Come. See Morriston, "God's Answer to Job," 350.

140. Twerski, "The Mystery of Suffering."

it cannot make any sense unless it fits in with the other 999 pieces which one does not have.

However, this reading seems to render the book pointless or perverse. One is to believe that God permits the Satan to inflict unbearable agony on the virtuous Job so that he could eventually appear before him, and by means of magnificent poetic imagery, browbeat Job into acceptance of this non-explanation? This view threatens to turn the Master of the Universe into a long-winded bully. There *must* be more to this text than this.

The fatal defect in Tradition's understanding of Job is that it cannot explain God's statement that Job has "spoken the truth about me" or the Almighty's harsh criticism of Job's friends. If God's "answer" to Job is simply "trust me," then what did Job get so right and the friends so wrong? Professor Berkovits goes so far as to acknowledge that Job was correct to claim that God acted unjustly towards him, and his friends wrong to deny it, but: "God taught [Job] that in the plan of a universal Creator there are other considerations, too, apart from justice alone, whose validity may be understood only from the viewpoint of the Creator alone."[141] Left unsaid is the nature of these "other considerations."

Various authorities have suggested interpretations that seek to elucidate the connection between God's elaborate description of his precisely calibrated world and Job's suffering. They are so numerous and varied that it is impossible to treat them all, so for purposes of illustration, the thoughtful proposal of Professor Robert Gordis (1908–1992)—an important and influential theologian in the Conservative movement—will be examined. He argues that Job's willingness to "recant and relent" is caused by his recognition that:[142]

> [J]ust as there is order and harmony in the natural world, though imperfectly grasped by man, so there is order and meaning in the moral sphere, though often incomprehensible to man . . . When man steeps himself in the beauty of the world, his troubles grow petty . . . The beauty of the world becomes an anodyne to man's suffering (emphasis in original).

However, Professor Wesley Morriston, a respected philosopher of religion, seems correct to assert that Gordis's reading suffers from two serious

---

141. Berkovits, "The Biblical Idea of Justice," 151. See also Kugel, *How to Read the Bible*, 638–41.

142. Gordis, *The Book of God and Man*, 133.

flaws. He notes first that the analogy is unpersuasive because, "If we are worried about someone's moral character, it is of no help to be shown a wonderful picture that he has painted."[143] In other words, God's universe can be both beautiful *and* grossly unjust. Secondly, Morriston argues that "it isn't at all clear what Gordis has in mind when he speaks of 'order and meaning in the moral sphere,' or how this kind of order is supposed to be different from 'order and harmony in the natural world.'"[144] Thus, one continues to wonder what satisfying answer God has given Job.

One plausible answer to Morriston's critique centers on the human attribute of moral autonomy discussed in chapter 2. The beauty of God's creation, its "order and harmony" (in Gordis's words), rests on his solicitude in providing for the unique needs of *all* the species in the natural world, of which human beings are just one. However, in sharp contrast to all the other animals, human beings do not live "by bread alone." Only persons can sensibly be said to have free will, and thus moral agency. Humans are the only beings that can self-consciously sacrifice their own well-being for the greater good, but the price of this freedom is that some persons will act viciously. Like the poor, to some extent, evil and injustice will always be with us.

Accordingly, it would not merit a *Dayenu!* if only our physical needs are satisfied. The special and precious gift that God has bestowed on humans is the opportunity to obey the Torah's command: "justice, justice, shall you pursue." However, God cannot, as a matter of elemental logic, ensure that the Aristotelian ideal of justice is satisfied, that everyone gets what they deserve, while simultaneously upholding free will and the laws of nature.[145]

Thus, what Job gets right is his bitter complaint that the old bromides offered by his friends are insulting. The world is morally chaotic, and terrible things happen to virtuous people, while evildoers live long and prosper. He is convinced by God's majestic defense of the world as the best one possible, given the constraint just mentioned. This interpretation has the

143. Morriston, "God's Answer to Job," 346.

144. Morriston, "God's Answer to Job," 346.

145. Of course, in addition to human predators, natural disasters kill and maim countless people as well, but this is the impersonal operation of physical laws, constituting great unfairness but not injustice. But this, too, may be seen as gist for the mill of human ingenuity powered by regard for human life. As the Talmud avers, "he who saves one life, it is as if he saved the entire world." M. Sanh. 4:5 and b. Sanh. 37a." See the earlier discussion in chapter 4, note 90 regarding "one life.".

virtue of crediting the Almighty with a meaningful reply to Job, and one that is consistent with the Torah's essential philosophy.

Hopefully, this book's brief and limited review of the canonical texts is sufficient to show that, far from preaching dogma, they present divergent positions on critical ethical and theological questions, stimulating and challenging the attentive reader to think through these issues for themselves. As Moshe Greenberg (1928–2010), a leading rabbi and scholar of the Conservative movement, has written, the canon contains contradictions because "[t]he religious sensibility absorbs or even affirms the contradictions embodied in these books. That may be because these contradictions are perceived to exist in reality."[146]

Or, as James Sanders (1927–2020), an influential Christian bible scholar, puts it:[147]

> Honesty demands recognition of the Bible's internal dialogues . . . how impossible it is to limit God or reality to any one set of propositions. To insist that the Bible is harmonious or even homogeneous had led to diabolical abuses . . . How the Jewish canon came together formally as a closed collection of texts, and how these texts were read with *and* against each other evolved over centuries.

Scripture teaches that humans are endowed by our Creator not only with certain unalienable rights but also with the capacity for empathy, a love of justice, and an aptitude for moral reasoning. It seems that multiple biblical voices are calling on humanity to achieve our divinely inspired ends by constantly questioning the received wisdom in search of something better.

---

146. Greenberg, "Reflections on Job's Theology," 332.

147. Sanders, "The Integrity of Biblical Pluralism," 162–63. See also Clines, "Introduction to the Biblical Story," 74–75.

7

Making Peace with the Torah's Immoral Commandments

As noted in the introduction, the Torah contains many manifestly horrific commands and laws that cannot be reconciled with humankind's current moral knowledge, including capital punishment for such victimless crimes as Sabbath desecration, fornication, homosexuality, and so on, and the decree of genocide not just against the Amalekites but also their descendants down through the ages. These passages have led many thoughtful people to a conclusion like the one voiced by Professor Dan Baras, a contemporary academic philosopher: "The Torah includes immoral norms, including norms that unjustly harm people, and it inculcates harmful values."[1] This chapter will examine a range of popular responses that have been offered by leading Jewish theologians to this devastating accusation and explain why they are unsatisfactory. Instead, these immoral commands should be conceptualized from the critical rationalist perspective that sees persistent error, including in ethics, as an unavoidable step in getting closer to the truth.

---

1. Baras, "A Moral Argument," 313.

Making Peace with the Torah's Immoral Commandments

Background

Before going further, it is important to observe that the Rabbis were themselves deeply troubled by the dubious ethics undergirding many of the Torah's mitzvot, and took steps to ameliorate their harsh effects, a process that was continued by the leading medieval commentators. Thus, as previously discussed, the Rabbis held that a Great Sanhedrin that executed criminals more frequently than once every 70 years should be regarded as destructive or murderous. Similarly, it seems clear that the Rabbis blanched at the genocidal mandates regarding the Amalekites and Canaanites, as the Mishnah includes various laws meant to avoid unnecessary wars and to ensure that they would be waged justly, and these regulations do *not* expressly exclude the Canaanites or Amalekites.[2] Maimonides was even more explicit, holding that peace terms would have to be offered even to the Amalekites and that, in any case, God's command to exterminate them, including their descendants down through the ages, was now a nullity, since history had scattered them to the winds and no reliable means of identification is possible.[3]

Nevertheless, these embarrassing laws are still "on the books," awaiting the revival of a Great Sanhedrin unconstrained by secular authorities for their potential enforcement. And there are at least a few prominent ultra-Orthodox rabbis who have called for the re-establishment of such a court.[4] Moreover, as Professor Baras argues, the absence of current enforcement does not appear to absolve God from issuing such commandments

---

2. See Lamm, "Amalek and the Seven Nations," 211–13. It is worth noting that just as there is no meaningful extra-biblical evidence for the existence of Moses, the patriarchs, etc., there is no historical evidence that the Israelites actually *committed* genocide against these tribes or even conquered them in the way described in Jewish Scripture. With respect to the Amalekites, there is real doubt regarding the historicity of any such tribe or nation. See Abramsky and Sperling, "Amalekites," 2:28–31. Similarly, contrary to the accounts of massacres in the book of Joshua, there is no reliable historical evidence that the conquest (if that is even the right term) of Canaan took the form of a well-organized military campaign or was any more brutal than was customary in those times. Finally, as discussed in chapter 5, very few, if any, gay people, Sabbath violators, fornicators, etc., were executed by religious courts.

3. See Lamm, "Amalek and the Seven Nations," 216; and Korn, "Moralization in Jewish Law," 7–9.

4. See Weiss, "Plan to Revive Biblical Sanhedrin."

in the first place, even in ancient times.⁵ How could a supreme being, whom believers hold to be perfectly good, do so?

The Crux of the Problem

In order to understand the grave difficulty rabbis and scholars across the theological spectrum have in formulating an acceptable apology for the Torah's repellent commandments, it is necessary to appreciate its source. Given the current state of Jewish philosophy, there seems to be an inescapable trade-off between distancing God from the Torah's abhorrent mitzvot by revisionist accounts of Revelation and deflating one's conception of him as the awesome, omnipotent God of Abraham, Isaac, and Jacob. In other words, to the extent these odious mandates are understood as God's eternal will, expressed at Sinai, it becomes increasingly difficult to defend the idea of his perfect justice. Conversely, if such commands are the mere norms of the ancient Israelites subsequently recorded in the Pentateuch by human authors, it invites the question why this is not also the case with respect to the progressive aspects of the Torah, and thus God fades into the metaphysical background.

This dilemma is evident in the wide range of theological responses to the Torah's immoral mitzvot surveyed below, starting at, for lack of better terminology, the extreme "left" and "right," and then moving on to more mainstream alternatives. These conceptions typically have their origins in the writings of the rabbis and scholars associated with particular Jewish denominations. However, it would be a serious mistake to *identify* such models with these movements, as the latter evolve over time, are internally heterogeneous, and often bleed over into each other's "territory." Finally, a Popperian solution is proposed that seems to land on the "sweet spot."

Dodging the Question

First, consider a theology that denies the existence of a *personal* God. As explained by Neil Gillman (1933–2017)—a prominent religious philosopher affiliated with Conservative Judaism—a personal God acts⁶

---

5. See Baras, "A Moral Argument," 325; and Solomon, "Relating Truthfully," 4.
6. Gillman, *Encountering God in Judaism*, para. 3.

Making Peace with the Torah's Immoral Commandments

> with intent, purpose, and concern toward and about individual human beings . . . [An impersonal] God is one who acts blindly, by rote, without focus or intentionality . . . who does not have an inner life. This metaphor of a personal God is concretized in the many more specific biblical metaphors for God: God is a shepherd, a parent, a teacher, a lover, a sovereign, a judge, a spouse. These are all relational qualities: a shepherd needs sheep, a sovereign needs subjects, a lover needs a beloved. They all capture the sense that God is personally and intensely involved in relationships with people.

If God is an impersonal force, then a theistic *revelation* of any sort is impossible, and all Scripture was written by men simply under the illusion that they are transmitting God's message. Accordingly, the Almighty is no more to blame for the Torah's immoral commandments than gravity is to be faulted when airplanes fall from the sky and, by the same token, no more worthy of praise for its positive, uplifting narratives and noble moral teachings.

On such a view, Jewish Scripture has no greater claim to our attention or affection than any other well-written literature that happens to appeal to us. Ritual and worship offer no hope for connecting with anything greater than oneself and thus achieving the sort of spiritual elevation and transcendent experience that many people find in other streams of Judaism. This approach also abandons any claim that Judaism might make regarding the unique or special nature of its relationship with the Almighty, and may well strike one as an exceedingly enervated, shriveled version of the faith.

At the other extreme lies the belief that the Revelation is historical fact. God has the right to command us because he is omniscient, omnipotent, and omni-benevolent. The Pentateuch is, perhaps with the exception of some minor scribal errors and its final verses (written by Joshua), a verbatim transcript of God's words to Moses on Mt. Sinai. The laws should be punctiliously obeyed because humans are, in comparison to the Almighty, insignificant and ignorant. The Jewish people should accept, as a matter of faith, that these apparently immoral mandates serve some greater purpose that is beyond the ability of humans' finite minds to comprehend.

Even putting aside the obvious objection to the Torah's historical accuracy, this worldview disregards the profound respect for humankind's moral autonomy that informs and animates much of Scripture (see chapter 2). It also flies in the face of the near-unanimous rejection by the leading Jewish rabbis and scholars throughout the ages of Divine Command Morality (DCM); that is, the opinion that, "an act is right because (and only because) God commanded it."[7] As Professors Sagi and Statman conclude: "In sum, not only does DCM enjoy no significant support in Judaism, but the prevailing view in the world of the sages is that morality is autonomous."[8]

Unfortunately, traditionalist rabbis adopt DCM through the "back door." That is, they affirm that morality exists independently of God's will but nevertheless hold that God never actually does nor orders anything that is immoral, even if our finite minds are unable to comprehend his ways.[9] However, this view is pure dogma, as no counterexample can ever falsify it. Moreover, it requires moral agents to disregard their own carefully considered judgment, a stance inconsistent with the supreme value the Torah and the Rabbis assign autonomy.

Having surveyed the two opposite ends of the theistic spectrum, consider next theories that recognize the existence of a personal God and accept that both God and man had *some* role in the authorship of the Five Books, while varying dramatically in the relative involvement of the two sides and the circumstances under which these texts were produced. Thus, these conjectures differ widely in their allocation of responsibility for the Torah's specific content, and accordingly the image of God they imply.

Progressive Revelation

One explanation is that of "progressive revelation," which accepts the existence of a personal God but denies that he gave *any* commands to humankind at Sinai or elsewhere. By this view, the Torah was entirely written by men, inspired by their understanding of God's essence, but not revealed by him. The idea is that persons are able through their moral reasoning to *discover* God's will over time, in the same way that scientists continuously refine their theories regarding the laws of physics and doctors improve their treatment of disease. This investigation is the responsibility of every individual Jew, and because ritual is not grounded in reason, there is no expectation of observance unless the individual finds it meaningful.

Because this theory rejects any notion of revealed and binding laws, God obviously bears no responsibility for the indefensible ones nor, it would

7. See Sagi and Statman, "Divine Command Morality," 40.

8. Sagi and Statman, "Divine Command Morality," 54. See also Kaufmann, *The Religion of Israel*, 75.

9. See Statman, "Modern Orthodoxy and Morality," 7–13.

seem, for the laudable ones. However, this exoneration comes at a very high price. As Louis Jacobs observes, "'progressive revelation' . . . tends to set up the *Zeitgeist* as the final arbiter in religious and moral affairs. It leaves the content of revelation vague and undefined. It comes perilously close to a belief in a God who is constantly changing His mind."[10] Although this theory is commonly described by its proponents as "progressive revelation," it seems more accurate to label it "continuous discovery," as God is doing none of the work in this process. Thus, it seems likely that, when Jacobs refers to "revelation" in this quotation, he understands it in terms of the "discovery" model.

Rudolph Otto's coinage of "numinous" was referenced above to describe the experience of the holy and sacred. Intriguingly, as one authority notes, Otto appears to have been strongly influenced by traditional Jewish theology:[11]

> The various aspects of the numinous as described by Otto correspond to the complementary categories of "love of God" and "fear of God" in Jewish thought, and more especially to the feelings evoked and emphasized by the liturgy of Rosh Hashanah and the Day of Atonement (the "Days of Awe").

Unfortunately, denying any active role to God in the communication of divine truth seems anything but numinous.

Indeed, it may reasonably be asked what purpose Judaism serves if one excludes from it everything reason cannot confidently affirm? Once we start down this road, where does it end? Why observe Shabbat, *kashrut* (the dietary laws), *brit milah* (circumcision), the three ancient pilgrimage festivals (Passover, Shavuot, and Sukkot), or the High Holidays? What about Judaism's well-known "particularism" (roughly, the idea that Jews have a special relationship with and obligations to fellow Jews that are not owed, or at least not owed to the same degree, to gentiles)? This seems a textbook case of "throwing the baby out with the bathwater." Accordingly, it seems clear that the belief system just described offers a pale and tepid conception of God's majesty and authority that would not inspire the sort of religious commitment and fervor that would ensure Jewish continuity over future generations.

---

10. Jacobs, *A Jewish Theology*, 202.
11. Werblowsky, "Otto, Rudolph," 15:518.

Continuous Revelation

There is another family of theories regarding revelation that acknowledges God's active participation, whether at Sinai or at other times and places. From this perspective, Matan Torah did not take the form of God dictating laws to Moses but rather consisted of human authors receiving some form of divine communication, much as biblical prophecy is understood.[12] This conjecture posits that the received text of the Torah, including its mitzvot, reflects the inability of persons, however inspired they may be, to fully grasp and accurately record God's communication. Accordingly, it is appropriate for rabbis and *posekim* throughout the generations to revise these laws to recover God's true intent.

These would, of course, include the nullification of horribly immoral laws and commandments. Thus, Benjamin Sommer, a prominent Bible scholar, holds that the Torah's account of God commanding the Jewish people to exterminate the Amalekites stems from humankind's inability to faithfully "translate" the Almighty's words, resulting in "a gross misunderstanding of the divine will."[13] Accordingly, it is the Jew's duty to correct these errors, in his words, "to work with the wheat in order to produce flour."[14]

Heschel, the Orthodox-trained rabbi greatly admired by the Reform and Conservative movements, appears to take a similar stance regarding the relative responsibility of God and man for the Torah:[15]

> Revelation is not *vicarious thinking*. Its purpose is not to substitute for but to extend our understanding . . . The full meaning of the

---

12. The difference between a text written by a person receiving divine revelation and one written by someone inspired by God lies in the extent to which we may appropriately attribute the content of the communication to God relative to the human author. Revelation is generally thought to be a more explicit and reliable transmission of God's will than mere inspiration. Either way, as Heschel observes, "it has often been maintained that what reached the ear of man was not identical with what has come out of the spirit of the eternal God," as the human recipient must somehow decode God's "message" with their own finite cognitive apparatus and then reduce it to human language. Heschel, "Understanding the Bible," 245. See also Dorff, *Conservative Judaism*, chapter 3D. Thus, both inspired and revealed texts my not accurately reflect God's intent and may require subsequent revision.

13. Sommer, *Revelation and Authority*, generally 235–41 and quoted on 236.

14. Sommer, *Revelation and Authority*, 239 (quoting the Midrash, *Seder Eliyahu Zuta*, ch. 2).

15. Heschel, "Understanding the Bible," 248.

Making Peace with the Torah's Immoral Commandments

> Biblical words was not disclosed once and for all. Every hour another aspect is unveiled. The word was given once; the effort to understand it must go on for ever. It is not enough to accept or even carry out the commandments. To study, to examine, to explore the Torah is a form of worship, a supreme duty. For the Torah is an invitation to perceptivity, a call for *continuous understanding*.

Thus, a theory of continuous revelation strives to both sustain divine authority—as all mitzvot, ethical and ritual, originate with God—while exonerating the Almighty because of our mutual failure to (fully) communicate.

In addition to acknowledging some form of divine revelation in the Torah's composition, this theory differs from "progressive revelation" in other meaningful ways. First, to maintain continuity with Judaism's core values, it mediates all revisions of halakhah through deep engagement with rabbinic history and its worldview. Second, since only rabbis and scholars have the requisite knowledge and sensitivity to undertake this task, they are accorded responsibility for judging when revision of halakhah is required.

While this model elevates our image of God relative to its "progressive revelation" rival, it places on its proponents the burden of explaining the nature of this mis- or incomplete communication. It seems odd that an omnipotent God that created the world and everything in it *ex nihilo*, rescued the Jewish people from Egyptian bondage with ten supernatural plagues, and is said by Tradition to "speak in the language of Man" cannot manage to get his point across, either at Sinai or elsewhere.

The theory is subject to a number of other telling objections offered by Jon Levenson,[16] surely one of the great authorities on the Hebrew Bible. While directed specifically against Sommer's proposal, it appears these criticisms apply, in whole or part, to most "continuous revelation" theories. First, if the content of God's revelation is to be continuously revised, who is to be entrusted with this task? Rabbis and scholars (and their communities), who scrupulously study the Talmud and strictly observe halakha in all its elaborate details; less rigidly observant rabbis and communities; those who are minimally and haphazardly observant; all those born to a

---

16. See Levenson, Review of *Revelation and Authority*.

Jewish mother and converts; outstanding secular Jewish philosophers?[17] Any answer seems inescapably to be, as Levenson notes, "circular."[18]

> 17. This is not the place for a full discussion of this subject, but if liberalism is the best moral/political philosophy now available to humankind, then is seems clear that God's will cannot be reliably ascertained by the leaders of deeply illiberal communities who reject these values. Sadly, this label surely applies to Haredi and ultra-Orthodox rabbis and *posekim*, as those communities are intolerant, oppressive, and reactionary: textbook examples of what Popper calls "closed societies." They are rigid hierarchies, with the great Torah scholars, senior rabbis, and heads of yeshivot at its apex. These men (exclusively) have unquestioned authority and are reflexively obeyed. One consequence of this power dynamic is that allegations against them of sexual abuse, even of young children, are generally not reported to secular authorities and are often covered up. See Waks, *Who Gave You Permission?*; Otterman and Rivera, "Orthodox Jews Shun Their Own"; Wolfson, "Child Abuse Allegations"; and Za'akah.org, "Agudath Israel."
>
> The leadership not only coercively discourages the discussion and debate of all ideas that challenge the entrenched ideology and worldview but also exerts every effort to shield members even from exposure to them. See, e.g., Deen, *All Who Go*; Salkin, "The Scandal of Hasidic Education"; and Vizel, "The Anachronisms of Hasidic Yiddish," 19–27. Conformity to community norms, including fixed gender roles, is enforced by harsh, unrelenting social pressure, including shunning and outright ostracism. Dissenters are publicly shamed by the denial of various commonly granted religious privileges and discriminated against in business and employment; they will not be invited to community social events, their children will be deemed unsuitable for marriage to other community members, and so forth. See the personal histories recorded at the website of Footsteps.org, a nonprofit organization that assists Orthodox men and women "in their quest to lead self-determined lives."
>
> The illiberal nature of ultra-Orthodoxy is perhaps most starkly on display in the one place on earth where its leaders can enlist the irresistible power of the state in their service. As a result of the devil's bargain struck by Ben Gurion in Israel's most desperate hours, there is no separation of shul and state in a variety of contexts where it is taken for granted in all other liberal democracies. Moreover, even while enjoying lavish state subsidies, the ultra-Orthodox are exempt from the military service required of all other Israeli Jews. See Zakheim, "Transforming Israel's Chief Rabbinate." Moreover, the Chief Rabbis have said the most disgusting, vile, stomach-turning things imaginable about gentiles, gays, Blacks, and other streams of Judaism. See Heilman, "5 Shocking Quotes," for a small sample. Finally, as I write these words, the Haredi political parties are key components of a government coalition that seeks to eliminate the power of the Israeli Supreme Court to invalidate any important legislation enacted by the Knesset, thereby enabling a transient electoral majority to violate the fundamental rights of all Israeli citizens.
>
> In sharp contrast, Modern Orthodox communities, while fully observant, are not closed societies, as their members are deeply engaged with and capable of functioning in the secular world and their children generally receive a quality secular education, including postsecondary if so desired. Accordingly, they make the fully informed decision to live an observant lifestyle and are not subject to the same onerous social pressure exerted in ultra-Orthodox communities. Further, they do not harbor the repulsive attitudes regarding less *frum* Jews and gentiles cited above, nor do they seek any privileges or advantages not equally available to other members of the wider society.
>
> 18. See Levenson, Review of *Revelation and Authority*.

Second, Levenson questions what assurance one can have that whatever group is entrusted to decide halakhah understands God's message correctly. The only apparent objective measure is whether the community's interpretations have survived over time, but he then asks: "Might a small minority not be in the right against the vast majority, even the vast majority of those who consider themselves observers of the law?" The answer is surely "yes." And therefore, he concludes: "So far as I can see, this [proposal] does not identify revelation or the will of God: it identifies a winner."[19]

Finally, in responding directly to Sommer's suggestion that the genocidal decree against the Amalekites was a gross misunderstanding of God's will, Levenson notes that this excuse, in effect, proves too much; that is, it arbitrarily aligns God's will with man's present moral inclinations:[20]

> Since in the Deuteronomic conceit the speaker of that ghastly command is Moses, one would have to say that the Shepherd of Israel, to revert to the rabbinic title, grossly misunderstood God's wordless revelation to him. *Bonus dormitat Moyses* [even Moses nods]. But I question whether any notion of divine revelation can withstand a theology in which unpalatable or offensive norms are simply ascribed to human error and the currently palatable or acceptable norms are ascribed, I assume, to the genuine will of God. Suppose God wanted to send a message at odds with understandings of morality in a given cultural situation. Could he ever get it past a screen like that one?

The self-evident answer to this query is "no."

A postmodern version of the continuous revelation concept has been propounded by Professor Tamar Ross, a Modern Orthodox academic philosopher and professed feminist. Her public writings strongly suggest that she rigorously observes traditional halakha in practice, while theologically she is far out of the Orthodox mainstream. While the overall thrust of her 2004 book, *Expanding the Palace of Torah*, is a critique of Orthodox Judaism's rigid and unjust gender roles, much of what she says is relevant to the broader discussion here of the Torah's other repugnant laws.

Professor Ross agrees with many thought-leaders of the more liberal streams of Judaism that "historical evidence cannot leave the traditional picture [of the Torah's origin] intact."[21] Accordingly, she seeks to salvage its

---

19. See Levenson, Review of *Revelation and Authority*.
20. Levenson, Review of *Revelation and Authority*.
21. Ross, "Orthodoxy and the Challenge," 265.

transcendent significance and meaning for observant Jews by "developing a concept of God that blurs the sharp distinction between the natural and supernatural, and between God's existence and human initiative."[22] Ross describes her work as a "first step in this direction" by offering an interpretation of the Sinaitic revelation that "break[s] down the strict dichotomy between divine speech and natural historical processes."[23]

Ross makes no bones about her commitment to postmodernism. Thus, in response to the criticism of her work by a more radical feminist that Ross is willing "to engage with the internal language of tradition and its appeal to metaphysics" and thus harbors "some residually fundamentalist understanding," Ross replies that this critic "did not take sufficient note of my post-liberal orientation."[24] She also makes it clear that she does not subscribe to a "modernism" based on "the assumption of rigid and stable notions of truth, supported by a universal, neutral, and objective rationality that serves as their justification."[25]

Accordingly, rather than simply admit that Chazal's version of Sinai is false (as history), and therefore adopting an alternative theory of transmission or an interpretation of the Bible as sacred fiction, Prof. Ross accepts the postmodernist perspective. As described by Helen Pluckrose, one of its best-known critics, it holds that: "objective knowledge is inaccessible and what we consider knowledge is actually just a cultural construct that operates in the service of power."[26] If objective knowledge is impossible, one need not take a stand on the veracity of the Revelation.

As Ross explains her strategy:[27]

> By blurring distinctions between the natural and the supernatural, the finite and the infinite, I contend that it is possible to relate to the Torah as a divine document without being bound to untenable notions regarding the nature of God and God's methods of communication or denying the role of human involvement. Such a view

---

22. Ross, "Orthodoxy and the Challenge," 277.
23. Ross, "Orthodoxy and the Challenge," 277.
24. Ross, "Orthodoxy and the Challenge," 278.
25. Ross, "Orthodoxy and the Challenge," 265, note 3.
26. Pluckrose, "On Activist Scholarship." Since withering critiques of postmodernism have already been written by others (see, e.g., Pluckrose and Lindsay, *Cynical Theories*; Sokal and Bricmont, *Fashionable Nonsense*; and Hicks, *Explaining Postmodernism*, this study will make no further comment on this worldview.
27. Ross, "Orthodoxy and the Challenge," 278.

> allows the religiously committed to understand that the Torah can be totally human and totally divine at one and the same time.

Unfortunately, it seems that elemental laws of logic dictate that Ross's last sentence above can no more be true than the claim that a figure can simultaneously be both round and square. It seems this perspective would be *especially* problematic for the religiously committed, who customarily refer to the Five Books as *Torah Emet* (Torah of Truth).

Whatever happened or did not happen at Sinai, Ross follows other proponents of "continuous revelation" in holding that its teachings will unfold over time, presumably including the Jewish Community's responses to problematic commandments. In her words, they will be disclosed through the ongoing "rabbinical interpretation of the texts . . . and through the mouthpiece of history . . . particularly what happens to the Jewish people."[28] By this account, the history of the Jewish people and the construction and use they make of their sacred texts "are essentially another form of ongoing revelation, a surrogate prophecy."[29]

However, Ross's proposal to blur the distinction between objective truth and subjective belief does not appear to escape the problem, described above, of radically diminishing God's authority and majesty. By surrendering Judaism's claim to objective truth, even as literature or moral philosophy, she robs the faith of its inspirational power and emotional appeal, *especially* for the observant. Remarkably, Ross acknowledges this peril in *Expanding the Palace of Torah*, where she observes that "Torah can function as the source of a living religion based on passion and commitment only to the degree that it makes some compelling appeal to truth and a connection with the divine."[30]

---

28. Ross, "Orthodoxy and the Challenge," 278.

29. Ross, "Orthodoxy and the Challenge," 278.

30. Ross, *Expanding the Palace*, 161. Yoel Finkelman, an Orthodox rabbi and scholar, expresses this concern quite eloquently in his critique of Ross's proposal:

> I fear that adoption of this theology will lead to a bland and insipid religion, reduced to social policy, communal politics, and literary metaphor. The elemental power of faith in the living, personal, and demanding God who reveals Himself in the sacred words of His Torah which He dictated directly to Moses is replaced with functionalism, metaphor, and sociology . . . If I need revelation, it is not to give a divine seal of approval to ideas that I might believe without it. If God matters at all, it is because He can teach me what I could not know myself, can demand of me more than I would demand of myself, can call me to task for failing to live up to His uncompromising demands.

Finkelman, "Review Essay," 9.

Furthermore, there is seemingly nothing in Ross's hypothesis that exonerates God from issuing the genocidal commands and other egregious mandates discussed above. Perhaps cumulative revelation permits us now to disregard or reinterpret them, but why were they given in the first place? Could God not have accelerated humanity's moral progress with better norms? Ross does not directly address this question, merely noting that one of the things prompting doubt in certain traditional circles regarding the received account of the Sinaitic revelation is its "questionable morality."[31] Perhaps this omission is the result of such matters not being even cognizable within the postmodernist purview. Finally, Professor Ross's theory still seems subject to the above-mentioned objections of Professor Levenson regarding the community to be entrusted with the revisionary process and the reliability of its editorial choices.

Traditionalist Versions of Continuous Revelation

As discussed at the beginning of this chapter, it may appear that Chazal's understanding of Revelation saddles God with total responsibility for the problematic mitzvot. If one were examining these commands in a vacuum, uprooted from their narrative "soil" and without knowing the history of rabbinic pluralism and tolerance, one might well conclude that authentic Judaism is morally bankrupt. However, as argued to this point, implicit in the Rabbis' halakhic philosophy is the view that God's commands must somehow be squared with secular morality's understanding of the right and good.

No doubt aware of the powerful tension between the Torah's repugnant commandments and humans' moral instincts, a number of otherwise impeccably *frum* rabbis and philosophers have begun to articulate interpretations of the Sinaitic narrative intended to harmonize traditional Judaism with our best moral theories.[32] Two of the more influential examples of such theories are critiqued below.

The late Rabbi Dr. Norman Lamm (1927–2020), a highly respected Modern Orthodox scholar and longtime dean of Yeshiva University, addresses the decree against the Amalekites head on in his 2007 article

---

31. Ross, "Orthodoxy and the Challenge," 263, 265.

32. The venue for much of this activity is the website TheTorah.com, and a survey of new theories regarding revelation is presented in the post by the editorial staff, "Current Approaches to Revelation and Torah."

"Amalek and the Seven Nations: A Case of Law vs. Morality." He does so while explicitly rejecting DCM, as he says in this same text that "morality is not dependent upon religion, and that the Torah's commands must accord with moral considerations."[33] Lamm's analysis starts with a thought experiment in which he imagines the moral dilemma facing a halakhically observant Jew who somehow learns with certainty that a friend is a descendant of the Amalekites.[34] While Rabbi Lamm affirms the historical truth of the Revelation, he forthrightly acknowledges that Judaism's understanding of morality has evolved over the generations and that the command to kill the friend clearly appears morally indefensible in the modern person's eyes. Yet he denies that "contemporary concepts of morality are sufficient to override a Biblical commandment or for declaring Halakhah . . . 'optional.'"[35]

However, Lamm acknowledges that an evolution in moral consciousness may legitimately motivate a reconsideration of existing halakha and change the understanding of it, but only if "[t]he moral reasoning for which we attempt to circumvent a Biblical mandate . . . itself issue[s] from or [is] compatible with Torah and mitzvot."[36] Such a judgment must be made by "mature and responsible halakhic authorities who are, at the same time, sensitive to the currents of contemporary moral philosophy."[37] In the case of the command to exterminate the Amalekites and all their descendants, however remote, Lamm finds the requisite biblical authority in the Torah's insistence in the Sixth Commandment that "[t]hou shall not kill" and its general commitment to justice.[38] Thus, our current unconditional rejection of genocide "bespeaks a later development that always inhered latently in the Torah itself."[39]

Rabbi Lamm's proposal clearly does better than the previously considered alternatives in upholding Judaism as a numinous faith; however, it appears to come at a very steep price in other respects. First, as Levenson notes, it has no apparent limiting principle. In other words, as we have seen to this point, the Torah, both in its narrative units and law codes, enshrines many noble ethical principles. This would seem to give *posekim* a license to

33. Lamm, "Amalek and the Seven Nations," 234, n1.
34. See Lamm, "Amalek and the Seven Nations," 202, 217.
35. Lamm, "Amalek and the Seven Nations," 226.
36. Lamm, "Amalek and the Seven Nations," 226.
37. Lamm, "Amalek and the Seven Nations," 232.
38. Lamm, "Amalek and the Seven Nations," 228.
39. Lamm, "Amalek and the Seven Nations," 228.

revise troubling mitzvot whenever they conflict with humankind's current best secular ethics. If so, then human morality trumps biblical morality, which, again, renders God a rather imperfect being.

Second, as previously noted, it leaves unanswered the question why the Almighty gave these indefensible commands in the first place, and why they have never been nullified. Could not God have advanced man's moral progress by telling the world up front that genocide is terribly wrong? Lamm's theory is also subject to the two other objections raised by Levenson against "continuous revelation." Namely, it fails to provide a principled answer regarding the selection of those to be assigned the task of revising the unacceptable mitzvot or any assurance regarding the soundness of their conclusions.

Professor Samuel Lebens, a widely published Orthodox rabbi and academic philosopher also proposes a variant of the "continuous revelation" theory that remains within the boundaries of Tradition's Sinaitic narrative.[40] He recognizes that "The Bible endorses attitudes and actions that *strike us today* as unethical. This provides us with reason for doubting that it is true, and thus that it comes from God" (emphasis added).[41] The Almighty's intentions are not exclusively found in the "Earthly Torah" (the one that Jews study and read aloud during services), says Professor Lebens, but are revealed in the manner describe by Professor Ross above, bringing it ever closer to the "Heavenly Torah" (God's will).[42] Accordingly, he says, "the meaning of [the Torah's] words is radically undetermined. It is up to the tradition to unpack them in light of its own evolution, guided by *ruach hakodesh* (the holy spirit)."[43]

For Lebens, the implication of this ongoing process of rabbinical revision is that God did *not* endorse genocide, but:[44]

---

40. Professor Lebens accepts what he regards as the essential elements of the Jewish faith, broadly defined by the writings of the influential medieval Jewish philosopher Joseph Albo (1380–1444). As Lebens states, the three principles are: (1) God's existence, (2) that revelation occurs, and (3) that God fairly rewards and punishes everyone. See Lebens, *Principles of Judaism*, 2. This commits Lebens to some version of the traditional account of the Sinaitic revelation, although not the stenographic one. See Lebens, *The Principles of Judaism*, 183–84.

41. Lebens, *Principles of Judaism*, 217.

42. Lebens, *Principles of Judaism*, 186–88.

43. Lebens, *Principles of Judaism*, 218.

44. Lebens, *The Principles of Judaism*, 219.

God was willing to be *viewed* as endorsing genocide in ancient times as he sought to guide a barbaric world towards the light. To allow yourself to be viewed in such a way *is* pretty horrifying, but no more horrifying than the human situation to which God was addressing himself.

It is appears clear that Lebens cannot bring himself to say that God gave immoral commands at Sinai but merely (as quoted above) that they "strike us today" as such; or at another point, that "the Torah contains details in deep tension with many of our modern ethical beliefs."[45] This reticence appears to be due to Lebens' understandable conviction that God did not actually approve of these laws. Rather, he asserts that they were formulated as they are because humans were simply not ready for a more elevated ethics.

Nevertheless, those holding a traditional view of revelation will certainly *understand* them to be God's will, as they are forthrightly propounded in the Pentateuch and have never been "officially" nullified. Thus, theologians are entitled to ask why not. And, because Lebens' answer is that they are to be "continuously revealed," his conjecture is subject to the objections raised above against Professor Ross.

An Alternative Explanation

Approaching the Hebrew Bible as a corpus grounded in critical rationalism and respect for autonomy resolves many of the apparent anomalies that plague the theories outlined above (I use "Hebrew Bible" here because, as argued in chapter 1, contrary to Chazal's stance, there is no ontological distinction in the holiness of the various canonical texts). This strategy avoids the trade-off between excusing God for the Torah's horrific mitzvot and dramatically reducing his omnipotence, and thus our reverence. One can readily admit the immorality of certain mitzvot because there is a benign explanation.

That is, out of respect for the supreme value of moral autonomy, God elected to accept his chosen people where they stood, moral warts and all. Rather than instantly accelerate their progress to some arbitrary point along an infinite continuum, he gave them—and through them, all of humanity—a road map that would guide them to their final destination with a set of liberal values that honor persons as moral agents; instill

---

45. Lebens, *The Principles of Judaism*, 185.

open-mindedness and a problem-solving mentality; esteem pluralism and controversy; and so forth.

Indeed, one might hazard that God's greatest miracle was not one of the awesome supernatural acts described in the Torah but the creation of a species able to formulate and eventually adopt new ideas, theories, and ways of living, ensuring steady (if erratic) ethical progress over an infinite time horizon. Had God given the Israelites the absolute truth at Sinai, it would have left humanity with nothing to accomplish. Progress will inevitably come, but it will have to be earned the hard way.

Furthermore, this approach to the Bible's account of revelation avoids the need to posit some cumbersome and questionable process of "progressive revelation" or "continuous revelation." The Torah does not require ongoing revision by "experts" because moral progress is assured if we live by the values described there, which—as we have seen—were eloquently articulated by the Rabbis. For the same reason, there is no need to struggle with the question of which individuals or institutions are to be assigned the responsibility of revising halakhah, as this is the task of every Jew and gentile guided by Scriptural principles.

8

The Tragedy of Rabbi Eliezer

MANY OF THE THEMES sounded throughout this volume—moral autonomy, the value of controversy and epistemic humility, pluralism, and the evolution of the Oral Law—are encapsulated by the talmudic story centered on a dispute over the ritual status of a peculiar oven. This imaginary tale, known as the "Oven of Akhnai," is certainly one of the most thoroughly discussed narratives of its kind and a flat-out literary masterpiece.[1] It pits a lone dissenter against all his rabbinic colleagues and is split into two distinct parts separated by some unspecified number of intervening years.[2] This tale is set in the first or second century CE among the Rabbis of the great academy of Yavneh (located along present-day Israel's central coast), who, following the destruction of the Second Temple, developed the theological underpinnings of the Mishnah.

This chapter presents a detailed analysis of this text because its content strongly suggests that authors wrote it purposely as a political manifesto of sorts that tends to substantiate this book's overall argument. Although less well known, appended is another, more straightforward, story also

---

1. One reason to say so is that the text is amenable to a staggering variety of interesting, provocative interpretations. I have read only a microscopic sampling of the papers on it and therefore fear that the interpretation I offer here may have been anticipated by others. I can only plead that, if this indeed is the case, my failure to acknowledge their work is entirely unintentional.

2. b. B. Metz. 59b; and b. Sanh. 68a.

involving a lone dissenter, Rabba bar Nahmani, set in Babylonia some two centuries after the dispute over this (in)famous oven.[3] As will hopefully soon become evident, the latter narrative appears to be written as a sympathetic elaboration of certain themes found in the first, inasmuch as there are just too many parallels and cross-references to be coincidental. While these parables almost certainly depict real historical figures, there can be no doubt that they were written as didactic fiction designed to convey a particular viewpoint.

The Players

Before going further, it will be helpful to consider some biographical information regarding the relatively few characters in this drama and "epilogue," as they are not simply random individuals who happen to stumble into a dramatic situation; but their reputed personalities and halakhic commitments are key parts of this narrative.

> *Eliezer b. Hyrcanus.* One of the greatest Tannaim. He was quintessentially old school and a dyed-in-the-wool theological conservative. R. Eliezer had no interest in halakhic innovation or creativity, and when confronted with a doubtful matter, used his phenomenal memory to identify a "tradition": that is, a teaching or ruling supposedly handed down at Sinai, as described in *Pirkei Avot* 1:1.[4] The Gemara quotes him as saying, "I have never said anything that I have not heard from my teacher," and his master, the great Rabban Yohanan ben Zakkai, followed the same halakhic philosophy.[5] The implication is that they regard themselves as reliable links in the chain of transmission that can be traced back to the Revelation, a view the Talmud explicitly attributes to R. Eliezer.[6] Such was his reputation, that R. Yohanan said of his pupil, "If all the sages of Israel were on one side of a scale and R. Eliezer ben Hyrcanus on the other, he would outweigh them all."[7]
>
> *Akiva b. Yosef.* Undoubtedly one of the most famous and revered of all the Sages. Although he was a student of R. Eliezer for many years,

---

3. b. B. Metz. 86a.
4. See chapter 4 above and Linzer, "Rabbi Eliezer vs. Rabbi Akiva."
5. b. Sukkah 28a.
6. b. Hag. 3b
7. *Pirkei Avot* 2:8.

his approach to halakhah was entirely opposite, as he used his unrivaled brilliance and inventiveness to derive bold new legal interpretations from the most subtle and esoteric textual hints. As previously discussed, there is a well-known aggadah of Moses being magically transported to R. Akiva's future academy and being befuddled there by his brilliance. R. Akiva's scholarship and erudition was such that he attracted 24,000 students, but tragically they all died in a single year between Pesach and Shavuot of a plague "because they did not treat each other with respect."[8]

Rabban Gamliel of Yavneh. A respected scholar, but not in the class of R. Eliezer or R. Akiva.[9] Rabban Gamliel's importance lies in his role as the head (*Nasi*) of the Yavneh academy upon its formation. He was known as a strict monist, perpetually on guard to prevent the emergence of divergent halakhic views that would cause the Torah to become "two Torahs." He went so far in this quest for uniformity as to publicly humiliate his subordinate, R. Yehoshua, for holding dissenting opinions, including whether a particular prayer was mandatory or optional. This triggered a revolt by Yavneh's Rabbis, who removed Rabban Gamliel from his position as Nasi, although he was eventually reconciled with R. Yehoshua and reinstated.[10]

Yehoshua (or "Joshua") b. Chananiah. Another very important and influential Sage; was a contemporary of R. Eliezer; and R. Akiva's primary teacher. Yehoshuah served as the head of the *beit din* (religious court) at the Yavneh academy under the supervision of Rabban Gamliel. Prior to his humiliation by Rabban Gamliel in the episode mentioned above, he had acceded to the latter's views regarding the fixing of the Jewish calendar, despite being quite certain of the correctness of his own opinion. Chazal depicts him generally as a humanistic seeker of peace, since, in addition to the above, there are midrashic sources that

---

8. b. Yevam. 62b. According to the Jerusalem Talmud, R. Akiva was an enthusiastic supporter of Bar Kochba (see y. Ta'an. 4:5), and after his revolt against Rome in 135 CE failed, the former was, according to legend, tortured to death by Emperor Hadrian. Some modern rabbis and scholars speculate that his students were killed fighting the Romans, or to prevent them from doing so. However, this is not suggested in the Talmud nor other contemporaneous sources, and so appears irrelevant to the analysis of this story. For a brief history of the Bar Kochba rebellion, see Schiffman, "The Bar Kochba Revolt."

9. See Steinmetz, "Must the Patriarch Know 'Uqtzin?" 164, 181–82.

10. See b. Ber. 27b—28a and Steinmetz, "Must the Patriarch Know 'Uqtzin?" for her extended, insightful analysis of this narrative.

describe him as having more positive attitudes towards converts and gentiles than R. Eliezer.[11]

Imma Shalom. Imma Shalom was, according to Tradition, both a sister of Rabban Gamliel and the wife of R. Eliezer. Perhaps because she was raised in a household run by the head of a rabbinic dynasty, she was, for a woman, unusually well-versed in halakha.[12]

Rabba bar Nahmani (or "Rabbah"). A third-generation Amora (ca. 270–330 CE), he was a renowned scholar who served for 22 years as head of the Academy of Pumbedita, one of the two great Babylonian centers of learning. Under his leadership, the academy achieved its greatest reputation. He is generally referred to in the Talmud simply as "Rabbah."[13]

The Rabbis Declare Independence

The famous story known as the "Oven of Akhnai" is introduced in the Gemara as "apropos the topic of verbal mistreatment,"[14] which, as discussed below, is regarded by halakha as a grave offense.[15] This appliance was constructed with a series of horizontally cut segments, each separated by a mortar of sand, giving it a snake-like appearance (*akhnai* means "snake"). R. Eliezer holds that, because of its peculiar structure, it was a non-unified object and thus could not be rendered halakhically impure, while all the other Sages disagree.[16]

When his arguments are rejected, he calls upon nature itself to testify for him, proclaiming that "if the *halakha* is in accordance with my opinion, this carob tree will prove it," and the tree is then violently uprooted and displaced by unseen forces. However, his interlocutors are unmoved by R. Eliezer's demonstration. Other apparently supernatural testimonies to the correctness of his opinion also fail to convince. Finally, R. Eliezer appeals to Heaven, and "a Divine Voice (*bat kol*) is heard to say, 'Why are you differing

---

11. See Wald, "Joshua Ben Hananiah," 11:450–52.
12. See Gilat and Wald, "Imma Shalom," 9:741–42.
13. See "Rabbah bar Nahamani," 17:9.
14. b. B. Metz. 59a.
15. See *Pirkei Avot.* 3:11; and b. B. Metz. 58b.
16. See Ledewitz, "The Openness of Talmud," 356.

The Tragedy of Rabbi Eliezer

with Rabbi Eliezer, as the *halakha* is in accordance with his opinion in every place that he expressed an opinion?'"[17]

Undaunted, Rabbi Yehoshua gets to his feet and adamantly responds to the heavenly voice, quoting Moses' admonishment to his beloved people:[18]

> Surely, the Instruction which I enjoin upon you this day is not too baffling for you, nor is it beyond reach. It is not in the heavens, that you should say, "Who among us can go up to the heavens and get it for us and impart it to us, that we may observe it? . . . No, the thing is very close to you in your mouth and in your heart, to observe it."

R. Yehoshua is implicitly relying on the argument that God has foreseen the death of prophecy and the development of the Oral Law, and has already delegated legal decision-making to the Rabbis, with the majority to govern.[19] Accordingly, R. Eliezer is living in the past, and because he is in the minority, his opinion must be rejected, even if it is correct in God's eyes. This pericope is frequently cited for its rabbinic "declaration of independence," but this does not even begin to plumb its depths.[20]

The Persecution of Rabbi Eliezer

The story now takes an ominous turn. It seems that, soon after this heated dispute, Rabbi Natan (an esteemed colleague of the Yavneh Sages) happens to encounter the prophet Elijah and asks him God's reaction to the majority's refusal to follow the *bat kol*. The prophet reports that "The Holy One, blessed be He smiled [in other translations, "laughed"] and said: 'My children have triumphed over me; My children have triumphed over me.'"

When R. Eliezer still refuses to accede to the majority opinion, the other Sages, at the direction of Rabban Gamliel, ban him and gather and burn all the objects he had previously ruled "pure." R. Akiva, his former "beloved disciple," volunteers to give R. Eliezer the bad news, "lest an unseemly person go and inform him in a callous and offensive manner, and he would thereby destroy the entire world." When this illustrious Sage hears it, he weeps, and "as a result the entire world was afflicted: One-third of its

---

17. b. B. Metz, 59b.
18. b. B. Metz, quoting Deut 30:11–14.
19. See Exod 23:2.
20. See, generally, England, "Majority Decision vs. Individual Truth."

olives were afflicted, and one-third of its wheat, and one-third of its barley. And some say that even dough kneaded in a woman's hands spoiled."[21]

As Professor Jeffrey Rubenstein, a leading authority on aggadah, observes: "This cruel and extreme measure—to ostracize a sage and cut him off from the community of Torah—kindles God's wrath."[22] Accordingly, Rabban Gamliel, who, as the leader of the Yavneh academy, bears ultimate responsibility, finds himself on a boat suddenly threatened by great waves. He correctly attributes his predicament to his humiliation of R. Eliezer, and he entreats the Almighty to consider that he did not do this out of any personal motive but "for Your honor, so that disputes will not proliferate in Israel."[23] In other words, so that the internal divisions that led to the Roman invasion and destruction of the Second Temple would not reoccur. The waves abate, but this is not a pardon, only a stay of execution; perhaps God is offering him a final chance at redemption.

Following this incident, the Talmud informs the reader that Imma Shalom "would not allow R. Eliezer to lower his head and recite the *tahanun* prayer, which includes supplication and entreaties."[24] She fears, based on a tradition taught in her paternal grandfather's house, that—were her husband to bemoan his fate during this prayer—her brother would receive divine punishment because: "All the gates of Heaven are apt to be locked except for the gates of prayer for victims of verbal mistreatment."[25] One day, due to a miscalculation or an interruption, she is unable to prevent her husband from saying *tahanun*, and indeed Rabban Gamliel immediately dies. This *sugya* ends, and the tractate then moves without further ado to a discussion of the mistreatment of converts, and in this discourse cites, perhaps not coincidentally, a teaching by none other than R. Eliezer.

However, this story resumes in another tractate, with R. Akiva, R. Yehoshua, and other unnamed Sages visiting the still-ostracized R. Eliezer on his deathbed. Their purpose is not entirely clear; the presence of R. Yehoshua suggests that they are hoping for some sort of reconciliation, since he was a man who suffered many indignities at the hands of Rabban Gamliel for the sake of communal peace and unity.[26] If so, they are to be

---

21. b. B. Met. 59b.
22. Rubenstein, *Rabbinic Stories*, 81.
23. b. B. Met. 59b.
24. b. B. Met. 59b.
25. b. B. Met. 59b.
26. See b. Bereakahot 27b—28a. Rabbi Wolowelsky, the Dean of the Faculty at a

disappointed. After overhearing him berate his son and wife for neglecting Sabbath preparations in favor of a lesser mitzvah, the visitors are reassured that he is still of sound mind. Thus, they enter his parlor and, because halakhah forbids performing acts of loving-kindness for heretics (i.e., visiting the sick), they inform him that they have come for the purpose of learning Torah, careful to keep the mandated physical distance between them and the outcast.

Things quickly go south. When R. Eliezer asks why they have not previously come to learn from him, they tell him they have been too busy. This does not sit well:[27]

> Rabbi Eliezer said to them: I would be surprised if these Sages die their own death, i.e., a natural death. Rather, they will be tortured to death by the Romans. Rabbi Akiva said to him: How will my death come about? Rabbi Eliezer said to him: Your death will be worse than theirs, as you were my primary student and you did not come to study.

It is obvious that the author of this story is familiar with and consciously incorporating into it the famous legend of the "Ten Martyrs," whose refusal following the Bar Kochba rebellion to renounce their faith caused them to be hideously tortured to death by the Romans, as solemnly commemorated in the Ashkenazic Yom Kippur liturgy. R. Akiva is, by far, the most illustrious of these martyrs. However, this is talmudic folklore, and there is no independent evidence that substantiates it. Even traditional sources differ as to the identity of the victims and the timing and circumstances of their deaths. It is apparent that the author includes the Ten Martyrs legend in this story to imply that R. Akiva and his colleagues suffered martyrdom for their abuse of R. Eliezer.[28]

Eliezer, facing his impending death, then bitterly complains about how little of his Torah knowledge he has been able to pass on: "only like the tiny amount that a paintbrush removes from a tube of paint." He says, for example, that "I can teach three hundred halakhot with regard to a

---

Modern Orthodox yeshiva, argues that "the Rabbis had come to realize that they had erred in the way they treated R. Eliezer [and] . . . had come to apologize and lift the excommunication." He suggests that their leader, R. Yehoshua, "had apparently been transformed by the uprising against Rabban Gamliel and his tactics." Wolowelsky, "Truth and Consequences," 68.

27. b. Sanh. 68a.
28. See Wolowesky, "Truth and Consequences," 68.

snow-white leprous mark [*bebaheret*], but no person has ever asked me anything about them."²⁹

The Sages then get down to the ostensible business at hand, questioning the master, as he lay dying, about the ritual status of various objects:³⁰

> They asked him further: What is the halakha with regard to a shoe that is on a last? Is it considered a complete vessel, which needs no further preparation, and is therefore susceptible to impurity? Rabbi Eliezer said to them: It is pure, and with this word, his soul left him in purity. Rabbi Yehoshua stood on his feet and said: The vow is permitted; the vow is permitted; i.e., the ostracism that was placed on Rabbi Eliezer is removed.

Their final question seems intended to mirror the halakhic issue posed by the troublesome oven, and it may reasonably be inferred that these Sages were hoping R. Eliezer might have changed his mind, but it was not to be. The Gemara's conclusion that "his soul left him in purity" suggests a favorable attitude towards R. Eliezer's steadfastness. R. Yehoshua's commutation of the dead man's sentence rings hollow.

The Talmud reports that, when R. Akiva later encounters his teacher's funeral procession, he:³¹

> was striking his flesh in terrible anguish and regret until his blood flowed to the earth. He began to eulogize Rabbi Eliezer in the row of those comforting the mourners, and said: "My father, my father, the chariot of Israel and its horsemen" (II Kings 2:12). I have many coins, but I do not have a money changer to whom to give them, i.e., I have many questions, but after your death I have no one who can answer them.

R. Akiva's words and self-flagellation evidence a profound regret regarding his relationship with his mentor.

Respect for Persons Above All

We are now able to draw a number of conclusions regarding the meaning of this powerful and intricately crafted tale. As mentioned, it is introduced as "apropos the topic of verbal mistreatment," which it certainly is.

29. b. Sanh. 68a.
30. b. Sanh. 68a.
31. b. Sanh. 68a.

The Tragedy of Rabbi Eliezer

Halakhically, the sin of "verbal mistreatment" (*ona'at devarim*) is, in the most basic terms, harming someone with words: by, for example, deceiving, shaming, embarrassing, or humiliating them, and is judged a great wrong. Rabban Gamliel is twice guilty of this offense, against both R. Yehoshua and R. Eliezer.

The Bavli goes to great lengths to emphasize its gravity and the drastic measures one must take to avoid committing it, including the opinion that "[i]t is more comfortable for a person to cast himself into a fiery furnace, than to humiliate another in public to avoid being cast into the furnace."[32] This *sugya* is the source of the tradition cited by Imma Shalom that "[a victim of verbal abuse] who cries before God may rest assured that his prayers will be answered," for God does not forgive this injustice.[33]

By ostracizing R. Eliezer, his rabbinic peers knowingly cause him great suffering. Of course, they believe they are in the right. Rabban Gamliel defends the ban based on his monist halakhic philosophy, and the biblical principle of "majority rule" licenses the authorities to enforce conformity of belief and conduct. There is no denying that there may be cases where such coercion is warranted: everyone has to drive either on the left side of the road or the right, but not both.

However, as argued in chapter 5, the overall spirit of the Bavli, in which this narrative appears, is that of tolerance and pluralism. Recall from the discussion there that some Rabbis even hold that it is permissible for two courts in the same town to disagree on halakhic matters. Thus, those wishing to avoid the risk of eating impure food from snake-like ovens could simply cook their food in kosher ones and purchase exclusively from those who follow the same practice, as *frum* Jews do today.

Indeed, Professor Devora Steinmetz argues, based on her in-depth review of the pertinent talmudic sources, that R. Gamliel's strict monism was one of the chief reasons for Rabbis' revolt against him:[34]

> The patriarch here [Gamliel], is not taken to task for ignorance; he is taken to task for behavior which limits the growth and free expression of ideas . . . The BT [Bavli], which so clearly values both the process and the products of unfettered debate, disposes of the patriarch who rejects this value . . . the very arrangement at

---

32. b. B. Metz. 59a.

33. See Enkin, "Embarrassing Others," for a compilation of rabbinic pronouncements stressing the pernicious nature of *ona'at devarim*.

34. Steinmetz, "Must the Patriarch Know 'Uqtzin?" 188–89.

the narrative's conclusion—the division of teaching responsibilities between R. Gamliel and R. Elazar b. Azaria—guarantees that never again will a single voice dominate the *bet midrash*.

Even if, for some strange reason, there had to be uniformity regarding certain unusual ovens, there was certainly no excuse for Rabban Gamliel's humiliation of R. Eliezer by publicly burning all the items he had formerly ruled "pure." Accordingly, it is likely that when God states, "my children have triumphed over me," he is ruefully acknowledging that the Rabbis, as autonomous agents, would have to—since prophecy had ceased—take the law into their own hands. However, this was not a blank check, as the Almighty expects that the Rabbis would judge with fear, trembling, and tolerance, conscious of their own inherent fallibility and the potentially catastrophic consequences of their errors.[35] Thus, it is highly improbable that the author of this morality tale agreed with R. Gamliel that the ritual purity of snake-like ovens was a hill worth dying on.

This tale plainly condemns Gamliel's persecution of R. Eliezer, but what is the Gemara's attitude regarding the great R. Akiva? The most natural and consistent reading is that it is no less critical, but on other grounds. R. Akiva was not the Nasi of the Yavneh academy and thus bears less responsibility than Rabban Gamliel for the abuse of R. Eliezer; yet this story has the former suffering a far more gruesome fate. Accordingly, it is apparent that the author of this saga understands his sin to be of a different nature.

It appears that the most plausible interpretation is that, in addition to his role in the ostracism of Rabbi Eliezer, Rabbi Akiva is implicitly accused in this narrative of both dangerous intellectual arrogance and disrespecting his former mentor. This becomes clear when we recall Eliezer's deathbed prediction that, of all his visitors, he says to Akiva, "Your death will be worse than theirs, as you were my primary student, and you did not come to study." Indeed, Akiva admits that ignoring his former mentor was a mistake when, as noted above, he laments, "I have many questions, but after [Eliezer's] death I have no one who can answer them."

Recall the discussion in chapter 4 of the talmudic legend of God magically transporting Moses far into the future to visit R. Akiva's academy. The

---

35. The story brings to mind Justice Robert Jackson's cautionary observation regarding the fallibility of judges: "Reversal by a higher court is not proof that justice is thereby better done. There is no doubt that if there were a super-Supreme Court, a substantial proportion of our reversals of state courts would also be reversed. We are not final because we are infallible, but we are infallible only because we are final." *Brown v. Allen*, 344 U.S. at 443, 540 (concurring).

latter is glorified there as a Sage of such profound insight that God takes pains to personally decorate the letters of the Heavenly Torah with subtle clues to its innermost meaning so that R. Akiva can later decode them.[36] The above-referenced analysis concludes that its narrator's purpose is to deny that the Rabbis took liberties with the Torah's written text by implying that these rulings were there all along, waiting to be discovered.

At the conclusion of this story, Moses asks the Almighty the fate of this genius, and God shows Moses "that they were weighing Rabbi Akiva's flesh in a butcher shop [*bemakkulin*], as Rabbi Akiva was tortured to death by the Romans." When Moses begs for an explanation, "God said to him: Be silent; this intention arose before Me."[37] God's command appears to indicate a certain unease regarding Akiva.

The clear implication of these various elements is that the "Oven of Akhnai" narrative includes a not-too-subtle critique of R. Akiva, in effect a counter-narrative to the hagiography just mentioned. Given the Bavli's positive attitude toward controversy, the presence of dueling aggadic tales is scarcely surprising. Not only did Akiva slight his former master, but by failing to engage with Eliezer, he deprived himself of the fruits of constructive disagreement, prized by critical rationalists. As Rabbi Dov Linzer, a highly regarded *rosh yeshiva* (head of yeshiva), writes in his analysis of this story: "Laws that are derived based on the human intellect—analysis, derivation, inference, analogy, and abstraction—need to be tested against other laws to see if they are consistent, to see if they are good. This is the value of R. Eliezer's Torah."[38]

The "Oven" story also intimates a direct connection between the esoteric, highly conceptualized character of R. Akiva's halakhic philosophy and the sudden deaths of his 24,000 students (12,000 study partners) "because they did not treat each other with respect." Perhaps their master, although mesmerizing them with his halakhic legerdemain, failed to instill in them sufficient reverence for the less philosophically artful but more fundamental Torah command that he is known for citing: "love your fellow as yourself."[39]

---

36. See b. Menah. 29b.

37. b. Menah. 29b.

38. Linzer, "Rabbi Eliezer vs. Rabbi Akiva." Perhaps it is worth remembering at this point the inherent limits of human reason and the immense danger of exceeding them. Even the most monstrous ideologies are claimed by their proponents to be "scientific."

39. See y. Ned. 9:4.

Come Now, Let Us Reason Together

As has been seen, R. Akiva apparently came to believe that he had nothing more to learn from R. Eliezer. If his students came to suppose that they, too, were entitled to formulate bold new legal doctrines derived from their individual psychology and sense of justice, unconstrained by established tradition, one can readily imagine that disputes would multiply and intensify, ultimately resulting in a "lack of respect" grievous enough to violate the law against verbal mistreatment. Accordingly, the story strongly suggests that R. Akiva's halakhic method is too dangerous to be emulated, at least by mere mortals. As noted above, God declines to tell Moses why Akiva's flesh is weighed in a butcher shop; our author's proposed answer can be summarized in a single word: "arrogance."

Lest the interpretation of the subject narrative as a brazen rabbinic attack on this halakhic giant seem incredible, note that the Talmud itself warns us that men of great learning are subject to equally great temptation. Thus, when R. Abaye's suspicion that an unmarried man and woman want to be alone for immoral purposes is disproven, he is depressed because he feels he would have succumbed to the temptation. However, "a certain Elder came and taught him: Anyone who is greater than another, his evil inclination is greater than his. Therefore, Abaye should not feel regret, as his realization is a consequence of his greatness."[40]

A comparison with R. Eliezer's philosophy is instructive. He is depicted in our story as stubborn, cantankerous, and unpleasant, while R. Akiva is tactful, considerate, and diplomatic. Yet, it is the older Sage that is intellectually humble; his halakhic method is simply to recover and perpetuate the traditions that can be traced back to Sinai. Once identified, their content is objective and (for purposes of Orthodox theology) certain, although always subject to further interpretation. As seen in chapters 5 and 6, the Rabbis were willing to modify established halakha in light of changing social circumstances and progress in the community's moral knowledge.

That halakhic norms may evolve in no way diminishes their great value. They are largely the hard-won lessons of humanity's collective history. As the future Justice Oliver Wendell Holmes wrote in 1881: "The life of the law has not been logic; it has been experience . . . The law embodies the story of a nation's development through many centuries, and it cannot be dealt with as

---

40. b. Sukkah 52a.

if it contained only the axioms and corollaries of a book of mathematics."[41] In other words, R. Eliezer's truths should not be lightly abandoned.[42]

Come Now, Let Us Reason Together

This reading of the "Oven of Akhnai" appears to be supported by the less famous talmudic story involving Rabbah.[43] This brief tale seems intended to strongly discourage the sort of hubris that prompted the majority to excommunicate R. Eliezer and R. Akiva to snub him. Perhaps by design, the story of Rabbah's last days is included in the same tractate containing the first half of the "Oven" saga.

The Talmud interrupts a story about Rabbah that seems designed to highlight his scholarly excellence and to furnish a necessary plot point for what follows. We are then told, "At that moment, the Sages in the heavenly academy were disagreeing with regard to a halakha of leprosy."[44] According to established law, one suffering from this disease is considered ritually impure if the white splotch on their skin precedes the growth of a white hair from it, but pure if the order is reversed. The question up for debate in Heaven: What is a person's status when the relevant sequence of events is unknown? The Bavli informs us that:[45]

---

41. Holmes, *The Common Law*, 1.
42. As G.K. Chesterton so eloquently puts it in this oft-quoted passage:
    > In the matter of reforming things, as distinct from deforming them, there is one plain and simple principle; a principle which will probably be called a paradox. There exists in such a case a certain institution or law; let us say, for the sake of simplicity, a fence or gate erected across a road . . . nobody has any business to destroy a social institution until he has really seen it as an historical institution. If he knows how it arose, and what purposes it was supposed to serve, he may really be able to say that they were bad purposes, or that they have since become bad purposes, or that they are purposes which are no longer served. But if he simply stares at the thing as a senseless monstrosity that has somehow sprung up in his path, it is he and not the traditionalist who is suffering from an illusion.

    Chesterton, "The Drift from Domesticity," 39.
43. See b. B. Metz. 86a.
44. b. B. Metz 86a. According to Rabbinic tradition, the "heavenly academy" (or Academy on High) is a community comprised of the souls of deceased scholars awaiting the World to Come, when their souls and bodies will be reunited. It is a place of deep learning and study, modeled on the great earthly academies, with God as its Nasi. See Freedman, "Academy on High," 1:353.
45. b. B. Metz. 86a.

> The Holy One, Blessed be He, says: The individual is pure, but every other member of the heavenly academy says: He is impure. And they said: Who can arbitrate in this dispute? They agreed that Rabba bar Nahmani should arbitrate, as Rabba bar Nahmani once said: I am preeminent in the halakhot of leprosy and I am preeminent in the halakhot of ritual impurity imparted by tents.

The Angel of Death is then dispatched to harvest R. Nahmani's soul, but there is some delay because he is constantly engaged in Torah study, and by divine fiat, a soul may not be taken when doing something so noble. When the framing story takes a certain fatal turn, Rabbah's soul becomes available, and: "As he was dying, he said in response to the dispute in heaven: 'It is pure; it is pure.' A divine voice emerged from heaven and said: 'Happy are you, Rabba bar Nahmani, as your body is pure and your soul left you with the word: Pure.'"[46] For Rabbah, God then makes a miracle so that his corpse, located in a swamp, is found by his fellow Rabbis and properly buried. The Almighty further instructs, via a note sent from Heaven, that this great scholar's death must be mourned for seven days and not the conventional three.

It seems evident that the author of this brief tale wishes us to regard Rabbah as R. Eliezer's alter ego, as they are paired in several obvious ways. Both are described as halakhic authorities on matters of leprosy (recall R. Eliezer's deathbed remark regarding his untapped knowledge of the law governing "a snow-white leprous mark.") Both men's final words are "it is pure," and it is said of them that they died in purity. Finally, and perhaps most significantly, their opinions are opposed by all the other Rabbis offering a verdict on the matter.

However, as described above, while these "twins" both sincerely judge the object in question as ritually pure, their opinions are received in radically different ways by their peers, and this disparity seems to be the focus of the Rabbah narrative. R. Eliezer's verdict is rejected and scorned, and he is persecuted by his colleagues for not renouncing it, while the Heavenly Academy accepts Rabbah's contrary opinion as final. The parable involving Rabbah seems to represent a harsh criticism of Eliezer's treatment, as God himself models a completely different halakhic process.

When the Almighty finds himself to be a minority of one, he, like Eliezer, refuses to yield. Instead, he proposes a fair arbitration procedure acceptable to all the disputants that results in no ostracisms or

---

46. b. B. Metz. 86a.

excommunications. The Academy exhibits epistemic humility by agreeing to be bound by the judgment of someone with greater expertise. It turns out that the original dissenting opinion (God's) is proven correct. In contrast to the abuse suffered by R. Eliezer, Rabbah is accorded special honors upon his passing.

It is evident that these two talmudic narratives are together urging a liberal reading of Moses' pronouncement that the Torah is "not in Heaven." It seems that the "Oven" narrative is written to warn us against intolerance, including intellectual arrogance, while the Rabbah counterpart is intended to model the liberal ideal. Unlike Moses, we cannot simply call upon God when we have questions. As autonomous moral agents, we are charged with adapting the law to reflect our ever-expanding empirical knowledge and evolving moral consciousness. While innovation is required, it must never tip over into obstinance and oppression. God expects us to act justly and with humility, respecting the rights of others to think and act differently, pursuant to the basic principles outlined in chapter 2.

Finally, as Chaim Saiman, the author of a recent well-received book on halakhah, rightly observes in his commentary on the Rabbah tale, it is extraordinarily revealing of the rabbinic ethos that the highest pleasure and greatest reward the Sages can imagine is studying and debating obscure legal questions. As Professor Saiman puts it, "To the Talmud, ultimate perfection is God and the angels arguing over the intricacies of halakhah."[47] In other words, the greatest joy lies not in holding the truth in our hands but in searching for it. So, as the prophet Isaiah pleads on behalf of God following the denunciations quoted in chapter 6, "come now, let us reason together."[48]

---

47. Saiman, *Halakhah*, 3.

48. Isa 1:19. This is the King James Version's translation. The JPS translation is "Come, let us reach an understanding."

Glossary

Aggadah: The non-halakhic (non-legal) materials in the Talmud, Midrash, and other classical sources, consisting of metaphorical or allegorical interpretations of biblical stories; imaginative narratives; homilies; and legends and fantastic tales, that open a more philosophical pathway to the understanding of the divine will.

Amoraim: The rabbis whose discussions and debates are recorded in the Gemara, active roughly between 220 CE and 500 CE (the "Amoraic era" or period).

Babylonian Talmud (or "Bavli"): The Talmud composed and edited by many generations of Babylonian rabbis, with its final codification occurring in the late sixth or early seventh century CE. For several reasons, including its later redaction, more comprehensive coverage of the Mishnah's tractates, and more in-depth and nuanced discourse, the Bavli is universally regarded as more authoritative than the Jerusalem Talmud, and halakhic conflicts are always resolved in its favor. The organization of both Talmuds follows that of the Mishnah, consisting of six "orders" (broad subjects such as family law, holidays, civil and criminal law, and so on), and each order is further subdivided into more precisely delineated "tractates" (chapters), totaling sixty-three in all (in the Bavli).

Baraita: An ancient oral tradition, typically in circulation contemporaneously with those of the Mishnah, but codified in other ancient texts. They are often cited in talmudic debates and are almost equal in authority to the traditions recorded in the Mishnah.

Glossary

Chazal: An acronym derived from the Hebrew *chachamim zichronam levracham*, literally "rabbis of blessed memory." Typically used to refer to the sages and rabbis of the talmudic era.

Classic Jewish Sources: The oral traditions and texts available to the sages and rabbis of the talmudic era, including the *Tanakh*; the Mishnah; oral material recorded in the Babylonian and Jerusalem Talmuds; the Tosefta (less authoritative legal material not recorded in the Mishnah); early Midrashim; and the collections of halakhic midrashim.

Gemara: The second and by far lengthier of the Talmuds' two primary components, consisting of the rabbis' seemingly exhaustive analysis and elucidation of the Mishnah, as well as many aggadic narratives. The result is often an extended chain of dialectical argumentation that may diverge widely from the original question presented.

Geonim: The plural form of "Gaon," the honorific given to the heads of the two major Babylonian academies (yeshivas), Sura and Pumbedita (both in present-day Iraq), from the end of the sixth century until their closure in about 1040, referred to as the "Geonic era." The Geonim assumed the intellectual leadership of the Jewish world after the closing of the Babylonian Talmud and maintained it for roughly four centuries, when their influence began to fade with the ascendancy of other centers of learning.

Halakha: Often translated as "Jewish law," referring to the laws set down in the Mishnah, elucidated in the Talmud, then codified in the *Mishneh Torah* and *Shulchan Aruch,* and further refined and clarified by *posekim* (judges and legal authorities) until today. However, the discourse in these sources, especially in the Talmud, is frequently a vehicle for voicing ethical, theological, pedagogical, and philosophical perspectives.

Jerusalem Talmud (or "Yerushalmi"): The Talmud composed and edited by the Rabbis of Yavneh and other academies in what is present-day Israel. It was reduced to final form at roughly the start of the fifth century CE and lacks the final editorial layer found in the Bavli.

Midrash (Midrashim pl.): When capitalized, a genre of Jewish literature consisting of compilations of aggadah and exegesis by rabbis and scholars between the fourth and twelfth centuries of the common area ("midrash" designates a single story, homily or other unit within

Glossary

the compilation). These Midrashim often reference or incorporate aggadah from earlier eras. The largest and best-known compilations are collectively known as "Midrash Rabbah" (the English translation of "rabbah" is "great"), that are organized around a specific canonical book. Other important Midrashim are *Midrash Tanchuma* and *Pirkei DeRabbi Eliezer*. This definition excludes halakhic Midrashim that explain the derivation of laws from the Biblical commandments.

Mishnah: The earlier of the two primary layers of the Talmud, codifying ancient oral halakhic traditions that serve as the starting point for the Gemara's detailed elucidation and elaboration. Organized into six broad subject-matter categories ("orders"), then further subdivided into tractates within each order. It consists generally of concise statements the laws governing the conduct of Jews in common day-to-day circumstances, although it frequently includes conflicting legal opinions by named Sages, as well as relatively rare stories. Generally thought to have been reduced to writing around the year 200 CE out of fear that these traditions might be lost because of political upheaval.

Oral Law (or Oral Torah): According to Tradition, Moses not only received the written Torah at Mt. Sinai, but God also conveyed orally the answers to future questions that would arise in interpreting and applying these laws. Moses then passed these interpretive keys down to Joshua, who transmitted them to the elders, then to the prophets, and so on, in an unbroken chain until they were finally recorded in the Mishnah.

Rabbis: When capitalized, the rabbis, scholars, and legal authorities of the talmudic era.

Revelation: When capitalized, the biblical account of the giving of the Torah to Moses on Mt. Sinai.

Rishonim: The great rabbis and jurists active between the second half of the eleventh century CE and the publication of the *Shulchan Aruch* (1563).

Sages: When in initial caps, the scholars and legal authorities active in Eretz Israel ("Land of Israel") prior to the reduction of the Mishnah to writing.

Sugya (*sugyot* pl.): A passage in the Gemara consisting of an in-depth analysis and elucidation centered on a particular law, topic, or narrative set forth in the Mishnah.

Glossary

Talmud: The encyclopedic length texts consisting of the Mishnah, Gemara, and, with respect to the Babylonian Talmud, the editorial layer authored by the Stammaim.

Tannaim: The community of halakhic authorities spanning several generations who, according to Tradition, faithfully preserved and transmitted the Oral Law from teacher to student until it was reduced to writing in the Mishnah. These sages also compiled and transmitted the aggadic narratives, non-literal biblical interpretations, and homilies recorded in the early Midrashim. They were active from roughly the start of the common era until about 220 (the "Tannaitic era").

Torah: Generally refers to the Pentateuch (the "Five Books of Moses"), but occasionally is used, depending on the context, to denote the entire corpus of sacred texts.

Tradition: When in initial caps, those beliefs and doctrines formulated by Chazal and affirmed by the Orthodox rabbis until today.

Selected Bibliography

Abo-Eleaz, Mohy-Eldin E. "Did Kings Meet Each Other Face-to-Face During the Late Bronze Age?" *Ancient Near East Today* 11, no. 3 (March 2022). https://www.asor.org/anetoday/2023/01/kings-bronze-age-rumors.

Abramsky, Samuel, and S. David Sperling. "Amalekites." In *EJ* 2:28–30.

Alter, Robert. *The Art of Biblical Narrative*. Basic Books, 2nd ed. 2011.

———. *The Five Books of Moses/Torah*. Vol. 1 of *The Hebrew Bible: A Translation with Commentary*. New York: W. W. Norton, 2019.

———. *Prophets/Nevi'im*. Vol. 2 of *The Hebrew Bible: A Translation with Commentary*. New York: W. W. Norton, 2019.

———. *The Writings/Ketuvim*. Vol. 3 of *The Hebrew Bible: A Translation with Commentary*. New York: W. W. Norton, 2019.

Altman, Alexander. "Bible, Allegorical Interpretations." In *EJ* 3:643–45.

Angel, Hayyim. "The End of Prophecy: Malachi's Position in the Spiritual Development of Israel." *Conversations*, no. 9 (Winter 2011) 112–18. https://www.jewishideas.org/print/article/end-prophecy-malachis-position-spiritual-development-israel.

———. "The Meaning of the Book of Jonah." *Institute for Jewish Ideas and Ideals*, excerpted from *Vision from the Prophets and Counsel from the Elders: A Survey of Nevi'im and Ketuvim*, 163–72. New York: OU, 2013. https://www.jewishideas.org/article/meaning-book-jonah.

Babylonian Talmud. English from The William Davidson digital edition of the *Koren Noé Talmud*. Translation with commentary by Rabbi Adin Even-Israel Steinsaltz. https://www.sefaria.org/texts/Talmud/Bavli.

Baras, Dan. "A Moral Argument Against Absolute Authority of the Torah." In *Sophia* 60, no. 2: 307–29.

Barnett, Randy E. *Restoring the Lost Constitution*. Princeton: Princeton University Press, 2004.

Batnitzky, Leora, and Ilana Parder, eds. *The Book of Job: Aesthetics, Ethics, Hermeneutics*. Berlin: De Gruyter, 2014.

Baumgarten, Albert I., and S. David Sperling. "Scroll of Esther." In *EJ* 18:215–18.

Bazak, Amnon. "Replications and Contradictions in Tanakh, Part 1." *Fundamental Issues in the Study of Tanakh: Lesson 9. Israel Koschitzky Torat Har Etzion*, September 21, 2014. https://www.etzion.org.il/en/tanakh/studies-tanakh/core-studies-tanakh/replications-and-contradictions-tanakh-1.

Selected Bibliography

Beal, Zane. "Is Postmodernism Inherently Authoritarian?" *Quillette* (July 13, 2017). https://quillette.com/2017/07/13/postmodernism-inherently-authoritarian/.
Ben-Menahem, Hanina. "Controversy and Dialogue in the Jewish Tradition: An Interpretive Essay." In *Controversy and Dialogue in the Jewish Tradition: A Reader*, edited by Hanina Ben-Menachem et al., 1–41. New York: Routledge, 2005.
Berkovits, Eliezer. "The Biblical Idea of Justice" [1969]. In *Eliezer Berkovits: Essential Essays on Judaism*, edited by David Hazony, 129–52. Shalem Press: Jerusalem, 2002.
———. "Conversion and the Decline of the Oral Law" [1974]. In *Eliezer Berkovits: Essential Essays on Judaism*, edited by David Hazony, 89–102. Shalem Press: Jerusalem, 2002.
———. "The Encounter with the Divine" [1959]. In *Eliezer Berkovits: Essential Essays on Judaism*, edited by David Hazony, 215–314. Shalem Press: Jerusalem, 2002.
———. "Law and Morality in Jewish Tradition" [1959]. In *Eliezer Berkovits: Essential Essays on Judaism*, edited by David Hazony, 4–39. Shalem Press: Jerusalem, 2002.
———. "The Nature and Function of Jewish Law" [1983]. In *Eliezer Berkovits: Essential Essays on Judaism*, edited by David Hazony, 41–87. Shalem Press: Jerusalem, 2002.
———. "On the Return to Jewish National Life" [1943]. In *Eliezer Berkovits: Essential Essays on Judaism*, edited by David Hazony, 155–75. Shalem Press: Jerusalem, 2002.
———. "The Spiritual Crisis in Israel." [1979]. In *Eliezer Berkovits: Essential Essays on Judaism*, edited by David Hazony, 201–12. Shalem Press: Jerusalem, 2002.
Berman, Joshua A. *Inconsistency in the Torah: Ancient Literary Convention and the Limits of Source Criticism*. New York: Oxford University Press, 2017.
———. *Ani Maamin: Biblical Criticism, Historical Truth, and the Thirteen Principles of Faith*. Maggid Books, an imprint of Koren, 2020.
Blenkinsopp, Joseph. "The Documentary Hypothesis in Trouble." *Biblical Archaeology Society, Bible Review* (Winter 1985).
Blidstein, Gerald F. "Oral Law as Institution in Maimonides." In *The Thought of Moses Maimonides: Philosophical and Legal Studies*, edited by Ira Robinson et al., 167–82. Lewiston, NY: Edwin Mellen, 1991. https://www.academia.edu/36620757/Gerald_J_Blidstein_Maimonides_on_Oral_Law_Jewish_Law_Annual_no_1_1978_108_122.
Bishop, John, and Daniel J. McKaughan. "Faith." In *SEP* (Fall 2022 Edition). https://plato.stanford.edu/archives/fall2022/entries/faith/.
Brettler, Marc Zvi. *How to Read the Jewish Bible*. New York: Oxford University Press, 2007.
Breuer, Mordechai. "The Study of Bible and the Primacy of the Fear of Heaven: Compatibility or Contradiction?" In *Modern Scholarship in the Study of Torah: Contributions and Limitations*, edited by Shalom Carmy et al., 159–80. Lanham, MD: Rowman & Littlefield, 1996. http://www.ericlevy.com/Revel/Cosmogony/Breuer%20-%20Study%20of%20Bible%20and%20the%20Fear%20of%20Heaven.PDF
Byrne, Alex, and Ned Hall. Review of *Philosophical Analysis in the Twentieth Century*, by Scott Soames. *Boston Review* (October 5, 2004). https://www.bostonreview.net/articles/byrne-hall-necessaryotruths/.
Bultmann, Christopher. "Deuteronomy." In *The Pentateuch*, edited by John Barton et al., 187–219. New York: Oxford University Press, 2010.
Cardozo, Nathan Lopez. "The Deliberately Flawed Divine Torah." *TheTorah.com*, 2016. https://thetorah.com/article/the-deliberately-flawed-divine-torah.
Carlyle, Thomas. *On Heroes, Hero-Worship and the Heroic in History*. London: Chapman and Hall, 1840. https://books.google.com/books?id=kCo-AAAAYAAJ&printsec=frontcover#v=twopage&q&f=false.

Selected Bibliography

Chesterton, G. K. "The Drift from Domesticity." In *The Thing*, archived November 6, 2018 at the Wayback Machine, 35. London: Sheed & Ward, 1929. https://archive.org/details/in.ernet.dli.2015.475818/page/n35/mode/2up.

Childs, Brevard S. *Biblical Theology in Crisis*. Philadelphia: Westminster, 1970.

Christman, John. "Autonomy in Moral and Political Philosophy." In *SEP* (Fall 2020 Edition). https://plato.stanford.edu/archives/fall2020/entries/autonomy-moral/.

Clifford, W.K. "The Ethics of Belief." In vol. II of *Lectures and Essays*. London: Macmillan, 1879. https://people.brandeis.edu/~teuber/Clifford_ethics.pdf

Clines, David J. A. "Introduction to the Biblical Story: Genesis-Esther." In *Harper's Bible Commentary*, edited by James L. Mays, 74–84. San Francisco: Harper & Row, 1988.

Cohn, Gabriel H., and S. David Sperling. "Jonah, Book of." In *EJ* 11:388–90.

Coopersmith, Dina. "Miriam: Instiller of Faith, Enabler of Redemption." *Aish.com*. https://aish.com/women-in-the-bible-6-miriam/

Courtland, Shane D., et al. "Liberalism." In *SEP* (Spring 2022 Edition). https://plato.stanford.edu/archives/spr2022/entries/liberalism/.

Cover, Robert. "Nomos and Narrative." *Harvard Law Review* 97, no. 4 (1982) 4–64. https://openyls.law.yale.edu/bitstream/handle/20.500.13051/2047/Nomos_and_Narrative.pdf?sequence=2&isAllowed=y.

Crenshaw, James L. "Ecclesiastes." In *Harper's Bible Commentary*, edited by James L. Mays, 518–24. San Francisco: Harper & Row, 1988.

"Current Approaches to Revelation and Torah" (Staff Editors). *TheTorah.com*, 2013. https://www.thetorah.com/article/current-approaches.

Dane, Perry. "The Yoke of Heaven, the Question of Sinai, and the Life of Law." *University of Toronto Law Journal* 44 (1994) 353–400. https://papers.ssrn.com/sol3/papers.cfm?abstract_id=1714071.

Davies, G. I. "Introduction to the Pentateuch." In *The Pentateuch*, edited by John Barton et al., 16–53. New York: Oxford University Press, 2010.

Deen, Shulem. *All Who Go Do Not Return*. Minneapolis, MN: Graywolf Press, 2015.

Deguzman, Kyle. "What is The Rashomon Effect in Film? Definition & Examples Explained." *Studiobinder.com*, September 11, 2022, https://www.studiobinder.com/blog/what-is-the-rashomon-effect-definition/.

Didion, Joan. *The White Album*. Pocket Books, 1980.

Dienstag, Jacob I. "Moses Maimonides, as Halakhist." In *EJ* 13:385–88.

Dotan, Aron. "Masorah." In *EJ* 13:603–56.

Dorff, Elliot N. Chapter III(D) of *Conservative Judaism: Our Ancestors to Our Descendants*. United Synagogue, 2nd printing, 1978. Excerpted by Adath-Shalom.ca. http://www.houseofdavid.ca/dorff110.htm.

EJ (anonymous author). "Rabba Ben Nahamani." In *EJ* 17:9.

Eldar, Itamar. "The Kuzari and Rav Yehuda HaLevi: Lesson 22—The Karaites and the Oral Law, Part 1," March 18, 2015." *Israel Koschitzky Torat Har Etzion*. https://etzion.org.il/en/philosophy/great-thinkers/rihal-kuzari/karaites-and-oral-law-i.

Elman, Yaakov. "R. Zadok Hakohen on the History of Halakha." *Tradition* 21, no. 4 (Fall 1985) 1–26. https://traditiononline.org/r-zadok-hakohen-on-the-history-of-halakha/.

Elon, Menachem. "Codification of Law." In *EJ* 4:765–81.

Enkin, Ari. "Embarrassing Others." *OU Torah*. https://outorah.org/p/49535/.

Englard, Izhak. "Majority Decision vs. Individual Truth." *Tradition* 15, nos. 1–2 (Spring–Summer 1975). https://traditiononline.org/majority-decision-vs-individual-truth/.

Selected Bibliography

Falk, Marcia. "Song of Songs." In *Harper's Bible Commentary*, edited by James L. Mays, 525–28. San Francisco: Harper & Row, 1988.

Feldman, Marla J. "Why Advocacy is Central to Reform Judaism." *Union of Reform Judaism*, 2023, https://urj.org/what-we-do/social-justice/why-advocacy-is-central-to-reform-judaism.

Finkelman, Yoel. Review of *Expanding the Palace of Torah: Orthodoxy and Feminism*, by Tamar Ross. In *The Edah Journal* 4, no. 2 (2004) 2–25.

Fisch, Menachem. *Rational Rabbis: Science and Talmudic Culture*. Bloomington, IN: Indiana University Press, 1997.

Fitch, Robert E. "The Bond Between Christian and Jew: Their Common Ethic." *Commentary* (May 1954).

Frank, Anne. *The Diary of Anne Frank*. London: Hutchinson, 1986

Fraude, Steven D. "Literary Composition and Oral Performance in Early Midrashim." *Oral Tradition* 14, no. 1 (1999) 33–51. https://www.yumpu.com/en/document/view/4044840/literary-composition-and-oral-performance-in-early-midrashim.

Frederick, Danny. "A Regimented and Concise Exposition of Karl Popper's Critical Rationalist Epistemology (Version 3)." In *Against the Philosophical Tide*, 3–14. Yeovil, UK: Critias, 2020.

Freedman, Harry. "Academy on High." In *EJ* 1:353.

Freeman, Tzvi. "What is Torah? A Comprehensive Overview." *Chabad.org*, undated, https://www.chabad.org/library/article_cdo/aid/3361517/jewish/What-Is-Torah.htm.

Fretheim, Terrence E. "Jonah." In *Harper's Bible Commentary*, edited by James L. Mays, 728–30. San Francisco: Harper & Row, 1988.

Gattei, Stefano. *Karl Popper's Philosophy of Science: Rationality without Foundations*. UK: Routledge, an imprint of Taylor & Francis, 2008.

Gaus, Gerald F. "The Place of Autonomy Within Liberalism." In *Autonomy and the Challenges to Liberalism: New Essays*, edited by John Christman et al., 272–306. New York: Cambridge University Press, 2005.

Gilat, Yitzhak Dov. "Eliezer." In *EJ* 6:322–24.

Gilat, Yitzhak Dov, and Stephen G. Wald. "Imma Shalom." In *EJ* 9:741–42.

Gillman, Neil. *Conservative Judaism: The New Century*. Millburn, NJ: Behrman House, 1993.

———. *The Way into Encountering God in Judaism*. Woodstock, VT: Jewish Lights, 2004, excerpt published by *MyJewishLearning.com* as "God: A Great Personality," https://www.myjewishlearning.com/article/god-a-great-personality/.

Ginsberg, Harold Louis. "Tamar." In *EJ* 19:493.

Ginsberg, Harold Louis, and Marvin V. Fox. "Ecclesiastes." In *EJ* 6:88–90.

Ginzberg, Louis. Vol. 3 of *The Legends of the Jews*. Baltimore, MD: Johns Hopkins University Press, 1998 [1911].

Goldin, Judah H. "The Freedom and Restraint of Haggadah." In Geoffrey H. Hartman and Sanford Budick, eds., *Midrash and Literature*. New Haven: Yale University Press, 1986, 57–86. https://www.academia.edu/43907822/Judah_Goldin_The_Freedom_and_Restraint_of_Haggadah_in_Geoffrey_H_Hartman_and_Sanford_Budick_eds_Midrash_and_Literature_New_Haven_Yale_University_Press_1986_57_86?email_work_card=title

Golinkin, David. "Is Judaism Really in Favor of Pluralism and Tolerance?" *Responsa in a Moment* 9, no. 6 (June 2015). https://schechter.edu/is-judaism-really-in-favor-of-pluralism-and-tolerance-responsa-in-a-moment-volume-9-issue-no-6-june-2015/.

Selected Bibliography

Good, Edwin M. "Job." In *Harper's Bible Commentary*, edited by James L. Mays, 407–32. San Francisco: Harper & Row, 1988.

Gordis, Robert. *The Book of God and Man*. Chicago: University of Chicago Press, 1965.

Gorton, William. "Karl Popper: Political Philosophy." In *The Internet Encyclopedia of Philosophy*. ISSN 2161-002, https://iep.utm.edu/popp-pol/, last accessed December 25, 2022.

Gottwald, Norman K. "Book of Samuel." In *EJ* 17:758–63.

Grabianowski, Ed, and Melanie Radzicki McManus. "13 Overturned Supreme Court Cases." *HowStuffWorks.com*, June 24, 2022, https://money.howstuffworks.com/10-overturned-supreme-court-cases.htm.

Green, Arthur, ed. *Jewish Spirituality: From the Bible Through the Middle Ages*. Crossroad, an imprint of Herder & Herder, 1989.

Greenberg, Moshe. "Bible Interpretation as Exhibited in the First Book of Maimonides' Code." In *Moshe Greenberg, Studies in the Bible and Jewish Thought*, 421–45. Philadelphia: Jewish Publication Society, 1995.

———. "The Decalogue Tradition Critically Examined." In *Moshe Greenberg, Studies in the Bible and Jewish Thought*, 279–311. Philadelphia: Jewish Publication Society, 1995.

———. "Ezekiel." In *EJ* 6:635–44.

———. "Reflections on Job's Theology." In *Book of Job: A New Translation According to the Traditional Hebrew Texts*, 327–33. Philadelphia: Jewish Publication Society, 1980.

Guttmann, Julius. *Philosophies of Judaism: The History of Jewish Philosophy from Biblical Times to Franz Rosenzweig*. Translated by David W. Silverman. 1933. New York: Holt & Kegan Rinehart, 1964.

Halbertal, Moshe. "The History of Halakhah, Views from Within: Three Medieval Approaches to Tradition and Controversy." *Jewish Law and Modernity: Five Interpretations*, in Harvard Law School Gruss Lectures, 1–19. Cambridge, MA: Harvard Law School, 1994. https://www.academia.edu/38287534/Moshe_Halbertal_The_History_of_Halakhah_Views_from_Within_Three_Medieval_Approaches_to_Tradition_and_Controversy_in_Harvard_Law_School_Gruss_Lectures_Cambridge_MA_Harvard_Law_School_1994_1_19.

Halivni, David Weiss. "The Breaking of the Tablets and the Begetting of the Oral Law: A History of 'Torah Shebe'al Peh.'" In *Gershom Scholem (1897–1982): In Memoriam, Volume Two*, edited by Joseph Dan, 137–63. Jerusalem: Hebrew University Department of Jewish Thought, 2007. https://www.jstor.org/stable/23365226.

Harris, Jay M. "Talmud Study." The *YIVO Encyclopedia of Jews in Eastern Europe*. https://encyclopedia.yivo.org/article/46

Hayek, Friedrich A. von. "Freedom and the Economic System." Public Policy Pamphlet No. 29. University of Chicago Press, 1939.

Heilman, Uriel. "5 Shocking Quotes by Israel's Chief Rabbis." *Jewish Telegraphic Agency* (March 28, 2016). https://www.jta.org/2016/03/28/culture/5-shocking-quotes-by-israels-chief-rabbis.

Helfgot, Nathanial. "Minority Opinions and their Role in Hora'ah." *Mishpetei Shalom: A Jubilee Volume in Honor of Rabbi Saul (Shalom) Berman*, edited by Yamin Levy, 36–60. New York: KTAV, 2010. https://library.yctorah.org/files/2016/09/Minority-Opinions-and-their-Role-in-Horaah.pdf.

Heller, Joseph Elijah, and Leon Nemoy. "Karaites." In *EJ* 11:785–99.

Henderson, Leah. "The Problem of Induction." *SEP* (Winter 2022 Edition). https://plato.stanford.edu/archives/win2022/entries/induction-problem/.

Selected Bibliography

Herr, Moshe David. "Oral Law." In *EJ* 15:454–55.

———. "Pirkei De-Rabbi Eliezer." In *EJ* 16:182–83.

Heschel, Abraham Joshua. *The Sabbath: Its Meaning for Modern Man*. New York: Noonday, an imprint of Ferrar, Strauss, and Young, 1951.

———. "Halakah and Agadah." In *Between God and Man*, selected, edited. And introduced by Fritz A. Rothschild, 175–80. New York: Free Press, a division of Macmillan, 1965.

———. "The Meaning of Observance." In *Between God and Man*, selected, edited. And introduced by Fritz A. Rothschild, 181–86. New York: Free Press, a division of Macmillan, 1965.

———. "Understanding the Bible." In *Between God and Man*, edited by Fritz A. Rothschild, 241–50. New York: Free Press, a division of Macmillan, 1965.

Heschel, Susannah, "Theological Affinities in the Writings of Abraham Joshua Heschel and Martin Luther King, Jr." *Conservative Judaism* 50, nos. 2–3 (1998) 126–43.

Hicks, Stephen R. C. *Explaining Postmodernism: Skepticism and Socialism from Rousseau to Foucault* (expanded edition). Loves Park, IL: Ockham's Razor, 2011.

Hidary, Richard. *Dispute for the Sake of Heaven: Legal Pluralism in the Talmud*. Providence, RI: Brown University Press, 2010.

Holm, Tawny. "Moses in the Prophets and the Writings of the Hebrew Bible." In *Illuminating Moses: A History of Reception from Exodus to the Renaissance*, edited by Jane Beal, 37–57. Boston: Brill Academic Press, 2013. https://www.academia.edu/1826730/_Moses_in_the_Prophets_and_the_Writings_of_the_Hebrew_Bible_Pp_37_57_in_Illuminating_Moses_A_History_of_Reception_from_Exodus_to_the_Renaissance_ed_Jane_Beal_Commentaria_4_Leiden_Brill_2013_ISBN_9789004235779

Holmes, Oliver Wendell. *The Common Law*. Boston: Little, Brown & Co., 1881.

Holtz, Barry W. "Mishnah." In *Back to the Sources: Reading the Classic Jewish Texts*, edited by Barry W. Holtz, 177–212. New York: Summit Books, 1984.

Hossenfelder, Sabine. "Einstein's General Relativity." *BackReaction.blogspot.com*, August 17, 2019. https://backreaction.blogspot.com/2019/08/how-we-know-that-einsteins-general.html.

Houston, Walter J. "Exodus." In *The Pentateuch*, edited by John Barton et al., 92–127. New York: Oxford University Press, 2010.

Huemer, Michael. *Ethical Intuitionism*. New York: Palgrave MacMillan, 2007.

Ibn Ezra's Commentary on the Pentateuch. Translated and annotated by H. Norman Strickman et al. Brooklyn, NY: ArtScroll/Menorah, 1998–2004. https://www.sefaria.org/Exodus.6.2?lang=bi&aliyot=0&p2=Ibn_Ezra_on_Exodus.6.1.1&lang2=bi.

Jacobs, Jill. "Midrash Rabbah: Rabbinic Interpretations and Discussions of the Bible." *My Jewish Learning*. https://www.myjewishlearning.com/article/midrash-rabbah/.

Jacobs, Louis. "Halakhah, Development of Halakhah." In *EJ* 8:254–57.

———. *A Jewish Theology*. London: Darton, Longman & Todd, 1973.

———. *We Have Reason to Believe*, 3rd ed. London: Vallentine-Mitchell, 1965.

Jacobs, Louis, and David Derovan. "Hermeneutics." In *EJ* 9:25–29.

Jaffee, Martin S. "Oral Traditions in the Writings of Rabbinic Oral Torah: On Theorizing Rabbinic Orality." *Oral Tradition* 14, no. 1 (1999) 3–32. https://mospace.umsystem.edu/xmlui/handle/10355/64779.

Jeremiah, Book of. Commentary by Nosson Scherman. Brooklyn, NY: ArtScroll/Mesorah, 2014.

Selected Bibliography

Jerusalem Talmud. Translation and commentary by Heinrich W. Guggenheimer. Berlin: De Gruyter, 1999–2015. https://www.sefaria.org/Jerusalem_Talmud_Kilayim?tab=versions.

Jordan, Jeff. "Pragmatic Arguments and Belief in God." In *SEP* (Fall 2022 Edition). https://plato.stanford.edu/archives/fall2022/entries/pragmatic-belief-god/.

Kadari, Tamar. "Leah: Midrash and Aggadah." The Shalvi/Hyman Encyclopedia of Jewish Women. https://jwa.org/encyclopedia/article/leah-midrash-and-aggadah

Kadosh, David. "Decalogue, In Rabbinic Literature." In *EJ* 5:525–26.

Kahana, Menahem I. "Midreshi Halakhah." In *EJ* 14:193–204.

Kant, Immanuel. *Groundwork of the Metaphysics of Morals*. Translated and analyzed by H. J. Paton. 1948. New York: Harper & Row, 1964.

———. "On the Proverb: That May be True in Theory, but is of No Practical Use." In *Perpetual Peace and Other Essays*. Translated by Ted Humphrey. Indianapolis, IN: Hackett, 1983, 61–92.

Kaplan, Abraham. "The Jewish Argument with God." *Commentary* (October 1980).

Kaplan, Lawrence J. "Daas Torah: A Modern Conception of Rabbinic Authority." *Rabbinic Authority and Personal Autonomy in Traditional Judaism*, edited by Moshe Sokol, 1–60. Northvale, NJ: Jason Aronson, 1992.

Kaplan, Zvi. "Eruv." In *EJ* 6:483–85.

Kass, Leon R. "The Ten Commandments: Why the Decalogue Matters." *Mosaic* (June 2013).

Katz, Steven T. "Issues in the Separation of Judaism and Christianity after 70 C.E.: A Reconsideration." *Journal of Biblical Literature* 103, no. 1 (1984) 43–76. https://www.jstor.org/stable/3260313.

Kaufmann, Yehezkel. *The Religion of Israel: From Its Beginning to the Babylonian Exile*. Translated and abridged by Moshe Greenberg. Chicago: University of Chicago Press, 1960.

Kellner, Menachem. "Maimonides on the Decline of the Generations." In *Hazon Nahum: Studies in Jewish Law, Thought, and History*, edited by Yaakov Elman et al., 163–85. New York: Yeshiva University Press, 1997. https://www.academia.edu/36077289/Menachem_Kellner_Maimonides_on_the_Decline_of_the_Generations_in_Yaakov_Elman_and_Jeffrey_S._Gurock_eds._Hazon_Nahum_Studies_Presented_to_Dr._Norman_Lamm_New_York_Yeshiva_University_Press_1997_163-185.

Kermode, Frank. "Canons." *London Review of Books* 6, no. 2 (February 1984). https://www.lrb.co.uk/the-paper/v06/n02/frank-kermode/canons.

Kimelman, Reuven. "Judaism and Pluralism." *Modern Judaism* 7, no. 2 (May 1987) 131–50. https://www.academia.edu/en/38120896/Reuven_Kimelman_Judaism_and_Pluralism_Modern_Judaism_vol_7_no_2_May_1987_131_150.

———. "Prophesy as Arguing with God and the Ideal of Justice." *Interpretation* 68, no. 1 (2014) 17–27.

Klitsner, Judy. *Subversive Sequels in the Bible*. Philadelphia: Jewish Publication Society, 2009.

Knohl, Israel. *The Divine Symphony*. Philadelphia: Jewish Publication Society, 2003.

Korn, Eugene. "Moralization in Jewish Law: Genocide, Divine Commands, and Rabbinic Reasoning." In *The Edah Journal* 5, no. 2 (2006) 2–11.

Kraemer, David. "Composition and Meaning in the Talmud." *Prooftexts* 8, no. 3 (September 1988) 271–91. http://www.jstor.org/stable/20689217.

Selected Bibliography

Kruger, Thomas. "And They Have No Comforter: Job and Ecclesiastes in Dialogue." In *Reading Ecclesiastes Intertextually*, edited by Katharine Dell et al., 94–105. London: Bloomsbury, 2014. https://www.zora.uzh.ch/id/eprint/105645/.

Kugel, James. *How to Read the Bible*. New York: Free Press, a division of Macmillan, 2007.

———. "Not a Naïve Reading: An Interview with Prof. James Kugel." *TheTorah.com*, August 19, 2018, https://www.thetorah.com/blogs/not-a-naive-reading-an-interview-with-prof-james-kugel.

Lamm, Norman. "Amalek and the Seven Nations: A Case of Law vs. Morality." In *War and Peace in the Jewish Tradition*, edited by Lawrence Schiffman et al., 201–38. New York: Yeshiva University Press, 2007. https://repository.yu.edu/server/api/core/bitstreams/6b38bfed-036d-4e12-951f-c85317f81389/content.

———. Lamm, Norman. *Torah Umadda*. Jerusalem: Koren, 2010.

Laytner, Anson. *Arguing with God: A Jewish Tradition*: Lanham, MD: Jason Aronson, an imprint of Rowman & Littlefield, 1998.

Lebens, Samuel. *The Principles of Judaism*. New York: Oxford University Press, 2020.

Ledewitz, Bruce. "The Openness of Talmud." In *Duquesne Law Review* 41, no. 2 (2003) 353–61. https://dsc.duq.edu/cgi/viewcontent.cgi?article=3372&context=dlr.

Levenson, Jon D. Review of *Revelation and Authority: Sinai in Jewish Scripture and Tradition*, by Benjamin Sommers. *Marginalia* (December 28, 2018). https://themarginaliareview.com/bible-scholars-need-theology/.

———. *Sinai and Zion*, 2nd ed. New York: HarperOne, 1987.

Lichtenstein, Aharon. "Developing a Torah Personality: Lesson 6—Being Frum and Being Good: On the Relationship Between Religion and Morality" (based on addresses by Harav Aharon Lichtenstein, adapted by Rav Reuven Ziegler). *Israel Koschitzky Torat Har Etzion*, September 21, 2014. https://www.etzion.org.il/en/philosophy/great-thinkers/harav-aharon-lichtenstein/being-frum-and-being-good-relationship-between.

———. "Does Judaism Recognize an Ethic Independent of Halakhah?" [1975] Reprinted in *Leaves of Faith: The World of Jewish Learning, Vol. II*, 33–56. New York: KTAV, 2004.

Lichtenstein, Mosheh. "The Season of Repentance: Lesson 9—To Err is Human: The Human Element in Teshuva." *Israel Koschitzky Torat Har Etzion*, September 21, 2014. https://etzion.org.il/en/holidays/studies-repentance/err-human-human-element-teshuva.

Linzer, Dov. "Rabbi Eliezer vs. Rabbi Akiva: Two Models of Torah." *Yeshivat Chovevei Torah*, April 23, 2010. https://library.yctorah.org/2010/04/rabbi-eliezer-vs-rabbi-akiva-two-models-of-torah/.

Little, Daniel. "Philosophy of History." In *SEP* (Winter 2020 Edition). https://plato.stanford.edu/archives/win2020/entries/history/.

Luban, David. "The Coiled Serpent of Argument: Reason, Authority, and Law in a Talmudic Tale." In *Chicago-Kent Law Review* 79 (2004) 1253–88.

Magonet, Jonathan. *Form and Meaning: Studies in Literary Techniques in the Book of Jonah*, 2nd ed. Sheffield, EN: Almond Press, 1983.

Maimonides, Moses (Rambam). *Ethical Writings of Maimonides*, edited by Raymond L. Weiss et al. New York: New York University Press, 1975.

Malbim (Meir Leibush ben Yehiel Michel Wisser). "Malbim's Commentary on Exodus." In *Sifsei Chachamim Chumash Vol. 1*. Translated by Avraham Davis. Metsudah, 2009. Accessed via Sefaria.org.

Selected Bibliography

Mansoor, Menachem. "Pharisees." In *EJ* 6:30–32.

———. "Sadducees." In *EJ* 17:654–55.

Marcus, David. "Ezra." In *EJ* 6:651–52.

Matassa, Lidia Domenica. "Samaritans." In *EJ* 17:718–23.

Mazar, Eilat. "Is This the Prophet Isaiah's Signature?" In *Biblical Archaeology Review* 44, no. 2 (March/April May/June 2018). https://www.baslibrary.org/biblical-archaeology-review/44/2/7.

Medan, Yaakov. "Vayechi: Rachel's Death and Burial." *Studies in Parashat HaShavua with Rav Yaakov Medan: Lesson 25* on *Koschitzky Torat Har Etzion* (March 29, 2017). https://etzion.org.il/en/tanakh/torah/sefer-bereishit/parashat-vayechi/vayechi-rachels-death-and-burial.

Midrash Rabbah, Bamidbar/Numbers. Sefaria Community translation. Accessed via Sefaria.org

Midrash Rabbah, Bereshis/Genesis, Vol. I–IV. Edited and commentary by Chaim Malinowitz, Avrohom Kleinkaufman, et al. Brooklyn, NY: ArtScroll/Mesorah, 2017.

Midrash Rabbah, Deuteronomy/Lamentations, Vol. VII, 3rd ed. Translated by J. Rabbinowitz. London: Soncino Press, 1983.

Midrash Rabbah, Shemos/Exodus, Vol. I–II. Edited and commentary by Chaim Malinowitz, Avrohom Kleinkaufman, et al. Brooklyn, NY: ArtScroll/Mesorah, 2012.

Midrash Tanchuma. Translation by John T. Townsend. 1989. Recension by S. Buber. Edited and supplemented by R. Francis Nataf. Accessed via Sefaria.org.

Mill, John Stuart. *On Liberty*. London: J. W. Parker, 1859. https://archive.org/details/onlibertyxerooomilluoft.

Miller, J. Maxwell, and John H. Hayes. *A History of Ancient Israel and Judah, Second Edition*. Louisville, KY: Westminster, 2006.

Mishnah. Joshua Kulp translation. Accessed via Sefaria.org.

Morriston, Wesley. "God's Answer to Job" In *Religious Studies* 32 (1996) 339–56. https://www.academia.edu/647515/Gods_answer_to_Job.

Muffs, Yochanan. *Love and Joy: Law, Language and Religion in Ancient Israel*. New York: The Jewish Theological Seminary of America, 1992.

Mykytiuk, Lawrence. "53 People in the Bible Confirmed Archaeologically." *Biblical Archaeology Society*, September 13, 2022. https://www.biblicalarchaeology.org/daily/people-cultures-in-the-bible/people-in-the-bible/50-people-in-the-bible-confirmed-archaeologically/.

Nachmanides (Ramban). *Commentary on the Torah*. Translated by Charles B. Chavel. Brooklyn, NY: Shilo, 1976. Accessed via Sefaria.org.

Navon, Chaim. "Halakha and Morality, Part II." *Philosophy of Halakha: Lesson 5* on *Israel Koschitzky Torat Har Etzion*, September 21, 2014. https://www.etzion.org.il/en/halakha/studies-halakha/philosophy-halakha/halakha-and-morality-2.

Nelson, Richard. "Deuteronomy." In *Harper's Bible Commentary*, edited by James L. Mays, 209–34. San Francisco: Harper & Row, 1988.

Ngo, Robin. "Should We Take Creation Stories in Genesis Literally?" *Biblical Archaeology Society*, August 28, 2022. https://www.biblicalarchaeology.org/daily/biblical-topics/bible-interpretation/creation-stories-in-genesis/.

Nozick, Robert. *Anarchy, State, and Utopia*. Cambridge, MA: The Belknap Press of Harvard University Press, 1974.

Selected Bibliography

Otterman, Sharon, and Ray Rivera. "Orthodox Jews Shun Their Own for Reporting Child Sexual Abuse." *The New York Times*, May 9, 2012. https://www.nytimes.com/2012/05/10/nyregion/ultra-orthodox-jews-shun-their-own-for-reporting-child-sexual-abuse.html.

Otto, Rudolph. *The Idea of the Holy*. 2nd ed. Translated by John W. Harvey. 1923. New York: Oxford University Press, 1958.

Paul, Shalom M., and S. David Sperling. "Prophets and Prophecy." In *EJ* 16:556–80.

Pines, Shalom. "Free Will." In *EJ* 7:230–34.

Pirkei DeRabbi Eliezer. Translated and annotated by Gerald Friedlander. London: K. Paul, Trench, Trubner & Co., 1916. https://www.sefaria.org/Pirkei_DeRabbi_Eliezer.1?ven=Pirke_de_Rabbi_Eliezer,_trans._and_annotated_by_Rabbi_Gerald_Friedlander,_London,_1916&lang=bi.

Pluckrose, Helen. "On Activist Scholarship: An Interview with Helen Pluckrose." By Jason D. Hill, December 16, 2020. https://quillette.com/2020/12/16/on-activist-scholarship-an-interview-with-helen-pluckrose/.

Pluckrose, Helen, and James Lindsay. *Cynical Theories: How Activist Scholarship Made Everything About Race, Gender, and Identity*. Durham, NC: Pitchstone, 2020.

Polliack, Meira. "Rethinking Karaism: Between Judaism and Islam." In *AJS Review* 30, no. 1 (2006) 67–93. http://www.jstor.org/stable/4131638.

Popper, Karl. *The Logic of Scientific Discovery*, 2nd ed. New York: Routledge, an imprint of Taylor & Francis, 2002.

———. *The Open Society and Its Enemies, One Volume Edition*. Princeton, NJ: Princeton University Press, 2013 [1971].

Rabinowitz, Louis Isaac, and Stephen G. Wald. "Talmud, Jerusalem." In *EJ* 19:483–87.

Rabinovitch, Nahum Eliezer. "The Way of Torah." In *The Edah Journal* 3, no. 1 (2003) 2–34. https://library.yctorah.org/journals/edah-journal-marheshvan-5761-11-3/.

Rashi. *Commentary on the Talmud*. Sefaria Community translation, presented as interspersed, parallel comments to William Davidson Talmud, quoted at: https://www.sefaria.org/texts/Talmud/Bavli/Rishonim%20on%20Talmud/Rashi.

———. *Commentary on the Torah: Bamidbar/Numbers*. Translated and annotated by Yisrael Herczeg. Brooklyn, NY: ArtScroll/Mesorah, 1997.

———. *Commentary on the Torah: Bereishis/Genesis*. Translated and annotated by Yisrael Herczeg. Brooklyn, NY: ArtScroll/Mesorah, 1995.

———. *Commentary on the Torah: Devarim/Deuteronomy*. Translated and annotated by Yisrael Herczeg. Brooklyn, NY: ArtScroll/Mesorah, 1998.

———. *Commentary on the Torah: Shemos/Exodus*, 4th ed. Translated and annotated by Yisrael Herczeg. Brooklyn, NY: ArtScroll/Mesorah, 1997.

Riskin, Shlomo. "The Importance of Dissenting Views." *Jewish News*, July 2, 2019. https://www.jewishaz.com/religiouslife/the-importance-of-dissenting-views/article_1f3e2d16-9d0e-11e9-b00c-b79b84768527.html.

Robinson, W. C. "Elementary Law" and "Elements of American Jurisprudence," appendices (IV–V) to *A Sketch of English Legal History*, by Frederick William Maitland et al., edited with notes and appendices by James E. Colby, 213–20. Union, NJ: Lawbook Exchange, 1998.

Rosenbloom, Noah H. *Luzzatto's Ethico-psychological Interpretation of Judaism: a Study in the Religious Philosophy of Samuel David Luzzatto*. New York: Yeshiva University Press, 1965.

Selected Bibliography

Rosensweig, Michael. "Elu va-Elu Divre Elokim Hayyim: Halakhic Pluralism and Theories of Controversy." In *Tradition* 26, no. 3 (Spring 1992). https://traditiononline.org/elu-va-elu-divre-elokim-hayyim-halakhic-pluralism-and-theories-of-controversy/.

Ross, Tamar. *Expanding the Palace of Torah: Orthodoxy and Feminism*. Lebanon, NH: Brandeis University Press and University Press of New England, 2004.

———. "Orthodoxy and the Challenge of Biblical Criticism." In *The Believer and the Modern Study of the Bible*, edited by Tova Ganzel et al., 263–87. Boston: Academic Studies Press, 2019.

Roth, Leon. "Moralization and Demoralization in Jewish Ethics." In *Judaism* 11, no. 4 (1962) 291–302. https://www.leonroth.org/_files/ugd/01b672_ea5dcf3815e94ecd86f7d6b0a98bef55.pdf.

Rothkoff, Aaron. "Prosbul." In *EJ* 16:586–87.

Rowe, William L. *Philosophy of Religion: An Introduction*, 3rd ed. Belmont, CA: Wadsworth/Thomson Learning, 2001.

Rubenstein, Jeffrey L. *Rabbinic Stories*. New York: Paulist, 2002.

Sacks, Jonathan. "Faith Lectures: What is Faith? Part 1." Transcription. *RabbiSacks.org*, September 26, 2000. https://www.rabbisacks.org/archive/faith-lectures-what-is-faith/.

———. "A Sage is Greater than a Prophet." *RabbiSacks.org*, 2019. https://www.rabbisacks.org/covenant-conversation/shoftim/a-sage-is-greater-than-a-prophet/.

———. "Was Jacob Right to Take Esau's Blessing?" *RabbiSacks.org*, 2016. https://www.rabbisacks.org/covenant-conversation/toldot/jacob-right-take-esaus-blessing/.

Sagi, Avi. *The Open Canon: On the Meaning of Halakhic Discourse*. New York: Continuum, 2008.

Sagi, Avi, and Daniel Statman. "Divine Command Morality and Jewish Tradition." In *Journal of Religious Ethics* 23, no. 1 (1995) 39–67. https://www.jstor.org/stable/40015197?origin=JSTOR-pdf.

Saiman, Chaim N. *Halakhah: The Rabbinic Idea of Law*. Princeton, NJ: Princeton University Press, 2018.

Salkin, Jeffrey. "The Scandal of Hasidic Education—a Cry from the Heart." *Religion News Service*, September 13, 2022. https://religionnews.com/2022/09/13/hasidic-school-education-schools-new-york/.

Sanders, James. "The Integrity of Biblical Pluralism." In *Not in Heaven: Coherence and Complexity in Biblical Narrative*, edited by Jason P. Rosenblatt et al., 154–69. Indianapolis, IN: Indiana University Press, 1991.

Sarna, Nahum N. *Understanding Genesis*. New York: Schocken, an imprint of Penguin Random House, 1970.

Sayre-McCord, Geoff. "Moral Realism" In *SEP* (Summer 2021 Edition). https://plato.stanford.edu/archives/sum2021/entries/moral-realism/.

Schiffman, Lawrence H., "The Bar Kochba Revolt." *My Jewish Learning*, excerpted from Schiffman, *From Text to Tradition: A History of Second Temple and Rabbinic Judaism*. New York: KTAV, 1991. https://www.myjewishlearning.com/article/the-bar-kochba-revolt/

———. *From Text to Tradition: A History of Second Temple and Rabbinic Judaism*. New York: KTAV, 1991.

Schmid, Konrad. "Who Wrote the Torah?" *Institute for Advanced Study*, 2018. https://www.ias.edu/ideas/2018/schmid-torah.

Selected Bibliography

Schorsch, Ismar. "Our Journey in the Wilderness." *Jewish Theological Seminary*, June 4, 1994. https://www.jtsa.edu/torah/our-journey-in-the-wilderness/.

Schoville, Keith N., and S. David Sperling. "Song of Songs." In *EJ* 19:14–18.

Schwartz, Baruch J. "Does Recent Scholarship's Critique of the Documentary Hypothesis Constitute Grounds for Its Rejection?" In *The Pentateuch: International Perspectives on Current Research*, edited by Thomas B. Dozeman et al. Tübingen, DE: Mohr Siebeck, 2011. https://www.academia.edu/39296078/Does_Recent_Scholarship_s_Critique_of_the_Documentary_Hypothesis_Constitute_Grounds_for_Its_Rejection.

Seder Eliyahu Zuta, Chapter 2. Sefaria Community translation. Accessed via sefaria.org

Seeskin, Kenneth. "Maimonides." In *SEP* (Spring 2021 Edition). https://plato.stanford.edu/archives/spr2021/entries/maimonides/.

Segal, Benjamin J. *The Book of Esther: A Commentary and History*. Jerusalem: Schechter Institute of Jewish Studies and Gefen Publishing, 2023.

Segal, Jerome N. "God's Project." In *Philosophers and the Jewish Bible*, edited by Charles H. Manekin et al., 167–98. Bethesda, MD: University Press of Maryland, 2008.

Shapiro, Marc B. *Limits of Orthodox Theology: Maimonides' Thirteen Principles Reappraised*. Liverpool, UK: Littman Library of Jewish Civilization, in association with Liverpool University Press, 2011.

Sharon, Jeremy, and Sam Sokol. "Chief Rabbinate in Fierce Attack on Reform, Conservative Movements." *Jerusalem Post*, February 26, 2016. https://www.jpost.com/israel-news/politics-and-diplomacy/chief-rabbinate-in-fierce-attack-on-reform-conservative-movements-446143.

Shimon, Zvi. "Studies in Parashat HaShavua with Rav Zvi Shimon: Lesson 32 Shelach: Spy vs. Spy." *Israel Koschitzky Torat Har Etzion*, September 21, 2014. https://www.etzion.org.il/en/tanakh/torah/sefer-bamidbar/parashat-shelach/shelach-spy-vs-spy.

Simon-Shoshan, Moshe. *Ein Yaakov: World of Talmudic Aggadah*. "Lecture 1—What is Aggada in Classical Jewish Sources? *Yeshivat Har Ezion Israel Koschitzky, Virtial Beit Midrash (VBM)*. https://etzion.org.il/en/series/ein-yaakov-world-talmudic-aggada.

———. *Ein Yaakov: World of Talmudic Aggadah*. "Lecture 2—What is Aggada? Part II: Aggada in Medieval Thought" *Yeshivat Har Ezion Israel Koschitzky, Virtial Beit Midrash (VBM)*. https://etzion.org.il/en/series/ein-yaakov-world-talmudic-aggada.

Silber, Michael K. "Orthodoxy." In *The YIVO Encyclopedia of Jews in Eastern Europe*, September 14, 2010. https://yivoencyclopedia.org/article.aspx/orthodoxy.

Silberberg, Naftali. "What is the 'Oral Torah?'" *Chabad.org*. https://www.chabad.org/library/article_cdo/aid/812102/jewish/What-is-the-Oral-Torah.htm.

Sivan, Hagith. "Rachel Weeps in Ramah: Of All the Patriarchs, God Listens Only to Her." *TheTorah.com*, December 16, 2022. https://www.thetorah.com/article/rachel-weeps-in-ramah-of-all-the-patriarchs-god-listens-only-to-her.

Sokal, Alan, and Jean Bricmont. *Fashionable Nonsense: Postmodern Intellectuals' Abuse of Science*. New York: Picador, an imprint of St. Martin's Press, 1999.

Solomon, Norman "Relating Truthfully to Morally Problematic Torah Texts." *TheTorah.com*, 2017, last updated March 26, 2024. https://www.thetorah.com/article/relating-truthfully-to-morally-problematic-torah-texts.

———. *Torah From Heaven*. Liverpool, UK: Littman Library of Jewish Civilization, in association with Liverpool University Press, 2012.

Soloveitchik, Joseph B. *The Lonely Man of Faith*. [1975] US: Doubleday, an imprint of Random House, 2006 [1965].

Selected Bibliography

Sommer, Benjamin D. "Did Prophecy Cease? Evaluating a Reevaluation." In *Journal of Biblical Literature* 115, no. 1 (1996) 31–47. https://doi.org/10.2307/3266817.

———. *Revelation and Authority: Sinai in Jewish Scripture and Tradition*. New Haven, CT: Yale University Press, 2015.

Sperber, Daniel. "The Great Synagogue." In *EJ* 19:383–85.

Spiro, Ken. "History Crash Course #32: Hillel and Shammai." *Aish.com*. https://aish.com/48943176/.

Statman, Daniel. "Modern Orthodoxy and Morality: An Uneasy Partnership." *International Journal for Philosophy of Religion* (February 2020). Accessed via https://www.academia.edu/41843586/Modern_Orthodoxy_and_Morality_An_Uneasy_Partnership?hb-sb-sw=15032033.

Steele, David Ramsay. "Are Critical Rationalists Completely Out of Their Minds?" In *The Conquistador with His Pants Down: David Ramsay Steele's Legendary Lost Lectures*, pp. 187–216. South Bend, IN: St. Augustine's, 2024.

Steinmetz, Devora. "Must the Patriarch Know 'Uqtzin? The *Nasi* as Scholar in Babylonian *Aggada*." In *Association for Jewish Studies Review* 23, no. 2 (1998) 163–89. https://www.jstor.org/stable/1486904.

Strauss, Leo. "On the Interpretation of Genesis." In *L'Homme* 21, no.1 (1981) 5–20. http://dx.doi.org/10.3406/hom.1981.368159.

Sullivan, Roger J. *Immanuel Kant's Moral Theory*. Cambridge, UK: Cambridge University Press, 1989.

Tanakh, A New Translation of The Holy Scriptures According to the Traditional Hebrew Text. Philadelphia: Jewish Publication Society, 1985.

Thompson, Charles. "Plessy v. Ferguson: Harlan's Great Dissent." In *Kentucky Humanities*, no. 1 (1996). Republished by Louis D. Brandeis School of Law Library. https://louisville.edu/law/library/special-collections/the-john-marshall-harlan-collection/harlans-great-dissent.

Thomson, Judith Jarvis. *The Realm of Rights*. Cambridge, MA: Harvard University Press, 1990.

Twain, Mark. "Concerning the Jews." In *Harper's Magazine* (March 1898). https://sourcebooks.fordham.edu/mod/1898twain-jews.asp.

Twerski, Abraham J. "The Mystery of Suffering." *Jewish Learning Institute.com*, excerpted from *Twerski on Chumash*. Mesorah Publications Ltd., 2003. https://lessons.myjli.com/faith/index.php/lesson-4/the-mystery-of-suffering/.

Unterman, Jeremiah, *Justice for All: How the Jewish Bible Revolutionized Ethics*. Philadelphia: Jewish Publication Society, 2017.

Vermes, Geza. *Jesus the Jew*. Philadelphia: Fortress Press, 1981.

Vizel, Frieda. "The Anachronisms of Hasidic Yiddish Biblical Coloring Books." *Artifacts of Orthodox Jewish Childhoods*, edited by Dainy Bernstein, 19–27. Teaneck, NJ: Ben Yehuda Press, 2022.

Waks, Manny. *Who Gave You Permission? The Memoir of a Child Sexual Abuse Survivor Who Fought Back*. Ft. Lauderdale, FL: Scribe US, 2017.

Wald, Stephen G. "Joshua Ben Hananiah." In *EJ* 11:450–52.

———. "Mishnah." In *EJ* 14:319–31.

———. "Talmud, Babylonian." In *EJ* 19:470–81.

Werblowsky, R. J. Zwi. "Otto, Rudolph." In *EJ* 15:518.

Wein, Berel. *Echoes of Glory: The Story of the Jews in the Classical Era, 350 BCE-750 CE*. Brooklyn, NY: ArtScroll/Shaar, 1995.

Selected Bibliography

Weinfeld, Moshe, and S. David Sperling. "Deuteronomy." In *EJ* 5:613–19.

Weiss, Steven I. "Plan to Revive Biblical Sanhedrin Receives Boost." *Forward*, June 10, 2005. https://forward.com/culture/3627/plan-to-revive-biblical-sanhedrin-receives-boost/.

Weiss, Susan. "5 Misconceptions About Jewish Law's Chained Women." *The Times of Israel*, March 16, 2022. https://blogs.timesofisrael.com/all-women-who-marry-in-an-orthodox-jewish-ceremony-are-chained-women/.

Wettstein, Howard. "Against Theology." In *Philosophers and the Jewish Bible*, edited by Charles H. Manekin et al., 219–45. Bethesda, MD: University Press of Maryland, 2008.

Wigoder, Geoffrey. "Christianity, Some 20th Century Christian Perceptions of Judaism and the Jews." In *EJ* 4:679–93.

Wolf, Arnold J. Excerpt from "The State of Jewish Belief." Symposium. In *Commentary* (August 1966). https://www.commentary.org/articles/jacob-agus-2/the-state-of-jewish-belief/.

Wolfson, Elijah. "Child Abuse Allegations Plague the Hasidic Community." *Newsweek*, March 3, 2016. https://www.newsweek.com/2016/03/11/child-abuse-allegations-hasidic-ultraorthodox-jewish-community-brooklyn-432688.html.

Wolowelsky, Joel B. "Truth and Consequences: A Talmudic Tale on Interpersonal Ethics." In *Conversations*, no. 8 (Autumn 2010) 61–70. https://www.jewishideas.org/article/truth-and-consequences-talmudic-tale-interpersonal-ethics.

Wurzburger, Walter S. "Orthodoxy." In *EJ* 15:493–94.

Wynn, Mark. "Phenomenology of Religion." In *SEP* (Winter 2022 Edition). https://plato.stanford.edu/archives/win2022/entries/phenomenology-religion/.

Yadin, Azzan. Review of *The Open Canon: On the Meaning of Halakhic Discourse*, by Avi Sagi. In *Journal of Semitic Studies* 55, no. 1 (Spring 2010) 291–92. https://doi.org/10.1093/jss/fgp054.

Yerushalmi, Yosef Hayim. *Zakhor: Jewish History and Jewish Memory*. Seattle, WA: University of Washington Press, 1996.

Yuval, Israel Jacob. "The Orality of Jewish Oral Law: from Pedagogy to Ideology." *Judaism, Christianity, and Islam in the Course of History: Exchange and Conflicts*, edited by Lothar Gall et al., 237–60. Berlin: De Gruyter, 2011. https://doi.org/10.1515/9783110446739.

Za'akah. "Agudath Israel and Child Sexual Abuse." *Za'akah*. https://www.zaakah.org/agudath-israel.

Zakheim, Dov S. "Transforming Israel's Chief Rabbinate." *Institute for Jewish Ideas & Ideals*, November 27, 2012. https://www.jewishideas.org/article/transforming-israels-chief-rabbinate.

Ziegler, Reuven. "The Thought of Rav Soloveitchik: Lesson 17: The Lonely Man of Faith, Presenting the Problem, Part 1." *Israel Koschitzky Torat Har Etzion*, February 19, 2019. https://www.etzion.org.il/en/philosophy/great-thinkers/rav-soloveitchik/lonely-man-faith-1-presenting-problem.

Zion, Noam. "Elu v'Elu: Two Schools of Halakha Face Off On Issues of Human Autonomy, Majority Rule and Divine Voice of Authority." *Shalom Hartman Institute*, 2008.

Subject Index

Aaron, 34, 82
Abraham. *See also Akedah* ("binding of Isaac"); Isaac; Sarah
    distressed by Sarah's demand, 107
    God's command to, 13, 14
    God's dialogue with, xiii, 105
    as a literary character, 4
    no evidence of the existence of, 2
    willingness to sacrifice Isaac, 32
Abraham b. David of Posquieres, 95
Abraham ibn Daud, 63
Abraham ibn Ezra, 36
"absolute truth and falsehood," 87
Abu Muhammad Ali ibn Ahmad ibn Sa'id ibn Hazm al-Andalusi, 63
academies, of Beit Hillel and Beit Shammai, 81n3
Academy of Pumbedita, 150
Academy of Yavneh, Rabbis of, 147
accountability, objective morality and, 26
Adam and Eve, 28
"Adam the first," 15n54
"Adam the second," 15n54
Adversary (Satan), 124, 127
aggadah
    Haggadah versus, 73–78
    of Moses being magically transported to R. Akiva's future academy, 149
    as non-halakhic (non-legal) materials, 163
    rich and extensive collection of, 10

aggadic tales, 157
agnosticism, 7
Akedah ("binding of Isaac"), 4, 5, 98
Akiva ben Yosef
    eulogizing Rabbi Eliezer, 154
    finding new meanings, 72
    fruits of constructive disagreement and, 157
    giving. Eliezer bad news, 151
    ignoring his former mentor, 156
    on Kohelet distrusted by earlier authorities, 115
    as a martyr, 153
    opposite approach to halakhah from Eliezer, 148–49
    supporter of Bar Kochba, 149n8
    visiting Eliezer on his deathbed, 152
Albo, Joseph, 144n40
"all swans are white" claim, 40
Almighty. *See also* God
    intentions of, 144
    meaningful reply to Job, 129
    on moral progress of humanity, 39
    as neither a tyrant nor a bully, 26
    refusing to yield as a minority of one, 160–61
    taught ethics by Moses, 36
Alter, Robert
    on biblical world as far from monolithic, 19
    on the book of Jonah, 121
    "genius" of, 114n75

Subject Index

Alter, Robert (continued)
    on ideology promoted by Ezra and Nehemiah, 123
    on Jonah, 99n3
    on prose fiction describing biblical narrative, 2
    on Qohelet, 114
    on Torah's narratives, 15
alternative revelation, 17–18
Amalekites, xiv–xv, 131n2, 139
American judicial system, dissenting opinions, 83–84
Amoraic era (Oral Law from Sinai), xix
Amoraim, 60, 66, 163
Amos, 111–12
Amram, 2
Anan b. David, 62
Ananites movement, 62
Angel, Hayyim, 70, 121
Angel of Death, harvesting R. Nahmani's soul, 160
angels, 27
"anti-traditionalism," Rabbis' defense of, xviiin13
Apocrypha, *halakhah* in the books of, 58n24
Aramaisms, in the book of Jonah, 117
Ashi, Rav, reduction of the Babylonian Talmud, 61
Ashkenazic Yom Kippur liturgy, 153
Assyrian Empire, 118
Assyrians, benign portrayal of, 120
atheists, arguments against the existence of God, 8
"attitude of reasonableness," 42
authenticity, of Orthodoxy, 21–22
autonomy, 26, 28

Babylonia, communal life in, 94
Babylonian academies (yeshivas), Sura and Pumbedita, 164
Babylonian exiles, return to the Holy Land, 32
Babylonian Rabbis, as permissive, 91
Babylonian Talmud ("Bavli")
    chain of transmission of the Oral Law and, 72n85
    closing of, 62, 95
    composition of, 61, 163
    as more authoritative than the Jerusalem Talmud, 72n85, 163
    original language of referred to "one life," 74n92
    pluralism as the dominant position voiced in, 92
    positive view of controversy, 83
    preference for pluralism, 91
    spirit of tolerance and pluralism, 155
King Balak and Balam, tale of, 77n97
Bar Kochba revolt, 59, 149n8
Baraita, ancient oral tradition codified, 163
Baras, Dan, 130, 131–32
bat kol (heavenly voice), truths of, 86
Bazak, Rav, 14
beit din (religious court), 86, 149
"belief in," as distinct from a "belief that," 7
Ben Gurion, devil's bargain struck by, 138n17
Ben-Menahem, 82, 83
Berkovits, Eliezer
    acknowledging Job was correct to claim that God acted unjustly, 127
    on the Almighty as a "hiding" God, 17
    on the codification of the Oral Law, 94
    on obedience to the non-rational commandments serving a moral purpose, 20
    on the Torah as animated by humanistic values, 88
    on Zionism as the last best chance to revitalize halakha, 97
Berlin, Naftali Zvi Yehuda ("Netziv"), 83
Berman, Joshua, 11n31, 63nn43, 44, 64n45, 65n51, 95n55, 97n60
Bible
    array of literary genres, 18–19
    incompatible viewpoints, 99
biblical controversy, 98–99
biblical metaphors, for God, 133
biblical scholarship, modern, 10–16
biblical texts, in conflict with dialectical interpretation, xviii

Subject Index

bitter waters, ritual of, 90, 101
blasphemer of the Holy Name, punishment for, 56
Blidstein, Gerald F., 64, 65
Boaz, 108, 123
"Book of the Law" (Torah), "discovered" by King Josiah, 100n7
"both these and these" language, of the heavenly voice, 65
Brettler, Marc Zvi, 103, 116
Breuer, Mordechai, 14–15
bribery, 102
Brown v. Board of Education of Topeka, 84
bulletproof theories, not searching for, 41
Bultmann, Christopher, 102
burning bush, 33

Cain, 28, 30, 31
Caleb, 34
Canaan, no reliable historical evidence of, 131n2
canon, as fractious, 98–129
canonical books, 16, 99, 110, 129
capital punishment, for victimless crimes, xv
Cardozo, Nathan, xvi–xvii
Carlyle, Thomas, 125n134
catastrophes, series of for Job, 124
Categorical Imperative, formulation of, 25
Cave of Machpelah, not the tomb of Rachel, 31
ceremonial practices, as worthless if offered with "unclean hands," 111
chachamim zichronam levracham acronym, for "rabbis of blessed memory," 3n9
character, importance of in God's eyes, 123
Chavah ("Eve"), fashioned from a rib of Adam, 13
Chazal
    acronym for "rabbis of blessed memory," 164
    affirming the identification of Jonah, 117
    on the Almighty creating 5,784 years ago, 3
    on the Golden Calf incident, 46
    on the Great Assembly, 57
    on Hillel and Shammai, 47
    interpretation of *Eruvin* 13b, 49
    on reading of Biblical texts, 4n12
    on residents of Nineveh returning to evil, 120n110
    understanding of Revelation, 142
    on Yehoshua, 149–50
Chesterton, G.K, 159n42
child sacrifice, replaced in Israel by animal sacrifice, 5
children, impossibility of "replacing" Job's murdered, 126n139
Childs, Brevard S., 99
Christianity
    adopted the entire Jewish canon, 9
    emergence of in Eretz Israel, 60
citizenship, equal distribution of the burden of, 45
Classic Jewish Sources, oral traditions and texts available to, 164
classic texts, respect for autonomy in, 30–39
"classical" or "literary" prophets, emphasized deviations from justice, 110n64
classical prophets, 110, 111, 111n65
Clifford, W.K., 5
Clifford's rule, 7
closed societies, 43, 138n17
codification
    legal, 95, 104
    liberalism and, 94–97
commandments of God
    achieving intimacy with God, 47–48
    apology for the Torah's repellent, 132
    attitudes about, 21n68
    squaring with secular morality's understanding, 142
    Torah's 613 as flawless, eternal, and immutable, xviii
    violating basic moral values, 38
Commentary on the Mishnah (Maimonides), 63–64
common sense or *sevara*, guidance by, 88
communal unity, through acceptance of diversity, 92

Subject Index

community, liberal principle of equal right and, 28
community norms, enforcing, 138n17
compulsion, Torah authority should never use, 34n42
"conjecture and refutation" process, of Popper, 41
Constitution of the US, Eighth Amendment, 53–54
"continuous discovery," "progressive revelation" as, 135
continuous revelation, 136–45
continuous understanding, Torah as a call for, 137
controversy
    biblical, 98–99
    embrace of, 80–83, 96
conventional wisdom, "crazy" ideas often supplanting, 7
corpse, ritual impurity due to contact with, 55
"counter-reformation," reaffirming biblical dogmatism, 97
courts, reversing the decision of a prior court, 86
Cover, Robert, 77
creation, different accounts of, 12
creation myth of Genesis, assigning Adam the dominant role, 105
creative powers and compassion, using humans,' 29
Crenshaw, James, 114
critical rationalism
    conceptualizing immoral commands from, 130
    examples in classic texts, 45–50
    of Popper, xviin13, 40–42
Cyrus II of Persia, 121

"D" (Deuteronomist) source, 11
daughters of Zelophehad, legal question posed by, 55–56
Deborah, 106
Decalogue. *See* Ten Commandments (Decalogue)
"declaration of independence," rabbinic, 151

Decline of the Generations (*yeridat hadorot*), xviii, 51, 66–69
Deuteronomic law, 100
"Deuteronomistic history," 3
Deuteronomy
    commandments in given to a new generation, 100–101
    drawing on popular oral traditions and folklore, 100n7
    marking an important theological shift, 111
    protecting the welfare of the seduced maiden, 103
    restriction of punishment solely to the offender, 104n33
    rolling back some harsh theology present in Exodus, 104
dialogue, thinly disguised invitation for from God, 46–47
Didion, Joan, 77n98
Dienstag, Jacob I., 95
disagreements, among the Tannaim, 57
"discovery" model, of "revelation," 135
dissenting opinion (God's), proven correct, 161
"divine chariot," Ezekiel's elaborate vision of, 116
Divine Command Morality (DCM), 133–34, 143
divine communication, Judaism's holy texts from, 19
divine destiny, overturning the rule of succession, 78
divine law, Christianity questioned the validity of, 61
divine will, gross misunderstanding of, 136
documentary hypothesis, 10–11, 12
doubt, faith consistent with, 7
dramatist, God as, 17
Dred Scott case, 84
Dworkin, Ronald, 24

"E" source, for "Elohim," 11
Ecclesiastes (Kohelet or Qohelet), 113, 114
"economic calculation problem," 44

Subject Index

economic system, serving the consumer, 44
Egyptian exile, duration of, 100n8
Eldar, Itamar, 63n41
Eleazar, Rabbi, 81
Eliezer ben Hyrkanus, 105n37, 148
    appeals to Heaven and a Divine Voice (*bat kol*), 150–51
    deathbed remarks, 153, 156, 160
    persecution of, 151–54
    as stubborn, cantankerous, and unpleasant, 158
    tragedy of, 147–61
    truths of should not be lightly abandoned, 159
Elitzafan, Korach's anger, 82
Elman, Yaakov, 70, 70n73
Elon, Menachem, 96
empirical evidence, warping or distorting, 3–4
English Masorti branch of Judaism, 11n32
Enlightenment values, Popper on, 43
epistemology
    of Popper, 42, 45
    precursor to Popper's, 87
"equal accommodation," as a pretext for racial discrimination, 84
equal protection clause, of the Fourteenth Amendment, 84
"equal right" formulation, of Kant, 45
Er, son of Judah, 108
Eretz Israel ("Land of Israel"), Jews persecuted in, 9
eruv, concept of, 86n26
eruvim (ritual enclosures), 86
Esau, 107, 107n51
Esther, 106, 115–16
Esther (book of), 113
the ethical, priority of, 88
ethical behavior, destiny of the people determined by, 112n69
Eve, 13, 14, 28, 105
evidence, faith and, 5–10
evil, always with us, 128
the Exodus, as a story, 9
Exodus (book of), 100, 102–3, 104, 111

Exodus and Deuteronomy, narratives differing in many details, 52
Expanding the Palace of Torah (Ross), 139, 141
"an eye for an eye," reinterpretation of, 89–90
Ezekiel (book of), 113, 116
Ezra, 122, 123

faith, evidence and, 5–10
Falk, Marcia, 115
fallibilism, Popper's concept of, 7, 41, 44
false testimony, convicting the innocent, 75
"feasibility" criterion, moral consequences of, 88
female biblical characters, 105–6
Finkelman, Yoel, 141n30
Fisch, Menachem, xviin13, 42
Five Books of Moses (Torah), 19, 134
flogging, interpretation of the laws of, 90
Footsteps.org, assisting Orthodox men and women, 138n17
Former Prophets, 3, 110n64
"fragmentary hypothesis," Pentateuch stitched together, 11
free will, 30, 30n22
freed Israelites, as profoundly immoral and corrupt, 100
friends of Job, bromides offered by as insulting, 128

Gaon, honorific, 164
"a garden in Eden," God places man in, 13
gates of prayer, unlocked for victims of verbal mistreatment, 152
Gattei, Stefano, 41–42, 43
Gaus, Gerald, 25
Gemara
    attitude of regarding the great R. Akiva, 156
    lengthier of the Talmuds' two primary components, 164
    on the number of prophets in biblical times, 69
    quoting Eliezer, 148
    quoting Rabbi Abbahu, 14

Subject Index

gender roles, in the Pentateuch, xv, 105–9
Genesis
    creation narrative in, 3, 4
Genesis (continued)
    discrepancies in, 13
    dual narratives of, 15n54
    first four chapters establishing autonomy, 26
    narrative inconsistency in the first two chapters, 12
genocide, 130, 143
Geonic era (Decline of the Generations), xix, 73
Geonim
    accepted the notion of Oral Law from Sinai, 64
    assumed intellectual leadership of the Jewish world, 164
    embarrassed by "wild" talmudic stories, 74
    feared religious autonomy advocated by the Karaites, 62–63
    as the plural form of "Gaon," 164
Gillman, Neil, 132
God. *See also* Almighty
    admission of error, 38
    boasting to "the Adversary" (Satan), 124
    carving the Decalogue in stone, 53
    conferring with ministering angels, 27
    conflict in Judaism's conception of, 4–5
    denying any active role to, 135
    eliminating only those who produced and worshipped the Calf, 46
    exacting punishment to the "third or fourth generation," 104n33
    expecting us to act justly and with humility, 161
    having the right to command us, 133
    hints delivered by His agents, 17
    human beings made in the image of, 25
    humanizing in order to model virtuous conduct, xiv
    involved in relationships with people, 133
    Jeremiah and, 32
    modeling a different halakhic process, 160
    Moses and, 34, 47, 98, 157, 158
    not in need of advice from his attendants, 27
    not needing mankind, 29
    not revealing the ultimate moral truth, 18
    nullifying his words, 39
    as open to disagreement and questioning, 47
    relenting for Rachel's sake, 33
    renounced the punishment of Nineveh, 119
    on Sarah's side, 107
    Satan and, 127
    selecting laws from the 613 of the Rabbis, 53
    sending a worm to destroy the plant, 119
    speaking to Job, 125, 126, 127
    teaching what I could not know myself, 141n30
    valuing autonomy above all else, 39
    viewed as endorsing genocide, 145
    will of, 134, 139
Golden Calf, 36–37, 45–47, 109
Goldin, Judah, 76
Golinkin, David, 93
Gordis, Robert, 127
Gorton, William, 45
grave offense, by halakha, 150
Great Assembly (or Great Synagogue), created by Ezra, 57
Great Sanhedrin, 131
Greenberg, Moshe, 129

ha-Cohen, Zadok, 67
Emperor Hadrian, 60, 149n8
haggadah, versus aggadah, 73–78
Hai, Gaon, head of the Pumbedita Academy, 73
halakhah (Jewish law)

in accordance with the opinion of Beit Hillel, 48
comprehensive system of, 61
disability of even Moses in the realm of, 56
living a life governed by, 21
modifying in response to new social conditions, xix
on performing acts of loving-kindness for heretics, 153
preserving the dignity of persons, 89
with regard to a shoe on a last, 154
of Shabbat observance, 54
tension with aggadah, 75
transformed from a common-law system to a statutory one, 95
translated as "Jewish law," 164
two disparate systems of developed, 57
ultimate perfection to the Talmud, 161
ultra-Orthodox adhering to, xvn8
understanding God's message correctly, 139
halakhic acceptance, of controversy, 82
halakhic arguments, of Korach, 82
halakhic decision-making, categories of, 86
halakhic innovation, 87–90, 148
halakhic method, 158
halakhic Midrashim, explaining derivation of laws, 165
halakhic questions, handed to Moses at Sinai, 54
halakhic "workaround," for creditors, 89
Halbertal, Moshe, 63
Halevi, Yehuda, 63
Halivni, David Weiss, 59, 64
Hananiah ben Hezekiah, 116
handiwork, of God has established balance, 125–26
hardship, prevention of unnecessary, 88
Haredi rabbis, as "closed societies," 138n17
Justice Harlan, as the Great Dissenter, 84
Hayek, F.A., 24, 44
Heavenly Academy, 159n44, 160

Heavenly Torah, God decorating the letters of, 157
Hebrew Bible, 19, 26
Helfgot, Nathaniel, 86
Heller, Yom Tov Lippmann, 67
Heschel, Abraham Joshua, 4, 21, 76n96, 136, 136n12
Heschel, Susannah, 20
Heshbon, destroying without offering peace to King Sihon, 39
Hidary, Richard, 61, 92, 94
hiddush (innovation), no space for, 69
"hiding" God, Almighty having to be, 17
Hillel the Elder, students of, 66–67
Hillelites, God's preference for the rulings of, 48
historical accuracy, of Torah, 1
historical evidence, not leaving the traditional picture intact, 139–40
history, incapable of producing a complete account, 2n4
Holmes, Oliver Wendell, 158
Holtz, Barry, 30n25
House of Hillel ("Beit Hillel"), 47–50, 85
human autonomy, explaining God's purpose in creating the world, 29
human beings. *See also* persons
created "in His image," 26
inclination for good and evil, 29
inherent limits of reason, 157n38
not living "by bread alone," 128
human morality, trumping biblical morality, 144
"humanitarian social ethos," Deuteronomy characterized by, 101
humility, psychology of, 42
husbands, controlling wives by biblical law, 105
hypothesis, falsifying by finding a single counterexample, 40–41

ibn Hazm, 63
illiberal communities, God's will not reliably ascertained by the leaders of, 138n17
imago Dei ("image of God"), moral agency and, 27

Subject Index

immoral commandments, making peace with the Torah's, 130–46
immoral mandates, 39, 133
immorality, consequences of, 104n33
impersonal God, acting blindly, by rote, 133
individual responsibility, rationale for, 26
injustice, always with us, 128
innovation, 161
institutions, depending on, 43
internal debates, in the canon, 113–29
internal divisions, not allowing to reoccur, 152
interpretations, of Torah verses, 14
intertextual conflicts, 99
intracommunal violence, regulated and reduced, 111
intra-pentateuchal controversy, 100–109
irrational things, believing in, 8
Isaac, 2, 4, 106, 107. *See also* Abraham
Isaiah, 3n7, 161
Ishmael, 106, 107
Israel, no separation of shul and state, 138n17
Israeli Chief Rabbinate, on assimilation of Jews, 22
Israelites
 acceptance of their eternal covenant with God, 51
 failure to heed their prophets' warnings, 121
Isserles, Moses, 91n43, 96
Izhbitza-Radzin rabbinical dynasty, of Eastern Poland, 70

"J" source, 11
Jackson, Robert, 156n35
Jacob
 buries Rachel "on the road to Ephrath," 31
 no evidence of the existence of, 2
 Rebekah and, 107, 108
 reminding God of the suffering he endured, 32
 set out for the houses of Torah study, 107n51
Jacobs, Louis, 11–12, 11n32

Jeremiah (book of), Rachel weeping for her children, 31
Jerusalem Talmud ("Yerushalmi"), 163, 164
Jewish calendar, fixing of, 149
Jewish canon, as an integrated and fundamental theological unit, 99
Jewish community, entire "heard" God speak at Sinai, 52
Jewish faith, essential elements of, 144n40
Jewish heroines, depicted in Scripture, 106
Jewish law, "moralization" of, 87
Jewish law and ethics, development of, xix
Jewish people
 Almighty's "partner" in purifying the world, 18
 in exile denied full self-governance, 96
 God expecting to rewrite portions of the play, 17
 history of, 9, 51, 141
 picking and choosing values aligning with secular ethics, 39
Jewish Scripture
 Christian Church's acceptance of, 60
 impact on Western civilization, 9
Jewish slaves, freed after six years of labor, 103
Jewish texts, dialectics of core, 42
Jewish theology, Otto strongly influenced by traditional, 135
Job, 98, 124, 125, 126
Job (book of), xix, 113, 114n74, 124–29
Jochebed, 2
Jonah, 117–18, 119, 121
Jonah (book of), xix, xixn17, 99n3, 113, 117–23
Joseph, 13, 105
Joshua, 34
Judaism
 authentic as essentially liberal, 23
 belief system promoting liberal, benign values, 6–7
 as a complicated religion, 10
 finding a mechanism to tame and appease God, 110

Subject Index

liberal values at its very core, 98
main "streams" of, 91
practice of forbidden by Rome, 60
sacred texts not enforcing intellectual conformity, 115
threat of Christianity to, 60
threatened by exigent external forces, 78
judges, fallibility of, 156n35
jurists, qualifications for modifies, 102
justice, 14, 44, 56
Justinian, 60–61

Kant, Immanuel, xiv, 25
Kaplan, Abraham, 29
Kaplan, Lawrence, 68n65
Kaplan, Zvi, 86n26
Karaism, 63
Karaite heresy, 61
Karaite theology, 62
Karaites, 62, 73–74
Karo, Joseph, xix, 96
kashrut, laws governing, 54
Kass, Leon, 53
Kaufmann, Yehezkel, 112
Kellner, Menachem, 66, 67
Kermode, Frank, 99
Ketuvim (Writings), xix, 19, 99n3
Kimelman, Reuven, 85n19, 91nn43, 44
kindness, outweighing strict justice, 104
King, Martin Luther, Jr., 20
Klitsner, Judy, 83n12, 105n34
Knohl, Israel, 4–5
knowledge, as cumulative, 71
Kohelet, 114, 114n74
Kook, Abraham Isaac, 67
Korach, controversy instigated by, 81–82
Korn, Eugene, 131n3
Kraemer, David, 93
Kugel, James, 102, 124–25

Laban, 32, 33
lamdanut (traditional casuistic study), 73
Lamm, Norman, 68–69, 142–43
laws, notion of revealed and binding, 134–35
Leah, 32

Lebens, Samuel, 21–22, 144
legal codification
  of Deuteronomy, 104
  stifling effect of, 95
legal requirements, relaxing for divorce, 90
Leibniz, on necessary truth, 41n4
Leiner, Mordecai Yosef, 70
leprosy, halakha of, 159
Levenson, Jon, 2, 137, 138–39, 142, 144
liberal society, 24, 80, 87
liberal subjectivism, 21n68
liberal values, xv
liberalism
  as the best moral/political philosophy available to humankind, 138n17
  codification and, 94–97
  critical rationalism and, 40–50
  defense of Judaism's essential, xvii
  defining, 23–24
  evident in Scriptural texts, xix
  of Popper, 42–45
liberty, restrictions on must be justified, 24
Lichtenstein, Aharon, xiv
Linzer, Dov, 157
literary prophets, 99, 110, 112
Lot and his immediate family, sparing, xiii
love poetry, interpreting as a metaphorical love story, 115
loving your fellow as yourself, as commanded in Leviticus, xiv
Luzzatto, Samuel, 18

Mabul (the Great Flood), sparing only Noah and his family, 106
Maimonides
  acting in accordance with instructions, 65
  as authoritative summaries of halakhah, 96–97
  on man knowing good and evil, 28
  on miracles, 16, 68n64
  in the *Mishneh Torah*, xix
  never sympathetic to R. Sherira, 67–68

Subject Index

Maimonides (continued)
    on offering peace terms, 131
    on producing courage, 101
    "Review of the Torah," 95
    "Thirteen Fundamental Principles of Faith," 63–64, 97n60
majority opinion, R. Eliezer refusing to accede to, 151
"majority rule," biblical principle of, 155
Malachi, 69–70
mamzer (illegitimate child), definition of, 93
man, creation of, 13, 27
mark, on Cain, 30
Marshall, Thurgood, 84
Matan Torah, 52, 136
matrilineal descent, halakhic doctrine of, 123
medieval elevation, of the Oral Law, 64
medieval Jewish commentators, on minority opinions, 86
medieval rabbis, rehabilitating God, 38
medrashic stories, on arguments between God and Moses, 46n24
Meir Leibush ben Yehiel Michel Wisser ("Malbim"), 36
Micah, 29, 112
midrash, 31–32, 164
Midrash (Midrashim), 164
"Midrash Rabbah," 165
Midrash Tanchuma, 165
Mill, John Stuart, *On Liberty*, 80
Minor Prophets, prophets in, 110n64
minority opinions, respect for, 83–87
"Minority Opinions and their Role in Hora'ah" (Helfgot), 86
miracles, denying the existence of, 16–17
Miriam, 108–9
Mises, Ludwig von, 44
Mishnah
    avoiding unnecessary wars and ensuring just, 131
    codifying ancient oral halakhic traditions, 165
    on ensuring witnesses testify truthfully, 74
    on every dispute for the sake of Heaven, 81
    exhaustive analysis and elucidation of, 164
    final reduction to written form, 59n27
    giving reasons why Adam was created alone, 75
    halakhah recorded in, 58n24
    organization of, 163
    original language of referred to "one life," 74n92
    on Sages questioning both Kohelet and the Song of Songs (Song of Solomon), 115
Mishnaic tractate *Eduyot* 1:5, on the opinion of a single person, 85
Mishneh Torah, synthesizing Jewish law, 96
mitzvot, 21, 47, 144
Moabites, 123
Modern Orthodox communities, as not closed societies, 138n17
"modernism," Ross and, 140
monism, 49
monists, 49, 149
monogamous marriages, preservation of, 90
moral agency, eliminating with constant miracles, 17
moral agents, xvi, xvii, 25
moral autonomy, 24, 38, 128, 145
moral consciousness, 143
moral considerations, 39
moral dilemma, 143
moral judgment, 39
moral law, 26, 30n23
moral philosophy, 4
moral principles, xvii, 23–24
moral reasoning, 100
moral suasion, 103
moral theories, 17
morality, 112, 143
Mordechai, 116
Morriston, Wesley, 127–28
Moses

Subject Index

asking God why he is upset over "that which is nothing," 46n24
beseeching God to remember how he was denied entry into the Promised Land, 32
bitter complaint to the Almighty after his and Aaron's initial demand of Pharaoh boomerangs, 35
character as his uniqueness, 110
decision to send spies into Canaan, 34–35
disregarding God's instructions, 33, 37
God transporting to visit R. Akiva's academy, 72, 156–57
imploring God to sheathe his sword, 46
interceding on behalf of his people, 36–37
leadership ordained by God, 82
misunderstood God's wordless revelation to him, 139
no evidence of the existence of, 2
patiently answers Korach's devious objections, 82
as a very humble man, 34n40
mother's milk, not boiling a kid in, 55
mourning, application of minority opinions, 86
Muffs, Yochanan, 17
Muhammad, Sages and Rabbis suppressing references to, 63
multiplicity of opinions, Bavli's positive view of, 92
murder, of Abel not premeditated, 31
myths, narratives of, 2n2

Nachmanides ("Ramban"), 16, 36, 64, 95
Nagel, Thomas, 24
Nahmani, Rabbi, God's acceptance on the halakhah of leprosy, 38n61
narrative, 4n12, 77
Natan, Rabbi, encountering the prophet Elijah and asks him God's reaction, 151
natural disasters, 128n145
"natural morality," xiv

Navon, Chaim, 38
necessary truth, 41, 41n4
needy, addressing the plight of, 102
"negative miracle," Decline of the Generations as, 68n64
Nehemiah, 122
Nelson, Richard, 101–2
Nevi'im (Prophets), 19
Newtonian physics, superseded by Einstein's general relativity, 17
Nineveh, King and people of repented, 118–19
Ninevites, not "know[ing] their right hand from their left," 120
Nissim Gerondi ("Ran"), 65
nitkatnu ha-dorot (degeneration-of-the-generations argument), 69
"non-classical prophets," 110n64
non-historical perspective, believers adopting, 15
non-Pentateuchal canonical books, 11n29, 19
nonsexist world, of the Song of Songs, 115
Nozick, Robert, 24, 25
"numinous" character, of religion, xvi

objections, raised by Moses, 33
objective knowledge, as impossible, 140
objectivity, attaining with the help of argument, 42
observance, activities of for Jews, 21
omnipotent God, not getting his point across, 137
On Liberty (Mill), 80
Onan, son of Judah, 108
"one life," on the supreme importance of, 75–76
The Open Canon (Sagi), 49
"open society," 42, 43
The Open Society and Its Enemies (Popper), 43, 44
open-mindedness, in Jewish theology, 47
Oral Law from Sinai (*Torah shebe'al peh*), xviii, 51, 54–66, 71, 76
oral traditions, authoritative unavailable to the Mishnah's redactors, 57

Subject Index

Orthodox communities, resembling closed societies, 43
Orthodox insistence, that every Jew do the same thing at the same time in the same way, 21n68
Orthodox Judaism, xviii, 51
Orthodox rabbinate, 22
Orthodoxy, 21–22, 94
Otto, Rudolph, xvi, 135
our image, after our likeness, strange language of, 27
"Oven of Akhnai" narrative
    critique of R. Akiva, 157
    pitting a lone dissenter against his rabbinic colleagues, 147
    presentation and analysis of the famous talmudic saga of, xx
    on the topic of verbal mistreatment, 150
    warning against intolerance, 161

"P" (priestly) source, 11
pagans, Jonah unable to accept God's mercy to, 120
parables, written as didactic fiction, 148
"particularism," of Judaism, 135
Pentateuch
    conflict between legal codes, 100
    conflict with prophetic books, xix
    final redaction of, 78
    holding a unique place as a divine work, 19
    no extra-biblical evidence for the existence of main characters, 2
    no overt references to the classical prophets in, 111n65
    studying to understand fundamental tenets of faith, xvii
    as a verbatim transcript of God's words to Moses on Mt. Sinai, 133
Pentateuchal texts, conflicts within, 99
Perez, son of Judah, 108
perfect being, God as, xvi
personal beliefs, unfounded, 5
personal God, 132–33, 134
persons. *See also* human beings
    respect for above all, 154–59

Pesach Sheni (Second Passover), 55
Pharisees, 58
philosophical arguments, in favor or against God's existence, 8
philosophical inquiry, as the surest path to the knowledge of God for Rambam, 68
philosophical literature, explicating and defending liberal values, 24
"piecemeal social engineering," of Popper, 44
Pirkei Avot (Ethics of Our Fathers), 56, 57
Pirkei DeRabbi Eliezer, 165
Plessy v. Ferguson, 84
Pluckrose, Helen, 140
pluralism, xvii, 49, 91–93
political choices, institutional checks for, 43
political process, revising detailed legal codes, 96
Polliack, Meira, 62
Popper, Karl, xviin13, 24, 40, 43, 80
posekim, 68, 138n17
positive effects, of unsupported beliefs, 6
postmodernist perspective, Ross accepting, 140
poverty, not exposing, 90
"primitive tribal" society, living in a charmed circle, 43
the "priority of the ethical," as following the ways of the good, 89
"private" space, creating, 86n26
profound social changes, response to, 101–2
progress, open-mindedness key to for Popper, 42
progressive revelation, 134–36, 137
"proofs," of God's existence, 8
property damage, overturning conventional law regarding, 90
prophecy, 69, 70
prophetic literature, 111
prophets, 19, 69, 110n64, 112
Prophets and Writings, books of, 77
proto-feminist text, Song of Songs as, 115
Proverbs, 113, 115
prozbul, Rabbi Hillel's creation of, 89

Subject Index

puzzles, concentrating on "solving" existing, 41

Qohelet, attraction to, 114
quantum mechanics, general relativity and, 17–18
"questionable morality," of the Sinaitic revelation, 142

Rabba bar Nahmani ("Rabbah"), 150, 159–61
Rabban Gamliel of Yavneh, 149, 151, 152, 155, 156
rabbinic assertion, of the Oral Law from Sinai, 56–59
rabbinic communities, legitimacy of different practices in, 93
Rabbis
    on the age of prophecy had ended, 78
    avoided adding a leap month to the calendar during a sabbatical (seventh) year, 89
    committed to tolerance and open-mindedness, 80
    declared independence, 150–51
    differentiated halakhah and aggadah by Amoraic times, 76
    distrusted controversy, 82
    embraced robust debate, disagreement, and dissent, 81
    "forced" to resort to reasoned argument, 57
    interpreted the Pentateuch's commandments in their best judgment, 72n84
    modified established halakha, 158
    placed value on autonomous moral judgment, 33
    reconciled systematic rationalism with the aggada, 74
    reluctance to enforce the death penalty, 88
    reoriented away from cultic practices in the diaspora, 22
    took the law into their own hands, 156
    troubled by dubious ethics of many of the Torah's mitzvot, 131
    when capitalized meaning legal authorities of the talmudic era, 165
    Yavneh's removed Rabban Gamliel from his position as Nasi, 149
Rabinovitch, Nahum, 34n42
Rachel, 31, 32–33
Ramah, 31n32
Ramban. See Nachmanides ("Ramban")
Rashi
    on the attribution of a doctrine to a particular individual, 86–87
    on God speaking at Sinai, 52
    on having a firm standing on truth, 71
    interpreting "playing" as idolatry, 106–7
    on men surrendering their jewelry, 109
    on "stiffnecked" people, 46
    on understanding the words "for yourself," 35
"Rashomon effect," after Akira Kurosawa's film, 15
Ravina II, reduction of the Babylonian Talmud and, 61
Rawls, John, 24, 25
reasonableness, attitude of, 42
Rebekah, 107–8
reforms, Popper favored small-scale, incremental, 44
regnant halakhah, canon bestowing divine sanction on, 54
Reines, Yitzchak, 49
responsibility, Cain attempting to evade, 30
revelation, 59n26, 133, 136–45, 136n12
    alternative, 17–18
    progressive, 134–36, 137
    Sinaitic, 13n42, 60, 66, 140
Revelation, when capitalized, the biblical account of the giving of the Torah to Moses on Mt. Sinai, 165
revisionary challenges, articulated to Judaism's longstanding principles, 99

Subject Index

revolutionary movements, dangers posed by, 44
"ricinus" plant, growing over Jonah, 119
right, as the limitation of each person's freedom compatible with the freedom of everyone, 25
Rishonim, as great rabbis and jurists, 165
Ritba, on the French Rabbis of blessed memory, 65
ritual, 20, 91, 113
Rome, "great revolt" against, 59
Ross, Tamar, 139–42
Roth, Leon, 87
ruach hakodesh (the holy spirit), guidance by, 144
Rubenstein, Jeffrey, 152
Ruth, 106, 123

Saadia Gaon. *See* Sherira ben Hanina
Saadya, Gaon, head of the Sura Academy, 73
Sabbath desecrator, method of execution for, 55
Sacks, Chief Rabbi, 14
sacred literature, infused with liberal values, xvi
sacrifices, meat from shared with "foreigners, orphans, and widows," 102
Sadducees, 58
Safed's illustrious rabbinic community, leader of, 96
Sages
    on the afflictions meted out to Adam and Eve, 105
    conflicting legal opinions by, 165
    disagreeing with regard to a halakha of leprosy, 159
    as greater than prophets, 69–72
    listed after Hillel and Shammai, 56–57
    looked askance at Ecclesiastes, 114
    needed to interpret texts and traditions, 70
    ostracizing kindling God's wrath, 152
    questioning Eliezer about ritual status, 154
    reversing legal rulings wrongly decided, 85
    as scholars and legal authorities, 165
Sagi, Avi, 42n7, 49, 134
Saiman, Chaim, 161
sake of Heaven, controversy for, 81
Samaria, 122n121
Samaritans, 123
Sanders, James, 129
Sanhedrin [High Court], executing a transgressor, 88
Sarah, 2, 106
Satan, 124, 127
Schiffman, Lawrence H., 58
Schorsch, Ismar, 101
scientific theories, 40, 41
scientists, estimating the age of the universe, 4
scriptural evidence, absence of for *Torah shebe'al peh*, 54–56
Scripture
    endorsement of norms, 98
    nature of, 18–20
    not depicting prophets as jurists, 56
    profound respect for moral autonomy, 133
    teaching the capacities of humans, 129
secular scholars, on the first eleven chapters of Genesis, 2
Seeskin, Kenneth 68n66
Sefer ha-Kuzari (Halevi), 63
self-centered demands, practicing saying "no" to, 20
self-sacrifice, of Rachel preceding Sinai, 33
Sen, Amartya, qualifying as "liberal," 24
"separate but equal" doctrine, 84
seven-year cycle, of tithing and remission of all debt instituted, 102
sexual abuse, allegations against leaders of closed societies, 138n17
Shabbat, different customs in various locales, 92
Shalom, Imma, 150, 152, 155

Subject Index

Shammai, 48, 85
Shapiro, Marc, 74n92
Shavuot, commemorating Matan Torah annually, 51
Shelah, son of Judah, 108
Sherira ben Hanina, 64
Sherira Gaon. *See also* Sherira ben Hanina
    Decline of the Generations theory and, 67
Shimon ben Lakish, death of, 81
Shimon ben Yochai, on allowing murder, 30
Shimon ben Yohai, on the office of High Priest, 34n40
ship's captain and crew, treating Jonah with scrupulous justice and dignity, 118
Shulchan Aruch ("Set Table"), 96
Sifre Deuteronomy, coming to know the One who spoke, 75–76
Sihon the Amorite, king of Heshbon, Moses engaging in battle, 37
Simon-Shoshan, Moshe, 74, 76
sin, Cain accountable for his, 30
Sinaitic narrative, harmonizing traditional Judaism with moral theories, 142
Sinaitic revelation, 60, 66, 140
sins of the fathers, visiting on the sons, 37, 38
slavery, Thirteenth Amendment's abolishment of, 84
snake-like ovens, morality tale on ritual purity of, 156
social attitudes, evolution of, 85n18
social problems, amelioration of, 44
Socratic dialogue, as key in Jewish theology, 47
Sodom and Gomorrah, as beyond redemption, xiv
Sodomites, unbounded wickedness of, 30
Soloveitchik, Joseph B., 15, 15n54
Sommer, Benjamin D., 29, 136
Song of Songs, 113, 115
sons of angels, early generations characterized as, 66
spoken word, forced into the straitjacket of a written mold, 94
Stammaim, 61–62, 166
Statman, Daniel, 134
steadfastness, towards R. Eliezer's, 154
Steinmetz, Devora, 155
"stiffnecked" people, defined, 46
stories, as an essential aspect of human consciousness, 77n98
Strauss, Leo, 8, 15, 15n54, 16n55
stringency, legal interpretations favoring greater, 48
strong claims, requiring strong evidence, 6
succession, issue of in the Bible, 78
sugya, 81, 92, 93, 155, 165
Sukkot, festival of, 89
supernatural power, unease regarding displays of God's, 16
"supplementary hypothesis," Five Books built up chronologically, 11

Talmud
    composed and edited by Babylonian rabbis, 163
    deep study of, 96
    departing from the Torah's literal words, 88
    followed by legal codes, 10
    of God being defied in halakhic matters, 38n61
    intense controversies during the Mishnaic period, 57
    on men of great learning subject to equally great temptation, 158
    new ways of learning, 97
    organization of following that of the Mishnah, 163
    Rabbis were deeply troubled by the oracles of Ezekiel, 116
    texts consisting of the Mishnah, Gemara, and part of the Babylonian Talmud, 166
talmudic era, 22, 164
talmudic narratives, 161
talmudic story, 71–72, 147
Tamar, 108

Subject Index

Tanakh, 19, 26, 98
Tannaim
    community of halakhic authorities, 166
    emphasizing importance of rituals and practices, 60
    era of activity of, 59
    as inferior to their predecessors, 66
    one of the greatest, 148
    teaching responsibilities, division of between R. Gamliel and R. Elazar b. Azaria, 156
Temple, destroyed by the Babylonians in 586 BCE, 121
Ten Commandments (Decalogue), xviii–xix, 51, 52–54, 55, 79
"Ten Martyrs," legend of, 153
theism, critics of, 6
theistic revelation, 133
theodicy, 30
theological framework, governing this study, 1–22
theology, denying the existence of a personal God, 132–33
theories, formulating bold new, 41
"these and these" language, of *Eruvin* 13b, 48–49
Thirteen Attributes of Mercy, Almighty proclaiming, 104
Thomson, Judith Jarvis, 25
thought crime, harmless mental lapses as, 5
tikkun olam, 20, 20n65
Torah
    account of the Golden Calf, 45–47
    containing details in tension with many modern ethical beliefs, 145
    describing events in supernatural terms, 52
    details in tension with many modern ethical beliefs, 130
    on different voices identified in the documentary hypothesis, 15
    "distasteful" elements of, xvi
    immoral mitzvot, 132
    insistence in the Sixth Commandment that "[t]hou shall not kill," 143
    in the language of people, 10
    literal reading of distracting from God's message, 3
    as literature, not history, 1–5
    new ways of learning, 97
    not requiring ongoing revision by "experts," 146
    oral study of as a factor supporting Jewish uniqueness, 61
    overturning of the "normal" order of succession, 77
    referred to the Pentateuch (the "Five Books of Moses"), 166
    reflecting inability to grasp and record God's communication, 136
    stressed the magnitude of Matan Torah, 52
Torah Emet (Torah of Truth), Five Books as, 141
Torah mitzvot, as repellant and problematic, xx
Torah shebe'al peh doctrine
    cornerstone of Chazal's commitment to, 56
    as a fixed halakhic principle in amoraic times, 58–59
    historical background to the claim of, 59–64
    rabbinic commitment to, 57, 78
    resistance to, 64–66
TheTorah.com website, 142n32
Tosefta, as less authoritative, 164
Tower of Bable story, enforcing uniformity of thought, 83
"tractates" (chapters), in the Bavli, 163
Tradition, 81, 127, 166
traditionalist rabbis, adopting DCM through the "back door," 134
Treatise on the Obvious Contradictions and Evident Lies in the Book Which the Jews call the Torah, 63
Tree of Knowledge episode, 16n55, 28, 105

Subject Index

truth(s)
    controversy conducive to arriving at, 82
    ejected from the debate as secondary, 27–28
    greatest joy in searching for it, 161
    idea of multiple, 86
    seeking, 50
truth discovery, advocated by critical rationalists, 27
truthful testimony, saving a life by as like saving an entire world, 75
Twain, Mark, 10n27
Twerski, Abraham, 126

ultra-Orthodox, 73, 138n17
uneducated Jews, not exposing illiteracy or ignorance of, 90
unfounded beliefs, acceptance of one or more, 6
uniform *halakhah*, handed down from generation to generation, 58n24
uniformity, quest for, 149
United States' federal system, with state courts, 94
universe
    as both beautiful and grossly unjust, 128
    God created *ex nihilo*, 16
unrepentant Israel, looking bad by comparison if non-Israelites repented, 121
Unterman, Jeremiah, 112n69
"Ur-manuscript" (or manuscripts), 100n7
utilitarianism, "saving one life" cutting against, 75

value systems, variety of in the Bible, 19
"venture" models, of faith, 7
"verbal mistreatment" (*ona'at devarim*), sin of, 155
"verisimilitude," Popperians notion of, 41n3
vicarious thinking, revelation as not, 136
virgin, Deuteronomy on the humiliation or moral degradation of, 103–4

Wald, Stephen, 75
"the way of peace," as one of the Torah's foremost values, 89
"weak pluralism," pluralists embracing, 49
Wein, Berel, 60
Wettstein, Howard, 5
"The White Album" (Didion), 77n98
wickedness and cruelty, capacity for, 30
Wilovsky, Yaakov Dovid ("Ridbaz"), 67
wisdom, 7, 70, 102
witness's responsibility, gravity of, 74
Wolf, Arnold Jacob, 21n68
Wolowelsky, Joel B., 152–53n26
women, portrayed in Exodus, 109
workers, receiving wages on the same day, 103
workings of the world, fine-tuned in a way far beyond human understanding, 125
Writings and Prophets, "troubling" texts within, 113–16

Yadin, Azzan, 49
Yavneh academy, Rabban Gamliel role as the head (*Nasi*) of, 149
Yefet ben 'Eli, 62
Yehoshua (or "Joshua") ben Chananiah, 38n61, 149–50, 151, 152, 153n26, 154
Yehoshua ben Karchah, 34n40
yeridat hadorot, 66, 68, 78
Yerushalmi, Yosef Hayim, xviin12, 93n48
"YHWH," overruling the numinous dimensions, 5
Yohanan, Rabbi, 81
Yohanan ben Zakkai, 90, 148
Yom Kippur, book of Jonah read aloud during, 117
Yom Tov Ishbili ("Ritba"), 65
Yuval, Israel, 60

Zadok of Lublin, 70, 71
Zerah, son of Judah, 108
Zion, Noam, 85

Scripture Index

HEBREW BIBLE

Genesis

	3, 4, 13, 15n54, 31, 106, 107
1	xvi, 12, 13
1–2	14
1:3	12n34
1–11	105
1:26	27
1:27	xvin10, 12n35
2	12, 13
2:2	12n36
2:2–3	3n8
2:5–6	12n37
2:7	13n38
2:17	28n11
2:18	13n39, 105n35
2:19	13n40
2:21–22	13n41
3:16	105n36
3:16–17	23n12
3:22	28
4:9	30n21
4:11–15	30n20
4:14	30n26
4:15	31n27
6:11–13	106n38
11	83
11:1–9	83n11
11:8	83n13
11:31–32	13n44
12:1	13, 13n43
16:2	106n40
16:15	106n41
18:17–19	xiiin1
18:20–21	xivn3
18:23–25	xiiin2
21:1–5	106n42
21:10	106n43
21:11	107n45
21:12	107n46
22	4
25:19–23	107n48
25:27	107n49
25:28	107n50
27:3–4	107n52
27:5–13	108n53
29:17	106n39
35:16–20	31n31
37:36	13n45
38	108, 108n55
39:1	13n46
48:7	31n31

Exodus

	13n42, 52, 87, 100, 101, 102, 103, 104, 105, 109, 111
2:4–10	109

Scripture Index

Exodus (continued)

3:4–22	33n37
3:5	46n27
3:10	33n38
4:12–13	33n39
5:6–9	35n46
5:22	35n47
6:1	35n48
12:40	100n8
15:20	108n57
17:14–16	xvn6
18:21	102n17
19:10–12	52n2
19:16–19	52n3
20:1–14	52n4
20:15	52
21:1–11	103n24
21:23	89
22:15–16	103n29
22:23	103n21
23:2	151n19
23:19	55n11
23:25–26	103n22
24:12	55
32:1–4	109n58
32:3	109n60
32:7	45n19, 47n29
32:9	46n20, 47n29
32:10	46nn21–22
32:14	46n23
32:32	46n25
32:33	46n26
33:3	46n27
34:6–7	37n56, 104n32
34:26	55n11

Leviticus

	56
24:10–14	56n15
24:19–20	72n84

Numbers

	82, 101
5:11–31	90, 101n11
9:6–12	55n13
12:3	34n40
13:1–3	35
13:2	35
13:17–33	35
15:32–35	55
16:1–35	82n5
20:9–12	98n2
21:1–2	109
22–23	77n97
27:1–7	56n14

Deuteronomy

xix, 3, 13n42, 35, 52, 87, 90, 100, 100n7, 101, 102, 103, 104, 104n33, 110, 111, 111n65, 112

1:13	102n18
1:19–40	35
1:23	35n44
2:24	37n57
2:26–27	37n58
4:2	xviii, xviiin14
4:12–13	53n6
5:9	104n33
6:18	89n38
10:1–4	53n6
14:21	55n11
15:1–2	102n15
15:9	89
15:13–14	103n23
15:15	103n25
15:18	103n26
16:11	102n16
16:14	102n16
17:9	65
17:11	xviii, 65
17:11–12	xviiin15
20:10	37n59
21:15–17	77n101
22:28–29	103n30
24:14–15	103n28
24:16	104n33
25:13–16	102
25:17–19	xvn6
26:12–13	102n15
30:11–14	151n18

Scripture Index

32:4	xv
34:10	56, 110n63

Joshua

	3

Judges

	3
4	106
5	106

1 Samuel

15:1–9	xvn6

1 Kings

12	122n121

2 Kings

2:12	154
14:25	117
22	100n7

Isaiah

	111
1:10–17	111n66
1:19	161n48
6	161

Jeremiah

	31, 111n65
31:14	31n32
31:14–16	31nn33–34

Ezekiel

	113, 116

Hosea

4:14	90

Amos

	111
5:21–27	112n67

Jonah

	xix, 99n3, 113, 117, 117n94, 118, 121, 121n112, 123
1:1	117n91
1:2	118n95
1:3	118n96
1:12	118n97
1:16	118n99
3:4	118n100
3:7–8	119n101
3:10	119n102
4:1	119n103
4:2	119n104
4:5	119n105
4:6	119n106
4:8	119n107
4:9	119n108
4:11	119n109

Micah

	112
6:7–9	112n68
6:8	29n19

Psalms

	114, 114n74
90:12	70

Proverbs

	113, 114, 114n74
2:20–22	89, 89n40
22:5	124n130

Job

	xix, 9, 113, 114n74, 124–29, 125n134
1:8–12	124n127
1:20–21	124n128
2:4–7	124n129
24:12	120n110
30:20–31	125n132

Scripture Index

Job (continued)

31:35–40	125n133
38:4–7	125n135
38:39–41	125n136
42:3–6	126n137
42:7	126n138
42:10	126n139

Song of Songs (Song of Solomon)

113, 115

Ruth

108, 123

Ecclesiastes

113, 114, 114n74, 115

Esther

113, 115, 116

Nehemiah

2:9–11	122n119

RABBINIC WORKS

Talmudic Literature

Mishnah

Eduyot

1:5	85, 85nn21–22

Pirkei Avot

1:1	56n17, 148
1:12	56n18
2:8	148n7
3:11	150n15
5:17	81n2

Sanhedrin

4	74, 74n91
4:5	128n145

Shabbat

1:4	81n3

Yadayim

3	115n76, 115n81

Jerusalem Talmud (Yerushalmi)

149n8, 164

Nedarim

9:4	157n39

Ta'anit

4:5	149n8

Babylonian Talmud ("Bavli")

xix, 95, 163, 166

Bava Batra

12b	70n72

Bava Metzi'a

	151n18
58b	150n15
59a	150n14, 155n32
59b	147n2, 151n17, 152n21, 152nn23–25
84a	81n4
86a	148n3, 159nn43–45, 160n46

Berakhot

9a	86n24
27b–28a	149n10, 152n26
36a	86n27
61a	14n49

Eruvin

13b	48n32
18a	14n49
46a	86n26

Gittin

36a–b	89n37
43a	71n76

Scripture Index

Hagigah
3b	148b6
13b	116n89

Hullin
7a–7b	74

Ketubbot
8a	14n49

Kiddushin
29b	74
30b	29n17

Makkot
2:7a	88n31

Megillah
7a	114n72, 116n86
14a	69nn69–70

Menahot
29b	72nn80–81, 157nn36–37

Mo'ed Qatan
18a	86n25

Sanhedrin
12a	89n35
37a	128n145
68a	147n2, 153n27, 154nn29–31
88b	57n26
111a	35n49

Shabbat
13b	116n88
30b	115n80
88a–89b	74
112b	66n57

Sotah
47a	90n42

Sukkah
26a	89n34
28a	148n5
52a	158n40

Yevamot
14a	92n45, 93n49
14a–b	81n3
62b	149n8

Yoma
4n10	4n10

Zevahim
102a	34n40
8b	10n28

Midrash (Midrashim)

Sifra Deuteronomy
49	75

Exodus Rabbah
42 §2, n35	47n29

Genesis Rabbah
8:3–8, n82	27n8
8:5	27nn9–10
22:9	30n24
22:12, n180?	31n28
22:12, n181	31n29
70:16	106n39

Lamentations Rabbah
Proem XXIV	31n30, 32n36

Numbers Rabbah
19:33	36n55

Scripture Index

Tanhuma

Korach
siman (chapter) 1	82n6
siman (chapter) 2	82n7

Pirkei DeRabbi Eliezer

43:8	120n110
45:4	109
49:13	105

Seder Eliyahu Zuta

ch. 2	18n62, 136n14

COMMENTARIES

Ibn Ezra on Exodus

36n51

Maimonides (Rambam)

Ethical Writings of Maimonides
87	16n56

Mishneh Torah ("Review of the Torah")
xix, 95, 164

Hilkhot Teshuvah
5:1	28n14

Nachmanides

Commentary on the Torah	36n52
Exodus 13:16	16n56

Rashi

Commentary on Babylonian Talmud (Ketubbot)
57a	86n29

Commentary on the Talmud (Gittin)
43a	71n77

Commentary on the Torah (Deut)
2:26	37n60

Commentary on the Torah (Exod)
4:10	34n41
6:1	36n50
12:40	100n8
20:15	52n5
24:12	53n7
32:2	109nn61–62
32:9	46n28

Commentary on the Torah (Gen)
21:9	107n44
21:12	107n47
25:27	107n51

Commentary on the Torah (Num)
13:2	35n43

ISLAMIC LITERATURE

Ibn Hazam

63

www.ingramcontent.com/pod-product-compliance
Lightning Source LLC
Chambersburg PA
CBHW070737160426
43192CB00009B/1479